MEDIA, FEMINISM, CULTURAL STUDIES

The Sacred Cinema of Andrei Tarkovsky
by Jeremy Mark Robinson

Lip Tyler
by Thomas A. Christie

The Cinema of Hayao Miyazaki
Jeremy Mark Robinson

Stepping Forward: Essays, Lectures and Interviews
by Wolfgang Iser

Wild Zones: Pornography, Art and Feminism
by Kelly Ives

'Cosmo Woman': The World of Women's Magazines
by Oliver Whitehorne

The Cinema of Richard Linklater
by Thomas A. Christie

Valerian Borowczyk
by Jeremy Mark Robinson

Andrea Dworkin
by Jeremy Mark Robinson

Cixous, Irigaray, Kristeva: The Jouissance of French Feminism
by Kelly Ives

The Erotic Object: Sexuality in Sculpture
From Prehistory to the Present Day
by Susan Quinnell

Women in Pop Music
by Helen Challis

Detonation Britain: Nuclear War in the UK
by Jeremy Mark Robinson

Julia Kristeva: Art, Love, Melancholy, Philosophy, Semiotics
by Kelly Ives

Luce Irigaray: Lips, Kissing, and the Politics of Sexual Difference
by Kelly Ives

Helene Cixous I Love You: The Jouissance of Writing
by Kelly Ives

Feminism and Shakespeare
by B.D. Barnacle

FORTHCOMING BOOKS

GHOST IN THE SHELL

GHOST IN THE SHELL

IT FOUND A VOICE... NOW IT NEEDS A BODY

GHOST IN THE SHELL
MAMORU OSHII
POCKET MOVIE GUIDE

JEREMY MARK ROBINSON

Crescent Moon

First published 2024.
© Jeremy Mark Robinson 2024.

Set in Book Antiqua, 9 on 12 point.
Designed by Radiance Graphics.

British Library Cataloguing in Publication data available for this title.

ISBN-13 9781861719256

Crescent Moon Publishing
P.O. Box 1312, Maidstone, Kent
ME14 5XU, U.K.
www.crmoon.com
cresmopub@yahoo.co.uk

CONTENTS

ACKNOWLEDGEMENTS

To Masamune Shirow.
To the authors and publishers quoted.

PICTURE CREDITS

Illustrations are © Masamune Shirow. Kodansha. Seishinsha. Kadokawa. Hakusensha. G.O.T. Co., Ltd. Harumichi Aoki/ Seishinsha. *Canopri Comic*. *Hobby Japan*. Manabu Kiowa. Viz. Cosmo Engineering. Tokuma Shoten. Tokuma International. Hakuhodo. Geneon. Dark Horse Comics. Studio Ghibli. Toho. Production I.G. Optimum Releasing.

Images are used for information and research purposes, with no infringement of copyright or rights intended.

NOTE

This book uses material that also appears in the companion volume, *The Art of Masamune Shirow: Volume 2: Animé*.
The three volumes are:
The Art of Masamune Shirow: Volume 1: Manga.
The Art of Masamune Shirow: Volume 2: Animé.
The Art of Masamune Shirow: Volume 3: Erotica.

We are the robots.

Kraftwerk

Colour sketch for the first Ghost In the Shell manga

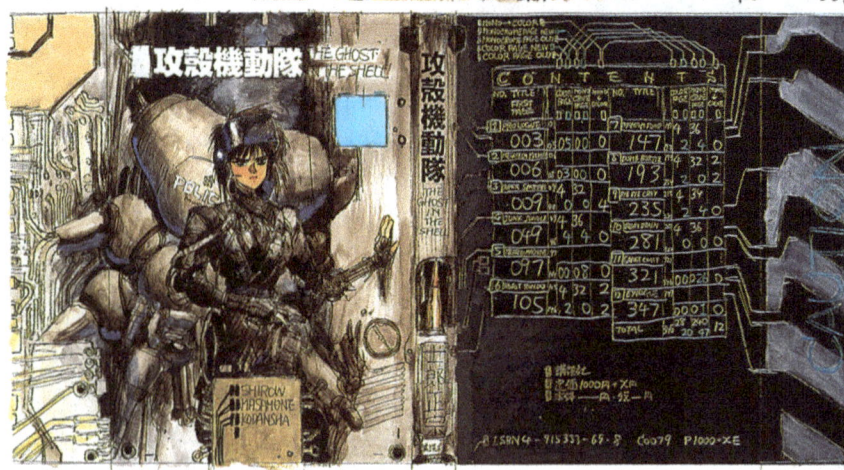

Rough draft for the tankobon (collected in Intron Depot).

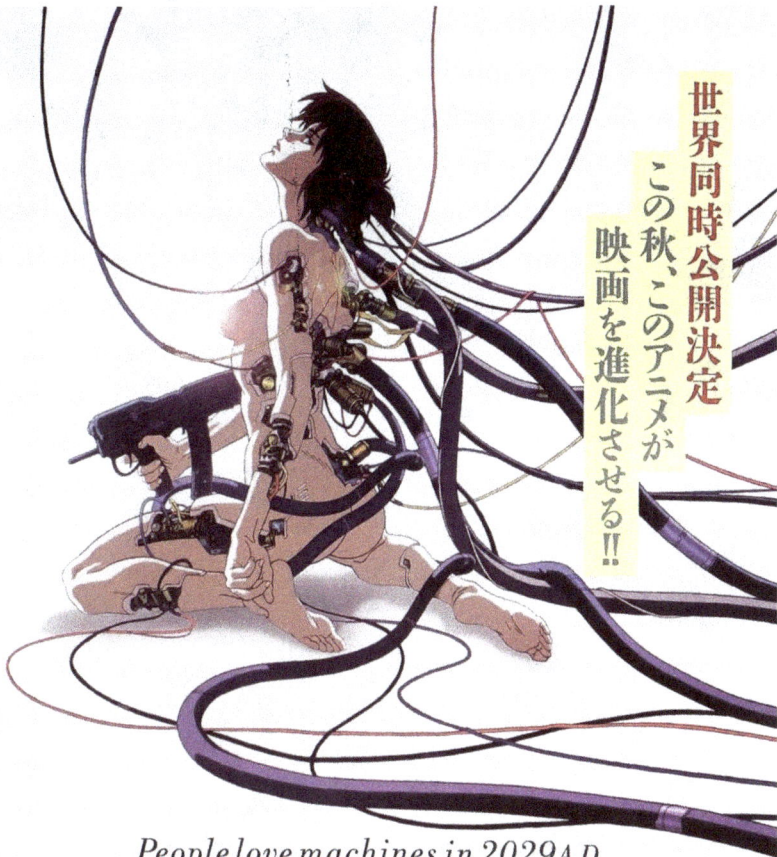

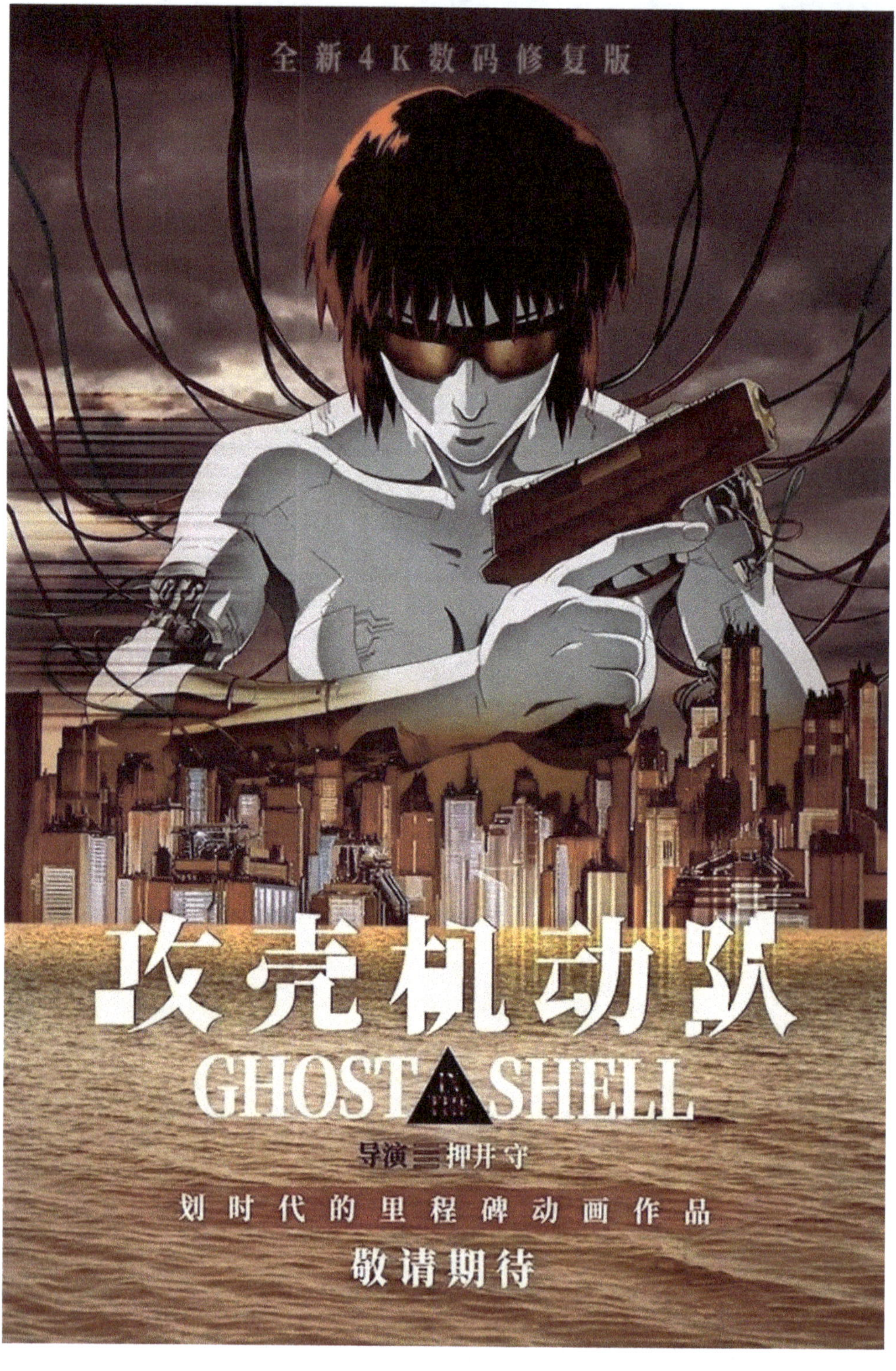
全新4K数码修复版
攻壳机动队
GHOST IN THE SHELL
导演 押井守
划时代的里程碑动画作品
敬请期待

PART ONE

MASAMUNE SHIROW

士郎 正宗

ROUGH

075

01

MASAMUNE SHIROW:
BIOGRAPHY AND WORKS

BIOGRAPHY.

Famously regarded as something of a recluse,[1] Masamune Shirow (not his real name, which is Masanori Ota), was born on November 23, 1961 in Higashinada, Kobe, Hyogo, and grew up in Kobe[2] (where he still lives. Kobe, pop. 1.5m, is 15 miles West of Osaka, in Kansai). He studied art (traditional techniques, like oil painting) at Osaka University, and his well-known *Appleseed manga*, which started out as a *dojinshi* (fan-based) work, was published in 1985 (by Seishinsha; later animated in a number of versions, beginning in 1988). During this time Shirow worked as an art teacher for five years.[3] Biographical information about Shirow is difficult to find outside of the published, official biogs, which are all short and all repeat the same data. (There's nothing on his background, his parents,[4] his marital status, etc).

Not only are there very few photographs publicly available of Masamune Shirow,[5] he has also declined to do TV interviews and audio interviews. When interviewed, journos tend to have to travel to meet him (in Kobe), rather than him travelling to Tokyo. You can spot the occasional satirical self-portrait in his *manga*, however:[6] sometimes as an octopus, sometimes as a *mangaka*. There are thus no filmed interviews with Shirow, and no audio interviews, on radio or in other audio formats.

Why are many *manga* artists and writers (and *animé* staff, too) so private? – to the point that photos of them are hard to find (let alone video footage)? Several reasons have been put forward. (1) *Mangakas* are

---

1 Shirow's media image is of a reclusive loner, rather like the Puppet Master and the Laughing Man in *Ghost In the Shell* (J. Clements, 2009, 309).
2 Kobe features prominently in the incredible *animé* series *Earth Maiden Arjuna* (dir. Shoji Kawamori, 2001).
3 How cool would it be to have the author of *Appleseed* and *Ghost In the Shell* as your art teacher!
4 In the 1990s he was looking after his ageing father.
5 Just one is widely available online. But is that really Masanori Ota?
6 Tho' not as many as Toshio Maeda (*Urotsukidoji*), who's fond of sending himself up.

private, often shy people;[7] they like to keep their personal lives separate from work. (2) They are not comfortable with being in the public spotlight. (3) They are workaholics, and being well-known could impinge on their work schedules (they wouldn't want to be approached by *otaku* – or anything or anybody that would take them away from their work).

Private, retiring, shy *mangaka* include the author of *Death Note* and *Bakuman* (Tsugumi Ohba), Kentaro Miura (*Berserk*) and Himoru Arakawa (*Fullmetal Alchemist, Silver Spoon*). And when a photo is required for publicity purposes, a *mangaka* will often draw a silly self-portrait instead (Arakawa pictures herself as a black-and-white, spotted cow, for example – she harks from rural Hokkaido). There *are manga* artists, tho', who're happy to be seen and interviewed: Katsuhiro Otomo, Hayao Miyazaki, Masashi Kishimoto, Hiro Mashima, Tite Kubo, etc.

It is striking, though, that someone so well-known, who's such a great artist, can avoid appearing – for his entire career – in newspapers, magazines, books, web pages, TV documentaries, filmed or radio interviews, photographs, articles, essays, etc.

So Masanori Ota – a.k.a. Masamune Shirow – remains a mystery: is he married? With kids? Is he straight? Gay? Is he a woman? Or a cyborg? (Shirow mentions he has a brother-in-law,[8] so presumably he has (or had) a sister).

Shirow-sensei started out writing fan stories (which he got into thru friends at Osaka University of Arts). Most comic artists are self-taught. Fans create *dojinshi manga*, which can range from simple home-made publications to high quality productions. Some *dojinshi* artists go on to become professional *manga* artists and writers. *Dojinshi* creators are often part of a group called *saakuru*.[9] While companies in the West often pursue copyright infringement (especially in the litigious U.S.A.), fan publications are more tolerated in Japanese culture. Most *dojinshi* portray existing *manga* characters; and often *dojinshi* are erotic (thus, many *dojinshi* depict well-known *manga* characters having sex).

Shirow-sensei was not one of those *mangaka* who drew comics as a child, starting out by copying by their favourites (*Dragon Ball* or *Tetsujin 28*, say). Shirow painted and drew as a child, but only really got into *manga* when he went to Osaka to study.

Like many successful *mangaka*, Masamune Shirow has produced a host of miscellaneous material, to be used for promotional work, for ads, for posters, for calendars, for collector's cards, and for the title and contents pages of *manga*. Plus commercial work, covers/ illustrations for novels, numerous magazine covers, designs and ideas for many *animé* shows, advice and designs for video games, designs for phone cards, etc. Shirow's work has also appeared in digital form in formats such as I-Phone, Android, I-Pad, E-books, websites and streaming.

In *Intro Depot: Ballistics*, Masamune Shirow portrays the familiar

7 If they do interviews, they still prefer to remain anonymous, without showing their faces (in either print, online or video interviews – some interviews are audio only).
8 In the notes to *Ghost In the Shell*.
9 It was estimated that there were 50,000 *manga* circles in Japan in the 1990s (F. Schodt, 2002, 37).

anxiety of the workaholic artist, which many *mangaka* can relate to:

> Maybe in my heart of hearts I just want to escape, since I spend so much time locked up in my studio. Yet when I do take a trip somewhere, I feel antsy without any work to do.

Among the elements and interests in the art of Masamune Shirow are: insects; tanks; guns and weaponry; utopias; political systems; nature; *mecha*; new technologies (with cyborgs, artificial intelligence and nano-robots a speciality); the future; alternative societies; and sexy warrior women.

In a 1995 interview, Shirow noted:

> Emphasizing a combination of females and mecha, as I do, is something that's been around for a long time, and neither the idea of computer brains nor Special Forces units are themselves new, either. But as with cooking, even if the ingredients are the same, the way they are mixed together and the goal of the person doing the mixing creates a different flavor. In that sense, if the result of cooking can be called original, so, too, can my work. I always try to draw manga that are true to myself.

Masamune Shirow started out as a *manga* fan, and has mainly worked on his own ('I personally like working alone'): he has not been an apprentice or assistant to established *manga* artists, tho' he has employed assistants – such as Hagane Kotetsu (actually a pseudonym for Shirow, or 'the other Shirow', the evil twin, as he calls him),[10] and Pure.[11]

WORKS.

The impact of the work of Masamune Shirow[12] has been immense in *animé* and *manga*: *Ghost In the Shell* alone led to not one but two classic movies, two outstanding TV series (plus a third, the *Arise* series), and spin-off movies. Add to that the live-action *Ghost* of 2017, and more *Ghosties* on the way. Then there's the *Appleseed* computer-assisted animations and *Appleseed* cel animation, plus *Black Magic, Real Drive, Ghost Hound* (*Unseen World*) and *Dominion: Tank Police*. It all adds up to a remarkable presence in TV and cinema.

The 'golden age' of Masamune Shirow's output would be the mid-1980s to the early 1990s, the era of his most celebrated works (*Ghost In the Shell, Appleseed, Dominion: Tank Police, Orion, Black Magic*, etc). This was also the period of the first *animé* adaptations of Shirow's *manga* (culminating in the *Ghost In the Shell* movie of 1995).

In the West, the *Appleseed manga*, Shirow's first big hit in comics, was published initially by Eclipse Comics and Studio Proteus (1988-1992),

---

10 Since 'Kotetsu's' departure, Shirow has been working on his own.
11 Pure produced the *manga Pixy Junket* (Seishinsha, 1992).
12 In the West, we're reading Shirow in translation. It gets irritating at times when Shirow's dialogue is translated into quippy, North American English – 'jeez', 'man', 'uh', 'crap' (and in *Appleseed* Briareos always calls Deunan 'girl').

and then in four volumes by Dark Horse[13] (in 1995), with the titles: 1. *The Promethean Challenge*, 2. *Prometheus Unbound*, 3. *The Scales of Prometheus* and 4. *The Promethean Balance*.

Among Masamune Shirow's early works are: *Areopagus Arther* (1980), *Atlas* magazine; *Yellow Hawk* (1981), *Atlas* magazine; *Colosseum Pick* (1982), *Funya* fanzine and (1990), *Comic Fusion Atpas* fanzine; *Pursuit* (1982), *Kintalion* fanzine; *Optional Orientation* (1984), *Atlas* magazine; *Battle On Mechanism* (1984), *Atlas* magazine; *Metamorphosis In Amazoness* (1984), *Atlas* magazine; *Alice In Jargon* (1984), *Atlas* magazine; and *Bike Nut* (1985), *Dorothy* fanzine.

Other *manga* works include: *Gun Dancing* (1986), *Young Magazine Kaizokuban*; *Pile Up* (1987), *Young Magazine Kaizokuban*; and *Neurohard: The Planet of a Bee* (1992-1994), in *Comic Dragon*. Both *Gun Dancing* (1986) and *Pile Up* (1987) were detective stories published in *Young Magazine*. The *manga* were later released in a CD-ROM format (as 'e-manga'). Shirow has created many covers for magazines such as *Comickers*, *Young*, *B-Club*, *Newtype*, *Groove*, *Manga Max*, *Comic Box* and *Comic Gum* (many of which are republished in his calendars or other collections).

Masamune Shirow's other works include his first comic, *Black Magic M-66* (made into an animation in 1987),[14] and *Dominion: Tank Police* (1988, published in *Comi Comi*, and also animated, in 1988, *Dominion: Tank Police*, directed by Koichi Mashimo), with a sequel in 1992, in *Comic Gaia*. *Dominion Tank Police* revealed Shirow in a light-hearted mood, a departure from his usual more serious pieces – altho' there is a lot more humour in the *Ghost In the Shell manga* than in its animated adaptations.

A story set on Mars in the future seems to have been planned then abandoned by Uncle Shirow; it would probably have centred around a police team[15] or the private detectives in the *W Tails Cat*, *Galgrease* and *Galhound* books (with Poseidon Industrial featuring prominently as a setting). In the end, what we have are the fragmentary plots collected in the *W Tails Cat* and *Galhound* volumes, where the emphasis is on erotic scenarios and depicting the girls as glamorous pin-ups. (Based around a female cop team, the Mars story would've featured tons of *mecha* – robots, robot tanks, motorcycles, cybernetics, and of course guns a-plenty).

There are collections of images related to *Ghost In the Shell*, including: *Cybergirls Portfolio*, *Cyber-world*, *Cyberdelics* and *Pieces Gem 01 – Ghost In the Shell Data + Alpha*. Shirow, however, has produced more extra material featuring Deunan Knute of *Appleseed* than Major Motoko Kusanagi. And he has focussed more recently on a bunch of other female characters, rather than Motoko, such as Cyril Brooklyn and her chums at

13 Dark Horse, one of the publishers in the Occident of Shirow-sensei, was founded in 1986 (or 1988) by Mike Richardson (b. 1950). Early publications included *Outlanders* by Joji Manabe and *Godzilla #1*. Dark Horse became the third largest publisher of *manga* in the New World. Dark Horse has specialized in horror, sci-fi and action *manga*, and published *Akira*. Its other titles include *Oh My Goddess!* and *What's Michael?* Dark Horse also licensed properties such as *Star Wars*, *Buffy the Vampire Slayer*, *Aliens*, *Predator*, *The Incredibles* and *Indiana Jones*. Dark Horse's Western products included *Sin City*, *The Amazing Adventures of the Escapist*, *Barb Wire*, *Grendel*, *X*, *Hell-boy*, *Concrete* and *300* (many of these were published under the *Dark Horse Presents* label).
14 This featured Shirow as animation director, but the experience was not good.
15 The space police team, a.k.a. S.S.A.A.T. (they appear in many of Shirow's erotic works).

the detective agency on Mars (in the *W Tails Cat* and *Calgrease* series), and Toguihime, the warrior-princess in historical Nihon (in the *Hellhound* books).

Masamune Shirow has also contributed designs to *Blue Uru* (1992, unmade), *Landlock* (Yasuhiro Matsumura, 1996) and *Gundress* (Katsuyoshi Yatabe, 1999).[16] Shirow provided the story for *Ghost Hound* (a.k.a. *Unseen World*, Ryutaro Nakamura, 2007) and *Real Drive* (2008), more animated shows.

Masamune Shirow's interviews have been published in a huge number of magazines, including: *Melti Lemon, Young, Metal Kids, Comics Informational, B-Club, Comic Box, Cyber Comics, Out, Anime V, Super Game, Hobby Japan, Comickers, Groove, Screentone, Monthly Newtype, Afternoon, Magazine S, Canopri Comic, Comic Ryu, Videoboy, Kissui Bijin, D.M.M., Newtype A*, etc. (So he's happy to chat about his work, but not in video or audio form).

An exhibition commemorating the 25th anniversary of *Ghost In the Shell* was shown in Japan in 2014. It featured artwork by Shirow, *genga* and sketches from each of the animated versions of *Ghost In the Shell*, etc (an artbook was published, too).

Masamune Shirow is a geek's *mangaka*, an *otaku*'s artist. In Japan, *otaku* signifies a nerd, geek or obsessive fan, while in the West it simply means a fan.[17] The 1990s term *moe* is also employed (it means 'to sprout'); for Toshio Okada, a *moe* fan is obsessed, but an *otaku* learns the background and details. Magazines sympathetic to *otaku*-dom include *Monthly Shonen Ace, Dragon Age, Comic Gum, Ultra Jump* and *Dengeki Daioh*. *Otaku* culture has been famously celebrated in *animé* in *Otaku no Otaku* (1991), and later works such as *Comic Party* (1995), *Maniac Road* (2002), *Genshiken* (2002) and *Pretty Maniacs* (2004). *Otaku* elements crop up in *animé* such as *Eden of the East, Ghost In the Shell: Stand Alone Complex* (Aoi is an *otaku*), *Paranoia Agent* and *Neon Genesis Evangelion*.

Editors play a vital role in the development of *manga* and a *mangaka*'s work and career: for Masamune Shirow, his editor at Seishinsha in Osaka was Harumichi Aoki (Aoki was an important early supporter of Shirow: he invited Shirow to publish *Appleseed* after seeing his *dojinshi* work – and *Black Magic* in particular). Shigehiko Ogasawara was one of Shirow's long-time editors. (Although Shirow had assistants, he said that often the only visitors he got in Kobe were Aoki and Ogasawara).

Koichi Yuri (b. 1947) was one of the editors of Masamune Shirow's early output – Yuri worked for *Young Magazine*, where *Ghost In the Shell* was published (it was Yuri who asked Shirow for a flashier title than *Ghost In the Shell*; so Shirow came up with *Shell Squad*, a.k.a., *Mobile Armored Riot Police*. Thus, altho' *Ghost In the Shell* is known as *Ghost In the Shell* outside Japan, in Japan it is *Mobile Armored Riot Police* as well as *Ghost In the Shell*).

---

16 On *Gundress* and *Landlock*, Masamune Shirow was credited as a 'planning assistant': the shows were released partly to cash in on the success of *Ghost In the Shell*.
17 Retreating from society was a growing trend in the 1990s, dubbed *hikkomori* (the issue has also been explored in *animé*).

In his "Afterword" to *Appleseed* (volume one), Masamune Shirow acknowledged that he wasn't as prolific as the commercial *manga* artists working in Tokyo. He wasn't producing 20 or more pages for the weekly and 30+ pages for the monthly *manga* magazines. Instead, he was publishing once a year: 'I've been very lucky'. To produce *Ghost In the Shell*, Shirow said (in 1995) that it took him about forty days to draw forty pages (i.e., one chapter):

> For *Ghost in the Shell* I drew an average of forty pages per episode and it took me around forty days to do one episode. But the number of hours I can work, and the efficiency of my work fluctuates, so it's not always possible to do a page a day.

The fifth volume of *Appleseed* has been rumoured for a long time (Shirow-sensei tended to deflect questions about the 5th book apologetically – he had already moved on to other things).

The many publishers of the work of Masamune Shirow have happily exploited it in many formats. The *manga* have been published, for ex, in digest (*bunkobon*) and *Wideban* (wide edition) sizes, as limited editions (and collector's editions = *Kanzeban*), and as part of special sets. Shirow's work has been released with booklets, posters, CDs, puzzles, etc. In ring binders. As booklet posters. As CD-sized booklets or posters. In plastic folders.

It's worth remembering that much of Masamune Shirow's work has been published in series, not all at once: his *manga* works, for instance, such as the big three – *Ghost In the Shell, Dominion: Tank Police* and *Appleseed* – were published in chapters over a long period of time (as with almost all longer *manga*). Only *later* were they collected into volumes. Thus, not only did each comic alter over the months and then years of publication (like any *manga*), they were also adjusted when they were collected together and published as *tankobon* (for instance, pages would be left out, or added, or changed). There are further changes when comics are published for overseas editions; Shirow sometimes revises his *manga* considerably for the collected editions.

By the time of the success of the *Appleseed* and *Ghost In the Shell manga*, in the late 1980s/ early 1990s, Masamune Shirow's publishers and editors would've informed the *mangaka* that if he kept producing *manga* like that, he would be rich (and so would they!). Indeed, many fans of Shirow-sensei would be very happy if he had simply gone on drawing *Appleseed* and *Ghost In the Shell* – and *Dominion* and *Orion* and *Black Magic*. The thought of *Ghost In the Shell* and/ or *Appleseed* extending into a long-running *manga* series, like *Berserk*, *Urusei Yatsura* or *Oh! My Goddess*, is mind-boggling (tho' hoping for a 700-chapter *manga* like *Naruto* from Shirow is probably too much!). But just think where Shirow might've taken the stories of *Appleseed* and *Ghost In the Shell*, if someone had locked him in a room from 1991 to 2011, and told him to write, to draw, to make *manga*!

No doubt publishers and editors have over the years pleaded and begged Shirow Masamune to produce either: (1) more of *Ghost In the Shell* (and/ or *Appleseed*), or (2) something in a similar manner.

MASAMUNE SHIROW'S WORK SINCE THE 1980s.

Masamune Shirow has received plenty of negative criticism over the years. Some fans don't like his digital artwork, with its images manipulated in Photoshop, Lightwave or similar digital software (the plasticky, floaty look of digital imagery, like computer-assisted scenes in movies, aren't to everybody's tastes. It *looks* photo-realistic, but it's still a *cartoon*). Some fans hanker after the watercolour and gouache artwork. Some fans find his stories too obscure (in the later *Ghost In the Shell* outings, for instance), or muddled, or way too arcane. Some fans don't want the out-there porn, where man-beasts, monsters and aliens do naughty things with oiled, pneumatic, young women, and some find the emphasis on eroticism too much and too bizarre.

But there's no doubt that Shirow Masamune is the King of 'Fan Service' (despite *strong* competition from other *mangaka*!) – whether it's *mecha*, cybernetica, esoterica or erotica. And by now Shirow is a Super-Class-A artist in the hyperspace of digital art, an artistic version of the Super-Class-A hackers in his *Ghost In the Shell*.

'Fan service' in Japanese pop culture means delivering to audiences something fetishized and glamourized: *mecha* (robots and machines), for example, lovingly depicted, or something sexy – glimpses of underwear or parts of the body.

Masamune Shirow has been creating erotic art throughout his career, but in his later career, it has greatly increased in proportion to his other published work. Also, it hasn't changed too much for twenty or more years: posterbooks published in 2019 (such as *Greaseberries 4*), employ the same approach as pin-ups and erotica published in 2000. But erotica is what Shirow wants to do: 'I always try to draw *manga* that are true to myself.'

Masamune Shirow has published his erotic imagery and stories in anthology magazines of erotica such as *Canopri Comic* and *Comic Anrthurium*. In those magazines, Shirow's digital art sits alongside the usual porn comic strips of schoolgirls and teachers, brothers and sisters, mom and her son's best friend, gang rape in the school store room, etc. The *Pieces, W Tails Cat, Greaseberries, Galgrease et al* series are marketed as 'collections of Shirow Masamune's full colour indecent works', in individual, colour book form.

Notice, though, that none of the regular publishers of Japanese *manga* in the West – Viz, Dark Horse, Del Rey, Yen Press, etc – have produced English-translated editions of Shirow's erotica. There is a market for it – there are many collectors of Shirowania in the Western world – but maybe not enough of a market to justify publishing a full-colour[18] English edition. The troublesome nature of some of Shirow's erotica wouldn't put

18 Shirow would likely insist on full colour – he is picky about the colour reproduction of his works (which would also mean good quality paper, etc).

off many publishers of similar material. (Erotica is a long-established sub-genre of the comics market in Europe and the U.S.A., producing artists such as Manara, Altuna, Serpieri, von Gotha, Coq, Ferocius, Lemay, Noe, Molinari, etc).

The *Hellhound* series and the *Toguihime/ Japanesque* series in particular cry out for a Western/ English edition. This is some of Shirow's finest art, a unique, inventive and luscious Dream of Japan (you could leave out the more explicit erotica from *Hellhound*).

Negative reactions to Masamune Shirow's art include the wish that Shirow had spent more of his talents and time on projects 'worthy' of his skills, instead of so many erotic pin-ups, posters and mini-stories. A girl getting assaulted on a train by a black guy, a girl being gang-raped in a swimming pool, and lubed-up ladies being set upon by spiders and aliens just aren't up to Shirow's artistic standards for the critical complainers (tho' the girls changing into high fashion outfits and steam-punk accessories every ten seconds is very Shirowian, and the quality of the artwork is outstanding).

When you know just what Masamune Shirow is capable of, in terms of storytelling and conjuring up fantasy worlds, it can seem way below his talents to produce yet another Photoshop file of a girl pulling her panties up into her crotch. (But all of the paraphernalia surrounding that girl, the clothing, the accessories, the props, the furniture, etc, is amazing).

But wait – this is what Masamune Shirow *wants* to do, part of the time. He likes to produce erotica. And artists have depicted sexual acts for millennia. And a great artist has earned the right, perhaps, to do what the hell they like (or at least they've achieved the economic independence to be able to do that). Picasso, Renoir, Titian, Moreau, Fuseli, Schiele, Klimt, Ingres, Rodin, Correggio, Goya, Boucher, Cranach, Michelangelo, and thousands of other artists have created erotic material. Some other *manga* artists have produced erotica as a sidedline, such as: Kohta Hirano (*Hellsing*) and Sakurako Gokurakuin (*Sekirei*).

It's true that Masamune Shirow has probably spent more time on his erotic artwork than on the *Ghost In the Shell* and the *Appleseed mangas* put together! Instead of cyber-punk fantasies and urban thrillers, Shirow has, for many years now, been more interested in portraying pretty, young things in fetish gear being ogled and molested by monsters.

Masamune Shirow acts as the Great God of Digital Art, creating the template of a young woman and dressing her up in astonishing costumes and accessories. Shirow is very much like a puppeteer with his dolls – his art comes across sometimes like that old toy of childhood which had cardboard figures and paper clothes that you could cut out and pin to a figure (where you could endlessly switch round the combinations of items). Or like a doll with miniature clothes. Shirow's art is the digital version of playing with Barbie (with sex added).

To satisfy every fan or consumer is probably impossible – but many fans would be happy for Masamune Shirow to create as many erotic images as he likes – but only if he was also writing further installments of

Appleseed or *Ghost In the Shell,* or if he was conjuring up new sci-fi/fantasy stories.

We can all wish…

I wish – to pick just a few in the fantasy realm – that J.R.R. Tolkien hadn't spent so long fiddling around with his Middle-earth legends and had put them into published form (they were published after his death, unfinished and incomplete, as *The History of Middle-earth*).

And I wish that Robert E. Howard hadn't killed himself at the age of 30 (in 1936),[19] so we could have 100s of *Conan* and other fantasy tales.

In cinema, we lament the early deaths of F.W. Murnau and Andrei Tarkovsky; the persecution of Sergei Parajanov; and the long gaps between movies (and the struggle to find backing) of Orson Welles and Carol Theodor Dreyer.

The poster(book)s, pin-ups, calendars and other erotica produced by Masamune Shirow from the late 1990s onwards *do* tell stories – stories that can be evoked in a single image. A woman as a pirate on a galleon, a woman as a vampire surrounded by blood-drained victims, a woman as a secretary, etc. But these are not long-form *manga* stories, with many characters, with dramatic interactions and action scenes. They are one-off vignettes which emphasize one element above all: eroticism. (Or, you could argue, they stress design and art above all: these are images which call attention to themselves as artworks).

Who knew that Masamune Shirow would revert to the pin-up, nudie and *Heavy Metal*-style art and comics that he grew up on in the 1970s? Who imagined that Shirow-sensei would devote weeks and months of his precious time to creating images of sexy babes in clichéd scenarios out of the genres of horror, science fiction and fantasy (the big three)?

Well, yes – but Masamune Shirow had *already* been doing that with the *Appleseed* and *Ghost In the Shell* comics! There is erotic material *already* in the first *Ghost In the Shell* collected book and the four *Appleseed* volumes!

Here's another way of looking at this issue: maybe Masamune Shirow wanted to be an artist who creates erotic art all along, and the years of producing *Ghost In the Shell*, *Appleseed* and other *manga* were simply a side-show, something he got distracted by for a while (but also just happened to make him a millionaire).

For Jason Thompson in *Manga: The Complete Guide*, Masamune Shirow squanders his terrific ideas and scenarios in endless footnotes, obscure storytelling, and a depressing move towards erotica/ porn.

One of the popular views of Masamune Shirow in the Western world is that his *manga* work was outstanding in the 1980s and 1990s (tho' quirky, over-written and sometimes obscure), but that in the second half of his career he has sunk to the lows of producing weirdo porn.

---

19 Robert E. Howard was born in Peaster, Texas, in 1906. Howard spent most of his life in Cross Plains, Texas. He committed suicide in 1936 following his mother's death. Although literary critics often cite J.R.R. Tolkien as the creator of the sword and sorcery genre, Howard defined much of it with his *Conan* stories. These included "The Phoenix and the Sword", "The Scarlet Citadel", "The Tower of the Elephant", "Black Colossus", "The Slithering Shadow", "The Devil In Iron" and "Jewels of Gwahlur".

Yes, it's true, much of Shirow-sensei's work in the late 1990s until the present day has involved a *lot* of erotic material (erotic for some, porn for others). But this is not all that Shirow has been doing! Of course not: for ex, he has worked in *animé*, magazine covers, computer games, and novels.

(1) Shirow has advised on the two *Ghost In the Shell: Stand Alone Complex* TV series, the *Ghost In the Shell: Stand Alone Complex* spin-off movie *Ghost In the Shell: Solid State Society*, the *Ghost In the Shell: Arise* series (and movie), the *Appleseed* computer-aided remakes, the *Appleseed* TV series, and the *TANK S.W.A.T. 01* show.

(2) Shirow has creator credit on several *animé* series including: *Ghost Hound, Real Drive, W Tails Cat* and *Pandora In the Crimson Shell: Ghost Urn*.

(3) Shirow has continued with commercial commissions and design work.

(4) Shirow has created covers for books, and insert illustrations.

(5) Shirow has produced cover artwork for magazines (such as *Comic Gum* and *Canopri*).

(6) Shirow has made artwork, illustrations and covers for spin-off books from his *manga* (including *Black Magic, Appleseed, Real Drive, Dominion: Tank Police* and *Ghost In the Shell: Stand Alone Complex*).

(7) Shirow has produced further installments of the *Intron Depot* series (*Blades, Ballistics, Battalion*, etc).

(8) And Shirow has contributed to the designs and ideas of computer games based on his *manga*.

Further recent Shirow artwork includes: *Seven Traps, Cover Girl Fragments, Dead Drive,* and the *Shirow Masamune Studio Diary*.

✳

Meanwhile, other artists and writers have produced tie-in comics based on each of the animated adaptations of Shirow's works, including *Ghost In the Shell* by Akinori Endo (1995, 1998) • novels of *Ghost In the Shell: Stand Alone Complex* by Junichi Fujisaku (2004-05) • two comics for the *Stand Alone Complex* (in 2009) and *Arise* (in 2013) versions of *Ghost In the Shell* • *Black Magic* by Hideki Kakinuma (2005-08) • *Real Drive* by Yoshinobu Akita (2008) • *Appleseed XIII* by Yoshiki Sakurai (2012) • *Appleseed: Alpha* by Iou Kuroda (in 2014) • light novels and collections of short stories have appeared • a theatrical play (in 2015) • a tribute anthology to *Ghost In the Shell* by contemporary *mangaka* (in 2017) • a history of *Ghost In the Shell* in animated form, *Perfect Book* (in 2017) • art books for the live-action movie (in 2017) • and an original *manga* spin-off (in 2019). Shirow has produced artwork, including book covers, for some of those tie-in/ spin-off works.

RESEARCH AND INFLUENCES.

Masamune Shirow has probably been influenced by, well, everybody (like everybody else). It's easy to see just how much Shirow has consumed of books, TV shows, movies, photos, art and music (Shirow has remarked that he's of the TV generation, the baby boomer generation, and TV and movies have influenced him more than comics; he got into comics later, at university). Numerous influences are easy to detect: the usual North American sci-fi movies (*Alien, Blade Runner, RoboCop, War Games, 2001: A Space Odyssey, The Terminator,* etc).[20] The usual roster of sci-fi authors: Arthur C. Clarke, Phil Dick, Isaac Asimov, Robert Heinlein, etc. Reference and scientific books and magazines. *Akira* and Katsuhiro Otomo (an influence on *Appleseed*).[21] *Thunderbirds* and other Gerry Anderson adventure (and team) shows. And Osamu Tezuka (of course!).

Hayao Miyazaki was a big influence on Masamune Shirow – especially when he was making the *animé* of *Black Magic* (the influence of *Laputa: Castle In the Sky* and of course *Nausicaä of the Valley of the Wind* is enormous on all subsequent fantasy and sci-fi *animé* and *manga*. Miyazaki's *Nausicaä manga* likely influenced the style of Shirow's subsequent comics – such as the use of very dense panels, crammed with information, and the rounded, organic forms).

For research, Masamune Shirow consumes (imported) books on military hardware, on art and sculpture, on cars, on micro-machinery, on military robots, on insects ('I have quite a lot of books on bees'), on biotechnology, on Greek mythology, plus 17 or 18 magazines a month, and as many *manga* as imported books.[22]

As his notes on his images relate, Masamune Shirow has a vast library of imagery and material which he draws on to create his art. Some come from photographs, some from photos he's taken himself, some from photocopies, and some from books. The backgrounds are constructed, piece by piece, rather than being a complete photo (tho' Shirow will occasionally use a whole photograph – of something like a deep-sea submersible). Shirow is known for using a photocopier to generate interesting textures (such as photocopying rocks, metallic images or the cloth of *kimonos*). The humble photocopier is an often overlooked tool in the creation of *manga*; it's used for all sorts of tasks. In 1995, Shirow commented:

> I use a color copy machine and copy rock or metallic images onto a 'transparent film with an adhesive on one side' (reversing or flipping positive and negative images, altering colors, and changing sizes), and then cut and paste them into the drawing. I usually use acrylic paint and apply several thin layers.

For many Japanese *animé* filmmakers, Masamune Shirow included, *Blade Runner* has been a major inspiration, a storehouse of possibilities. No matter what you think of *Blade Runner*, its importance for Japanese *animé* is enormous. *Blade Runner* has influenced *Akira* (Katsuhiro Otomo, 1988), *Patlabor, Legend of the Overfiend*, and of course *Appleseed* and

---

20 *Animé* filmmakers have been hugely influenced from seeing a number of Western movies: *2001: A Space Odyssey, Blade Runner, Alien, Star Wars, The Terminator, Thunderbirds* and *King Kong* (and to a lesser degree *RoboCop* and Ray Harryhausen's monster movies).
21 Shirow has cited *Macross* as an influence.
22 Masamune Shirow, in T. Ledoux, 1997, 42.

Ghost In the Shell. And Mamoru Oshii has spoken repeatedly of the influence of *Blade Runner* on his cinema.

Probably the most influential aspect of *Blade Runner* was its *mise-en-scène*, copied and developed in many subsequent films, such as *Judge Dredd* (1995), *Brazil* (Terry Gilliam, 1985), the *Star Wars* prequels (1999-2005), the *Batman* series (1989-), *Twelve Monkeys* (Terry Gilliam, 1995), *Cyborg* (Albert Pyun, 1989), *Total Recall* (Paul Verhoeven, 1990), *Strange Days* (Kathryn Bigelow, 1995), *Johnny Mnemonic* (Robert Longo, 1995), *The Salute of the Jugger* (David Peoples, 1990), the *Matrix* series (1999-2003), and *The Fifth Element* (Luc Besson, 1997).[23] The influence continued in the 2000s and 2010s.

INFLUENCED BY MASAMUNE SHIROW.

There are numerous instances of the influence on Masamune Shirow's art on Asian and Western art and artists. Some of the obvious examples include: *Gunnm* (a.k.a. *Battle Angel Alita*) by Yukito Kishiro, a futuristic comic about a female cyborg/ robot which's really a footnote to *Ghost In the Shell*. The *Burst Angel* (2004) *animé* series is a mere replay of *Appleseed* and *Ghost In the Shell*, as is the *Vexille*[24] movie of 2007 and the *Psycho-Pass* series (2012).

Hyper Police (1994-, by Mee) was influenced by Masamune Shirow. *Pixy Junket* (1992), by one of Shirow's assistants, Pure, bears his imprint. *Silent Möbius* (1988-99, Kadokawa Shoten) by Kia Asamiya 'borrows liberally'[25] from Shirow. *Alice In Lostworld* (2000-01) was influenced by Shirow. There's an amusing *hommage* to Shirow in *xxxHolic* (by the Clamp collective), when the magical girls play with a Tachikoma tank toy.

In Western/ Hollywood cinema, Masamune Shirow's influence is easy to spot in the *Star Wars* prequels, in the *Matrix* movies, in *Avatar*, in *Minority Report*, in the *Avengers* series, and in many a superhero flick.

---

23 Other flicks linked to Phil Dick's work include *A Nightmare On Elm Street*, *Mulholland Drive*, *Fight Club*, *Vanilla Sky*, *Donnie Darko*, *Videodrome*, *Existenz*, *Being John Malkovich*, *Adaptation*, *Eternal Sunshine of the Spotless Mind*, *Dark City*, *The Truman Show*, *Gattaca* and *Memento*.
24 *Vexille* shamelessly combines *Appleseed* and *Ghost In the Shell* (and uses some of the same personnel, such as the voice of Batou, Akio Otsuka). We're back in a futuristic world of robots, androids, mobile suits, an *élite* S.W.A.T. team (called Sword), terrorism and info-war. Aside from some fun *James Bond*-scale stunts (like a plane slicing thru the whole wing of a mansion so the super-villain Saito can make his escape hanging onto it), and over-stuffed design work (robots're everywhere), the most compelling aspect of *Vexille* is the concept of a Japan that seals itself off from the rest of the world for ten years. This is a cyber/ digital version of Japan's self-imposed political isolation during the Edo period, vividly portrayed with 3-D graphics to evoke hi-tech barriers which prevent information – and people – from entering or leaving Nihon.
25 J. Thompson, 2007, 340.

Masamune Shirow a.k.a. Masanori Ota
(this is a rare photograph of Shirow).

Below: Shirow's home town Kobe (photo: I-Stock).

（マンガ基礎テクニック講座/1989/美術出版社）

Masamune Shirow's sketch of his studio in 1989.

Masamune Shirow's self-portrait, included
in the manga of Ghost In the Shell

●士郎さんに直撃 Q&A!

【攻殻の単行本2巻はいつ頃に?】

●1998年の中〜後半の労力ほとんどを使って仕上げる予定です。単行本1巻のように並べやすい内容ではないので、調整が難航しています。大幅な加筆、「外科手術」が必要になっていますね。可能な限り早く仕上げるべく努力してますので、もうしばらくお待ちください。

【これから発売予定の作品は?】

●「INTRON DEPOT 2」が1998年前半に青心社から出ます。1992年から1997年にかけて描いたイラストの内、ファンタジー系を中心にまとめた画集です。サブタイトルをつける予定です。いずれは「攻殻」1と2のカラー部分だけを集めた「ID・3」を講談社から出します。「攻殻」以外の1992年から1997年のメカ系イラストは「ID・4」になる予定ですが、これもそう遠くない将来に形にできると思います。
それと、青心社から出版される(仮)「イスラエル」という小説に格闘&エロ系カラーイラストを描きました。著者は「メガブレイド」の出海まこと氏です。

●攻殻Tシャツ&ポスター発売!

●講談社が漫画のキャラクターグッズ制作に本格的に取り組むことになり、「攻殻」ではTシャツと超大判ポスターを計画中。予約限定生産方式で、来年2月頃からヤンマガ誌上で告知&予約開始。「サイバデリックス」ほど高いものにはならんでしょう。

1997年、士郎さんは久々に漫画家であった。サイバやゲームやいろんな動きもあったけど、なんといっても一連載がYMにとっては記憶されるべき大事件だったよ。そして今回の赤BUTA……。士郎さん、来年も漫画家でいてくれよ〜!

●士郎正宗完全BIBLIOGRAPHY

「アップルシード1」	青心社	1985
「アップルシード2」	青心社	1985
「ブラックマジック」	青心社	1985
「ドミニオン」(絶版)	白泉社	1986
「ブラックマジック M66 絵コンテ集」	青心社	1986
「アップルシード3」	青心社	1987
「1988アップルシード・カレンダーブック」(絶版)	青心社	1987
「アップルシード4」	青心社	1989
「アップルシード・データブック」	青心社	1990
「攻殻機動隊」	講談社	1991
「仙術超攻殻オリオン」	青心社	1991
「INTRON DEPOT 1」	青心社	1992
「ドミニオン」(白泉社版の再刊+番外編を収録)	青心社	1993
「ドミニオンC1・コンフリクト編 第1話」	青心社	1995
「コミックガイア版 アップルシード総集編 士郎正宗ハイパーノーツ」	青心社	1995
「1997ドミニオン・カレンダー」(絶版)	青心社	1996
「攻殻機動隊 Cyberdelics」(ポスターBOX)	講談社	1996
「1998士郎正宗カレンダー GEMCAT」	青心社	1997
※青心社・問い合わせ先 ☎06-543-2718

●未確認!? 情報、乱れ打ち!

●秋に発売予定だったゲーム「攻殻」のアニメメイキングビデオは、4月発売予定。●Windows版ゲーム「ブラックマジック」、価格9800円(税別)でウィズから発売中。●「ヴァレリア・ファイル」シリーズ(谷甲州・作)のさし絵を士郎さんが執筆予定。中央公論社から。●富士見書房から発売中のトレーディング・カードゲーム「モンスター・コレクション」に士郎さんも少し参加。●講談社から「攻殻」のメカ系解析本とノベライゼイション第2弾が。

SHIROW NEWS!

Manga and artwork by Masamune Shirow.

TV and movies based on the work of Masamune Shirow

GHOST IN THE SHELL.

Masamune Shirow's *manga Kôkaku Kidôtai* (*Ghost In the Shell*)[1] – his signature work – was first published in 1989, in the Kodansha magazine *Young* (where *Akira, Initial D, 3 x 3 Eyes* and *Basilisk* also first appeared). Shirow maintained his distance from the world centre of *animé* and *manga*, Tokyo, remaining in Kobe. It's no surprise that Shirow (like most Japanese), hasn't travelled outside of Japan (he says he'd like to visit the U.S.A., but, ironically for such a *mecha* junkie, he's afraid of planes). 'I've never been overseas, but I do think it's necessary' (he said that years ago, but it's likely he still hasn't been outside Nippon).

In Japan, *Ghost In the Shell* is called *Kôkaku Kidôtai*, which means *Mobile Armored Riot Police* – a more suitable title, really, than the more poetic, abstract title of *Ghost In the Shell* (Shirow's preference – which became the subtitle). In Spanish, it's *Ghost in the Shell: Espectro Virtual*, in Italian, it's *Lo Spirito nel Guscio*, in Portuguese it's *O Fantasma do Futuro*, and in Polish it's *Duch w Pancerzu*.

The *manga* refers to artificial intelligence, medicine, science, British politics, a lot of Japanese politics, the *Bible*, Hayao Miyazaki, and writers such as A.E. van Vogt and Isaac Asimov. (More people consume science fiction in Japan than anywhere else. There are many science fiction clubs in Japan, often in schools and colleges[2]).

You'll hear (or read) certain words recurring in the *Ghost In the Shell* world: *ningen* (humans), *gosuto* (ghost), *robotto* (robot), *tamashi* (soul), *saibogu* (cyborg), and *mashin* or *kikai* (machine).

There are six animated movies of *Ghost In the Shell* and four TV series. All are from Production I.G., Bandai, Kodansha, Dentsu, Nippon TV and associated companies: two movies directed by Mamoru Oshii, three spin-off movies from the TV series directed by Kenji Kamiyama, and the *Arise* Original Video Animations, TV series and movie. Add the *manga* by Masamune Shirow to that, and the spin-off *manga* (which re-tell the *Ghost In the Shell: Stand Alone Complex* TV series), and the merchandizing and the video games, and the live-action flick of 2017 (from Paramount/ DreamWorks/ Reliance/ Shanghai Film/ Huahua/ Arad), and you have a pretty big franchise. (There are more *Ghost In the Shell* adaptations in the pipeline: a new (fourth) TV series was announced by Production I.G. in April, 2017, to be called *Ghost In the Shell S.A.C. 2045*; it bowed in 2020. Every few years, it seems, the President of Production I.G., Mitsuhisa Ishikawa,[3] announces, *right!*, it's time for another *Ghost* series).

That idea that Masamune Shirow had for *Ghost In the Shell* in his early twenties has made him a millionaire. It's 'The Franchise That Won't Quit'. Other producers and artists of *animé* and *manga* must look at the *Ghost In the Shell* franchise and think, *sh¡t, how does he do it?* After all, it's a multi-million earner from only three *tankobons*!

No – it's *one book*! – the entire *Ghost In the Shell* franchise has been

1 *Gosuto In Za Sheru* and *Kokaku Kidotai* mean *Ghost in the Shell* and *Mobile Armoured Riot Police*.
2 G. Poitras, 2001, 35.
3 Ishikawa says his favourite animated movie is *Ghost In the Shell*.

based in the main on just one volume of *manga*. Yes, just 350 pages for a franchise that's generated million$ and influenced so many people. The other two *Ghost* books came later (in 2001 and 2003), and, besides, most of the adaptations have drawn on that all-important first *Ghost In the Shell* comic.

Of course, Shirow-sama has had plenty of help: the *Ghost In the Shell* franchise has been exploited by Production I.G., Bandai Entertainment in the U.S.A., and Manga Entertainment in Europe for every cent it can muster: thus, the TV series and the movies have been sold singly and in box sets for home entertainment formats such as video, DVD and Blu-ray; the movies have been re-mastered and updated (*Ghost In the Shell 2.0*); the TV shows have been broadcast in Russia, Germany, Italy, Canada, Spain, Oz, etc; the *Ghost In the Shell manga* has been re-issued (including recently in large format books). Add games, novels, artbooks. And on and on it goes. Same with any big franchise. Look at the *Harry Potter* or *Star Wars* franchises for textbook examples of commercial exploitation; and of course, the Walt Disney corporation still leaves everybody else behind when it comes to finding new ways of drumming up $$$$$.

The *Ghost In the Shell* movies and TV shows explore numerous aspects of science fiction, and science fiction cinema. Cyborgs, robots and artificial intelligence or life is an obvious one. But also the significance of time and memory;[4] the sublime; the role of the individual in society; how societies should be policed; and metaphysics, the soul and the divine.

The *Ghost In the Shell* world boils down to four principal characters, really:

• Major Motoko Kusanagi (Atsuko Tanaka),
• Batou (Akio Otsuka)
• Togusa (Kôichi Yamadera),
• and their boss, Daiksuke Aramaki (Tamio Ôki).

Most of the time the *Ghost In the Shell* TV series (and the movies) stay with either Kusanagi and Batou, or the Chief and Kusanagi, or Batou and Togusa, or Togusa and Kusanagi. In the *animé* TV shows, Motoko often spends more time with Aramaki than Batou or Togusa, but Aramaki tends to appear only to set the narrative rolling – the exposition scene following the opening set-up scene (it's the same in the *Ghost In the Shell manga*). Or he'll appear halfway thru to head-up the operation which'll climax the show's Part B.

Some of the later *animé* adaptations of the *Ghost In the Shell manga* have *sidelined* Motoko Kusanagi: *Ghost In the Shell 2: Innocence*, for instance, focusses on Batou and Togusa, and *Ghost In the Shell: Stand Alone Complex: Solid State Society* followed that example. Yet for Masamune Shirow, Motoko is absolutely central to *Ghost In the Shell* – Shirow is mad about putting women in the central roles in his stories. In fact, Shirow has gone in the *opposite* direction from the *animés*, and made Motoko *even more* central to *Ghost In the Shell* (in the *Ghost In the Shell* sequel *manga*, for instance, Batou, Aramaki, Boma, Togusa *et al* are either

---

4 There are disquisitions on how memory has been externalized in the digital era.

relegated to cameos, or don't appear at all. The sequel is *The Motoko Kusanagi Show*).

Let's remind ourselves that the two best-known and most successful of Shirow's creations – *Appleseed* and *Ghost In the Shell* – feature *women* as the main character. And women of action, too. In the world of television and movies, that is very rare. (It continues in other works, such as *Dominion: Tank Police, Orion, Pandora In the Crimson Shell* and *Real Drive.*)

Shirow-sensei might've stopped publishing books of *Ghost In the Shell* stories in 2003 (with *Ghost in the Shell 1.5: Human-Error Processor*), but he didn't stop drawing Major Kusanagi and the gang. Motoko, for ex, was a regular guest star in Shirow's calendars.

Masamune Shirow has exploited aspects of the world of *Ghost In the Shell* in print media: the *Cybergirls Portfolio, Cyberworld* and *Cyberdelics* collections are images which focus on Motoko Kusanagi.

Each *Ghost In the Shell* tankobon, meanwhile, has been published in short (cut) editions and longer editions (some include appendices).

On a selfish, fan-based note, I would like to see Production I.G. sell the rights to *Ghost In the Shell*, and let's see a completely new bunch of companies have a go at Masamune Shirow's famous work. It would be great, for ex, to see a version of *Ghost* which *really* captures the goofy humour and joshing among the team at Public Security Section 9, instead of the usual too-serious approach. (There's more to *Ghost In the Shell* than a kick-ass cyborg girl who beats up bad guys and spends the rest of her time moping about and philosophizing). I'd like to see the *One Piece* or Toei Animation version of *Ghost In the Shell.*[5]

---

5 The closest animation to that is *Dominion: Tank Police.*

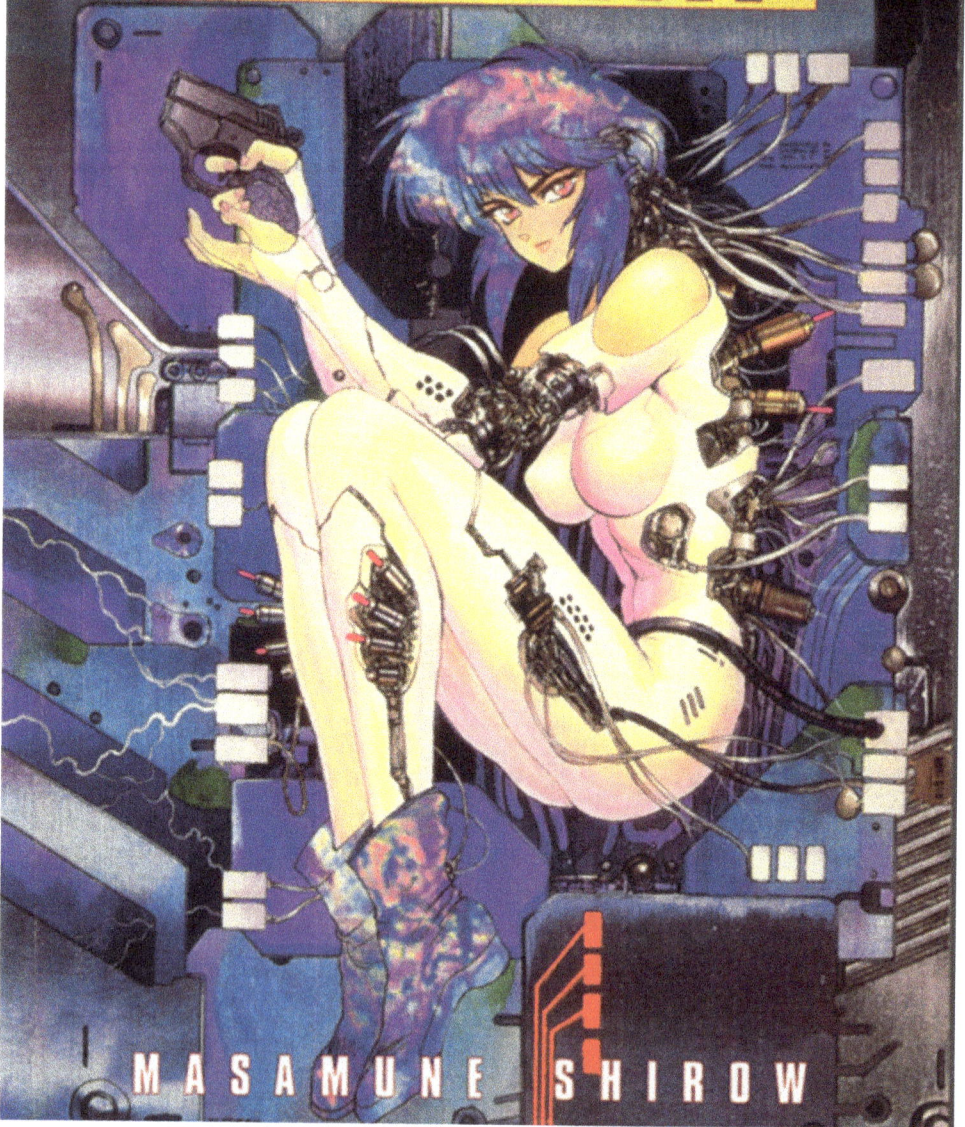

Masamune Shirow's first Ghost In the Shell manga
(on this page and the following pages)

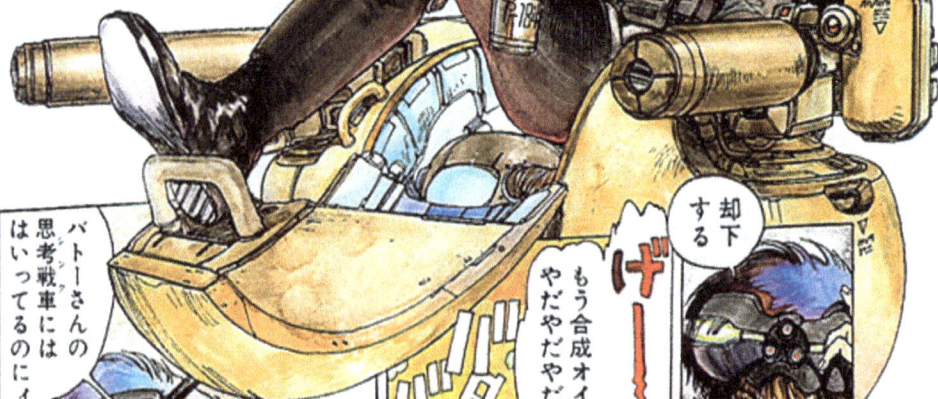

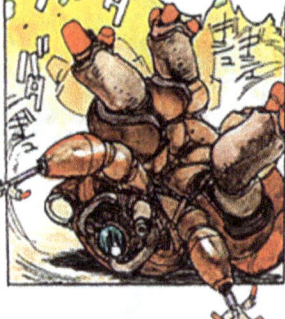

This page and over: pages from Masamune Shirow's follow-up
to Ghost In the Shell, Man-Machine Interface

IF ANY OF THE ANALYTICAL EQUIPMENT IN THE LAB SURVIVED, WE CAN USE IT TO CHECK THE CARCASSES. IF NOT, WE'LL HAVE TO REMOVE WHAT'S LEFT OF IT ANYWAY...
CRUDE. "ACQUIRED" FROM THE LOCAL MILITARY...?
WHILE YOU'RE AT IT, CAN YOU GET A SAMPLE FROM THE PIG'S BRAIN?
WE MIGHT NOT LUCK OUT, BUT WHY NOT JUST SEARCH FOR A PIG WITH AN EXPOSED BRAIN...?
YES, GOOD IDEA.
PSST
AREN'T YOU WORRIED ABOUT THE WASTE PROCESSING
CHECK OUT

Masamune Shirow's Ghost In the Shell 1.5: Human-Error Processor
(this page and following pages)

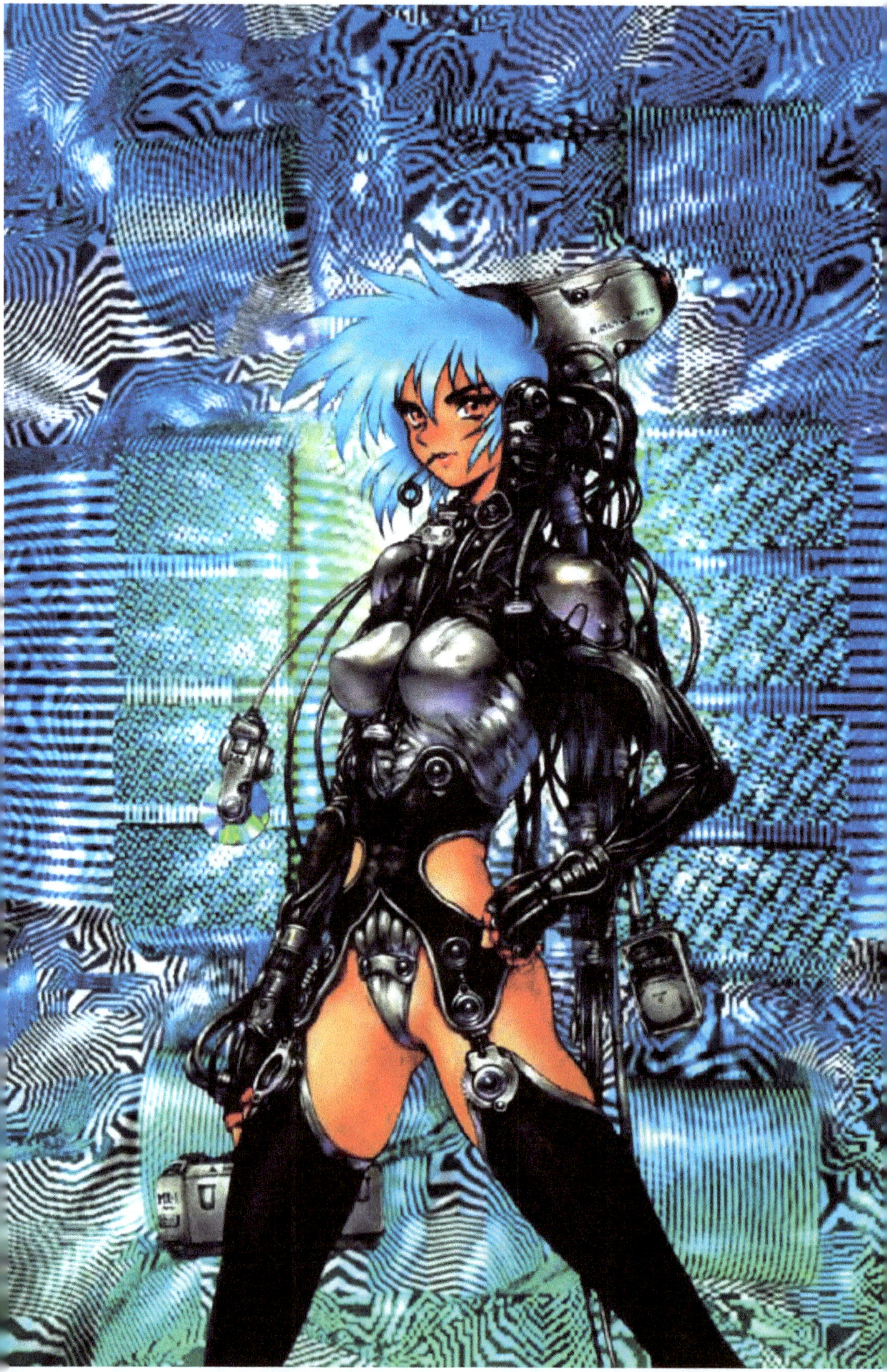

Heroic Calendar (2002), using characters from Ghost In the Shell.

MAX! LEX! STAY
ON GUARD
WITH *B-1* AND
EQUIP IT WITH
A STANDARD
COMBAT BODY.

AYE-AYE!

K-IK

SHSSSFT

Costumes in the
Ghost In the Shell
manga: hookers in
Etorofu in the sequel
(right).
Motoko in shrinkable
clothes: from mini to
pencil skirt! (above).

Motoko Kusanagi in the calendars, magazines and other material
(this page and over).

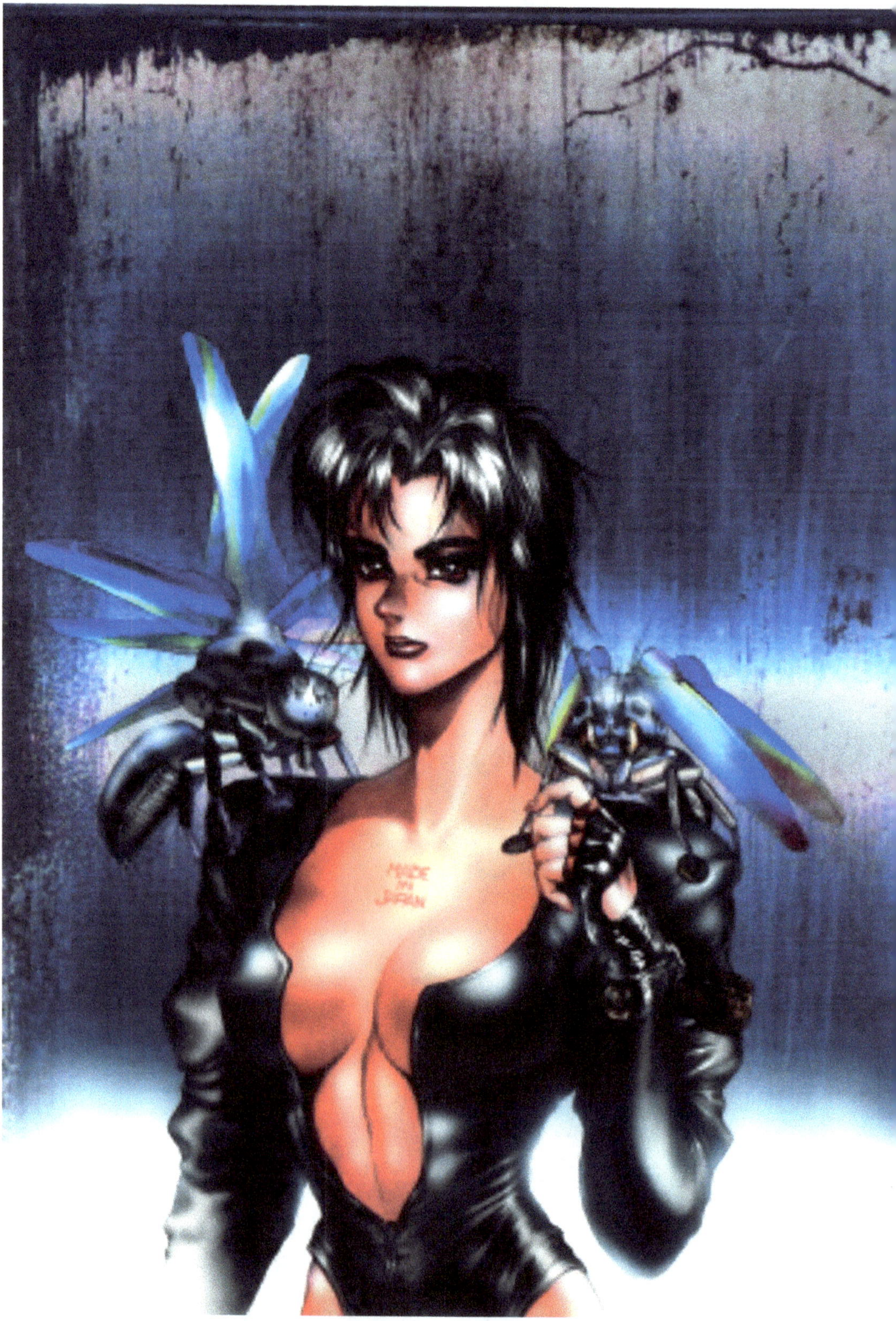
MADE IN JAPAN

MASAMUNE SHIROW'S WORKS IN *ANIMÉ*.

Among the works by Masamune Shirow that've been made into TV, Original Video Animations and movies are:

Black Magic (1987), Original Video Animation
Appleseed (1988), Original Video Animation
Dominion: Tank Police (1988), Original Video Animation
New Dominion: Tank Police (1994), Original Video Animation
Ghost In the Shell (1995), movie
Ghost In the Shell: Stand Alone Complex (2002-03), TV series
Ghost In the Shell: Stand Alone Complex: 2nd Gig (2004-05), TV series
Ghost In the Shell 2: Innocence (2004), movie
Appleseed (2004), movie
Ghost In the Shell: Stand Alone Complex: The Laughing Man (2005), movie
Ghost In the Shell: Stand Alone Complex: Solid State Society (2006), movie
Tank S.W.A.T. 01 (2006), Original Video Animation
Appleseed: Ex Machina (2007), movie
Ghost In the Shell: Stand Alone Complex: Individual 11 (2007), movie
Ghost Hound (2007), TV series
Real Drive (2008), TV series
Appleseed XIII (2011), TV series
W Tails Cat (2013), Original Video Animation
Appleseed: Alpha (2014), movie
Ghost In the Shell: Arise (2013-15), TV series/ Original Video Animation
Ghost In the Shell: The New Movie (2015), movie
Pandora in the Crimson Shell: Ghost Urn (2015-16), TV series
Ghost In the Shell (2017), live-action movie
Ghost In the Shell: S.A.C. 2045 (2020), TV/ net series

Masamune Shirow is one lucky *manga* artist: he has had *Ghost In the Shell* made into two classic movies by one of Japan's premier animation *auteurs*, Mamoru Oshii; he has had not one but two outstanding *animé* series made for TV from *Ghost In the Shell*; he's had three spin-off movies from the TV show; he's had not one but five *animé* adaptations of *Appleseed* (tho' the first, in 1988, is the best at capturing the *Appleseed* world); and other adaptations, such as *Black Magic* (made when Shirow was 26), and two versions of *Dominion: Tank Police*.

Lucky – because we all know how many less than stellar *manga* adaptations there are in *animé*. (However, several Shirowian adaptations are patchy – *Real Drive* and *Ghost Hound* – or downright dreadful: *Appleseed XIII* and *Tank S.W.A.T. 01*. In fact, adaptations of Shirow's work and concepts went off the rails between the mid-2000s and mid-2010s, with many shows being well below par: *Appleseed XIII, Ghost Hound, Real Drive, Tank S.W.A.T. 01, W Tails Cat* and *Pandora in the*

Crimson Shell: Ghost Urn. The *Ghost In the Shell: Arise* series of 2013-15 delivered a much-needed improvement in quality).

Masamune Shirow also has credits on other animations apart from his well-known pieces like *Appleseed* and *Ghost In the Shell: Gundress* (character design), *Hyakki Sho,* unmade (original creator), *Landlock* (original character design), *Real Drive* (original creator), *Ghost Hound* (original creator), *W Tails Cat* (original creator and designer), *Bounty Dog* (character design), and *TANK S.W.A.T. 01* (original creator).

The flow of creativity hasn't all been one way, from *manga* to *animé*: Masamune Shirow would very likely have been influenced by seeing the 1995 *Ghost In the Shell* movie – not least because the movie was a masterpiece. Imagine writing and drawing a *manga* as a 29 year-old starting out as a *mangaka* (Shirow was 29 in 1990), and watching a bunch of filmmakers in Tokyo turn it into this extraordinary, hi-tech action thriller! That's got to influence your later work, right?

ADAPTING MASAMUNE SHIROW'S WORKS

Masamune Shirow's involvement in *animé* adaptations of his work following the troubled *Black Magic* Original Video Animation has usually been in an advisory capacity, at a distance. But that includes story ideas, designs for characters and *mecha,* and other ideas.

Shirow has acknowledged that comics and television are two different ways of telling stories, and ideally he preferred animation that adapted *manga* as a stand alone work, drawing on the strengths of animation. In 1995, he said:

> I think there are ways to demonstrate and produce animation that are unique to animation. Also, in order to establish animation as a truly unique medium of expression, I think it's better to work from an original concept than to base the work on a manga, or, if producing animation based on a manga work, I think it's better to at least rewrite the story for the animation.

Shirow came to realize early on that adaptations of his comics into other media were fraught with issues (he had first-hand experience of this during the difficult production of *Black Magic*). So he developed a way of submitting a bunch of ideas and designs instead of finished stories, as he explained in 1993:

> If I create a regular 'story comic', it can't really be adapted to animation or games without radical changes. So, rather than offering a completed story to the various companies that have expressed interest in my work, I'm just putting together 'do-it-yourself' packages of various bits and pieces, such as mechanical and character designs, and basic storylines. So, from that, they can develop whatever they want, without feeling restricted by the existing work. (1994)

Many of the *animé* adaptations of the work of Masamune Shirow add psychodramatic and melodramatic elements that simply don't exist in the originals. To *Appleseed*, the writers added suicide and a troubled cop Karen Mawserus; to *Dominion: Tank Police*, the filmmakers focussed far too much on the villain Buaku's anxieties about his origins and being artificial; in the two *Ghost In the Shell* movies of '95 and '04, the Public Security Section 9 team mope like teenagers; and in the two *Ghost In the Shell: Stand Alone Complex* series narratives of suicide and self-loathing occur several times (which continues in the *S.A.C. 2045* series).

All of which reflects the concerns of the adapters and scriptwriters, and twist Masamune Shirow's stories to address issues like teenage alienation (the 'shut in' and *otaku* syndrome), social misfits, and, most disturbingly, self-harm and suicide. Yes, some of those issues *are* addressed by Shirow-sensei, but not in the same melodramatic manner, and certainly not in the same quantity. (There are far more evocations of self-hatred and suicide in the three *Ghost In the Shell: Stand Alone Complex* TV series, for instance, than in all of Shirow's *manga*).

The production teams behind the *Ghost In the Shell* franchise in TV and film are all mad, crazy *cinéastes*: executive producers Mitsuhisa Ishikawa and Shigero Watanabe, directors Kenji Kamiyama and Mamoru Oshii, and writers Dai Saito, Junichi Fujisaku, Yoshiki Sakurai, Shotaro Suga *et al*, have consumed movies by the ton and absorbed them: Jean-Luc Godard (*Breathless, Vivre Sa Vie, Alphaville, Pierrot le Fou*), Stanley Kubrick (*2001: A Space Odyssey, A Clockwork Orange, Full Metal Jacket*), Tsui Hark, Jackie Chan, John Woo (they love over-the-top Hong Kong action movie gunplay), Takeshi Kitano, Federico Fellini, François Truffaut, Akira Kurosawa (*The Seven Samurai, Yojimbo*), Martin Scorsese (*Taxi Driver, Raging Bull*), *The Terminator, Alien, Star Wars, RoboCop, Star Trek*, Hayao Miyazaki (*Laputa: Castle In the Sky, Princess Mononoke, Porco Rosso*), and of course *Blade Runner*.

As you study the adaptations of the *Ghost In the Shell manga* of Masamune Shirow, you are amazed at just how much of the comic made it into each movie and TV series. The filmmakers must've gone thru the *manga* literally 100s of times, to squeeze out every idea, detail and image. 'I looked at that book so much that it's all dog-eared now', remarked *mecha* designer of the *Ghost* TV series, Kenji Teraoka.

None of the adaptations of either *Appleseed* or *Ghost In the Shell*, two of the key franchises in the world of Masamune Shirow, have been able to translate his very distinctive character designs and figures into animation. They come close, but are never quite Shirowian through and through (Shirow's young women are a critical element in his *manga*, but the animated versions can't render them, and always make them too plump. The character designers have included Hiroyuki Okiura, Makoto Shimomura, Tetsuya Nishio, Takayuki Goto, Tetsuro Ueyama, Yumiko Horasawa, Hiroki Takagi, Noboru Furuse, Hiroyuki Kitakubo, Masaki Yamada, Kazuchika Kise, Takuya Tani and Ilya Kuvshinov).

It's a pity, but none of the video/ film versions of the *Ghost In the Shell manga* by Masamune Shirow have attempted to reproduce his crowded street scenes, where cyborgs and humans and robots jostle shoulders and spinal cords. Shirow, in full, post-punk *Star Wars*, *Blade Runner* and *Road Warrior* mode (the streets in *Blade Runner*, the cantina scene in *Star Wars*), loves to imagine ridiculous cyborgized augmentations for humans: weirdos with pipes running from a box on their shoulder into their nostrils; guys in biohazard suits; snooty folk holding opera glasses; a bozo with a *kawaii*, baby-shaped earring; and robots that're nothing more'n a tin box with flailing arms.

Only the home life of Togusa is depicted with any depth or detail in the *Ghost In the Shell: Stand Alone Complex* TV series and the *Ghost In the Shell* movies. The TV shows depict a family man with a wife and daughter (*Ghost In the Shell 2: Innocence* portrays Batou and his pooch, of course). Masamune Shirow's *Ghost In the Shell manga* goes *much* further in delineating the everyday lives of the principal characters. The audience gets no idea of what Aramaki, say, or Ishikawa, or even Major Kusanagi are like at home in the animated versions (the 1995 *Ghost In the Shell* movie has an eerie and hypnotic scene showing Kusanagi waking up in her apartment[1] – of course it has a *fab* view of the city outside the giant window – she lives alone, naturally (and it's beyond minimal, it's empty). And the 2004 *Ghost In the Shell* sequel has a lengthy sequence showing what life is like *chez* Batou – supping beer from cans and preparing food for dawgs is what it is).

If you know the *manga* of *Ghost In the Shell*, you will notice right away that the TV series *Ghost In the Shell: Stand Alone Complex* has consciously gone for something far, far more political and social than Masamune Shirow's cyber-thriller *manga*. The philosophical, meta-physical and scientific issues, so central to Shirow's *manga*, are still explored by the Japanese filmmakers (the adaptations have scenes with ministers and politicos), but they have grounded the three TV series of *Ghost In the Shell: Stand Alone Complex* very much in contemporary political and social issues.

One of the simple but crucial reasons that the two *Ghost In the Shell: Stand Alone Complex* TV series are so good is that the filmmakers have something to say (it helps that they know how to say it, too). Whereas in much of TV and cinema, the producers don't have much to say (but insist on saying it anyway).

However, the second *Ghost In the Shell* movie, *Ghost In the Shell 2: Innocence*, and the *Arise* version of *Ghost In the Shell* (2013-15), and the live-action movie of '17, don't have much to say that hasn't already been said before in the previous *Ghost In the Shell* outings.

The same companies have handled all of the animated versions of *Ghost In the Shell* – Bandai, Dentsu, N.T.N., Tokuma, Victor, Production I.G., etc. The *Arise* series was partly intended to be a new take on the *Ghost In the Shell* material, but ended up being essentially a prequel/origins story to the two *Stand Alone Complex* series. I'd like to see Toei

1 The shot holds and holds as Kusanagi walks offscreen then back into shot – a self-conscious, European New Wave motif which filmmakers such as Woody Allen have employed to an enormous degree.

Animation (*One Piece*) or A-1/ Satelight (*Fairy Tail*) or Studio Pierrot (*Bleach, Naruto*) or Madhouse (*Memories, Death Note*) or Studio Bones (*Cowboy Bebop, Fullmetal Alchemist*) tackle Masamune Shirow's cyberpunk comic.

I'd love to see Shoji Kawamori (*Macross, Escaflowne, Aquarion*), Noriyuki Abe (*Bleach, Arslan*), Yasuhiro Irie (*Fullmetal Alchemist*), Koji Morimoto (*Memories*), Tetsuro Araki (*Death Note*), Hayato Date (*Naruto*), or Konosuke Uda (*One Piece*) adapt *Ghost In the Shell*.

Live-action versions of *animé* and *manga* are occasionally produced, though seldom in the West. Inevitably, rumours of a live-action version of *Ghost In the Shell* have circulated from time to time (James Cameron and Steven Spielberg were linked to live-action remakes of *Ghost In the Shell*, and also *Akira*).[2] My question is always the same with remakes of classic movies: why bother? These are incredible movies.[3] Don't do it. Go think up your own story instead! (There is also a very mistaken assumption here that an <u>animated</u> version of a story isn't as 'important' or 'serious' as a <u>live-action</u> version. Live-action is culturally promoted above animation).

Also, you can bet that the ideas of making a live-action TV series of both *Ghost In the Shell* and *Appleseed* have been discussed many times in Tokyo. Shirow's most famous *manga* are ideal starting-points for a long-running TV series, or a shorter mini-series.

VIDEO GAMES.

Games are popular *animé* spin-offs – role playing games, card games, chess, jigsaw puzzles and board games are widespread in Japan (and you often see charas playing games in *animé*).

Video games are also tied in very closely with *manga* publishing: *manga* for elementary children, such as *Comic Bombom* and *Corocoro Comi*, have many game and *animé* tie-ins.

Masamune Shirow's art and storytelling is perfect for computer games (his three signature works, *Ghost In the Shell*, *Appleseed* and *Dominion: Tank Police*, are cop shows, ideal for shoot-em-up video games. It's not only Public Security Section 9 who blam-blam away, it's also the Tank Police of *Dominion* and the mobile suits of *Appleseed*). And we all know that the computer game industry generates billions, as *animé* producers in Japan know well.

Shirow-sensei has been involved with video games created from his works, including for PlayStation (*Ghost in the Shell, Yarudora Series Vol. 3: Sampaguita, Project Horned Owl* and *Gundress*), for PlayStation 2 (*Ghost in the Shell: Stand Alone Complex* and *Appleseed EX*),[4] for PlayStation Portable (*Ghost in the Shell: Stand Alone Complex* and *Yarudora Series Vol. 3: Sampaguita*), for Super Famicom (*Appleseed*), and games for Arcade, P.C. (*Aoki Uru, Black Magic, Emil Chronicle*), social media and cel phones, <u>flight simulator games</u>, and Nintendo D.S. There are also artbooks/

2 Rumours often turn out to be rumours, and often the rights have not been bought up.
3 As director Christophe Gans put it: '*Ghost In the Shell* is already perfect. What would you do, reproduce it frame for frame?'
4 There have been video games of *Appleseed* for PlayStation 2 (*Appleseed EX*), Super Famicom, online games, and cel phones/ social media.

guidebooks published for the computer games, and most of the games include Shirow's artwork and cover art. (Some of Shirow's work for video games was collected in *Intron Depot 5: Battalion*, 2001-09). So although film critics often deride action *animé* (including the shows based on Shirow's work) as being too much like shoot-em-up computer games, gaming has been part of Shirow's output for decades (and Shirow is a big fan of gaming himself).

COP SHOWS.

The cop show format is employed by Masamune Shirow many times: it is the basis of *Ghost In the Shell*, of course (the Japanese title of *Ghost In the Shell* is *Mobile Armored Riot Police*), but also *Dominion: Tank Police* and *Appleseed*. That means that Shirow's works are usually using the team format (*sentai*), which's common in sports *manga*, adventure *manga*, and giant robot *manga*.

Ghost In the Shell, in any of its manifestations, as *manga*, movie or TV series, is basically a cop show (if you call it *Mobile Armored Riot Police*, it explains what it's about much more than 'ghost in the shell'). Yes, it's a cyber-punk, hyper-space classic, with its philosophical musings on the digital realm, on life and death, on artificial life vs. organic life. But it's still a cop show. You've got the super-cop, Major Kusanagi,[5] her burly, gruff buddy, seen-it-all-b4 veteran, Batou, the sensitive, put-upon, long-suffering family man Togusa, the wry, seasoned, computer specialist, Ishikawa,[6] and of course the stern, patriarchal boss Daisuke Aramaki (who keeps the squad in line, and also juggles with being answerable to the politicos in command above him). As with all cop shows, there are mysteries to solve, murders to avenge, people to protect, bad guys to chase, civilian casualties to avoid, and politicians to out-manœuvre. (And, being a cop show, that means that *Ghost In the Shell* inevitably promulgates right-wing, pro-military, pro-government, and pro-State politics. The Major might pretend to be rebellious and independent, as in the *Arise* series, but she's working for the State, for The Man[7]).

Apart from Motoko Kusanagi, the *Ghost In the Shell* franchise employs two principal cops, the hulking Batou, a world-weary cop with cropped, white hair, blank, implanted eyes and a vast battery of weapons, and Togusa, a younger cop, with a family (and fewer technological additions to his body).

Batou is a type in Japanese animation of the guy who can't express his feelings – towards Major Kusanagi: these guys, as Gilles Poitras pointed out in *Anime Essentials*,

> have trouble clearly stating their feelings and struggle to express themselves to the one they love. It is not just men; female characters

---

5 As a character type, Motoko Kusanagi has numerous forebears in both Western and Japanese cinema.
6 The name Ishikawa in *Ghost In the Shell* might come from Goeman Ishikawa XIII, a samurai warrior sidekick of Lupin III. Goemon refers to a legendary thief character in Japanese culture, subject of *Kabuki* plays, such as *Ishikawa Goemon* of 1680 (G. Poitras, 2001, 42).
7 Shirow's own politics seem liberal and socially-conscious, but right of centre.

can also hold back or be confused by their emotions, as in the case of Madoka in *Kimagure Orange Road* or Kyoko in *Maison Ikkoku.* (2001, 56)

The cops in the *Ghost In the Shell* world're battling against crime, as cops've always done in the *policier* or thriller genre. Except the criminals in *Ghost In the Shell* are operating partly in cyberspace – hacking into networks, or creating viruses or dodgy software, or copying people's spirits, or selling e-brains on the black market. The cops're protecting society, as usual, and the Japanese nation, too; but a lot of their time is spent preventing attacks or countering attacks on minds, spirits and bodies.

Masamune Shirow makes computers and hacking sexy and thrilling: he takes working with computers far away from the clichéd image of lonely, spotty, fat slobs living in cheap motels, so it becomes beautiful super-babes in shiny, rubberized cat-suits who turn hacking into floating about in dreamy, golden realms like a slinky cat burglar.

PUBLIC SECURITY SECTION 9.

The *manga* of *Ghost In the Shell* portrays the creation of the Public Security Section 9 unit itself, with Chief Aramaki telling M. Kusanagi that they have been granted the budget for the kind of team they've been talking about. (Notice that critics and fans talk about Section 9, leaving out the all-important 'Public Security' part of the team's name. You could also say, 'Japanese Government Section 9'. The 'Public Security' bit reminds us that these are agents of the Japanese government. They're not rebels, or outsiders: they are cops – they *are* the State).

Public Security Section 9 is defined in the *Ghost In the Shell: Man-Machine Interface manga* thus:

> Section 9 of the Public Security Bureau is original to the *manga*.
> According to the information that I have on hand, the real Public
> Security currently consists of General Affairs (including special
> support troops), Section 1 (in charge of investigating student move-
> ments and radical activities), Section 2 (labor disputes and organized
> crime), Section 3 (right-wing activities), Section 4 (information
> gathering, statistics, etc), External Affairs Section 1 (in charge of
> investigating non-Asian foreigners), and External Affairs Section 2
> (Asian foreigners). (54)

Authority is seldom questioned among the Public Security Section 9 team in *Ghost In the Shell:* only three of the main characters ever question Chief Aramaki: Motoko, Batou and Togusa (which is quite the norm in Japanese pop culture. They *never* yell at Aramaki or even mildly grouse). It's intriguing that in the second *Ghost In the Shell* TV series, the Major doesn't voice her concern over the influence of Kazundo Goda as loudly or as often as Batou does (and Togusa too). Rather, Motoko seems to be going along with Aramaki, maybe opting to wait until Goda and his regime definitely does something immoral or wrong.

Similarly, within the hierarchy of the Public Security Section 9, no matter what they're up against, or how they're feeling, they all jump to attention when Aramaki or Kusanagi say *jump*. And Aramaki, too, doesn't argue with his superiors often, and also tends to go along with Prime Minister Yoko Kayabuki, in the *2nd Gig* series (Kusanagi reckons he might have a crush on her).

Masamune Shirow's heroes are heroes – they are not anti-heroes, nor are they villains. They fight on the side of 'right' (even if some of their methods are obscure, as with Motoko Aramaki in *Ghost In the Shell: Man-Machine Interface*). The Major, Batou, Deunan Knute, Briareos Hecatonchires, Leona Ozaki *et al* are not really flawed, either (tho' some of them have 'issues'). Detractors might carp that they're not fully-rounded characters, either. True – Shirow's charas tend to grow on you deeply only if you read and re-read his comics (that's when you take in all of the little details that Shirow packs into the corners of his *manga*). And they don't go thru many psychological changes – like most charas in *manga* and animation, they remain pretty much the same from start to finish.

GUNS.

Despite the scary amount of weaponry and gun-related violence on display in the *Ghost In the Shell* animations, and in a large amount of other *animé,* Japan has a low crime rate, and very low gun crime, according to Gilles Poitras (48 murders with hand-guns in 1979 compared to 9,848 in the U.S.A.).[8] As Poitras pointed out in *The Anime Companion*:

> Japan's Firearms and Sword Possession Control Law is the strictest
> weapons control law in the world. Police officers are not even
> allowed to carry firearms unless they are on duty, and many police
> never even draw their weapon during their entire career, much less
> ever fire their gun. (136)

But *Ghost In the Shell* is wholly a genre outing, and a cop show without guns ain't gonna fly – like a Western without horses, or a soap opera without scenes of people in bars, stores and hospitals wittering on and on and on about absolutely nothing.

Animé movies and shows fetishize guns to an extraordinary degree. Yes, of course that partly derives from the forms and genres that Japanese filmmakers have taken from North American cinema and Hong Kong cinema (everybody took from those American detective and *film noir* motifs, including the *sensei* himself, Akira Kurosawa). You can see the North American fetishization of weaponry in loads of national cinemas around the world. French cinema is the obvious example: for instance, there's always a gun lying around in a Jean-Luc Godard movie (in some of Godard's films, people sit around brandishing guns while reading books, which's classic Godardism – guns and books! The intellectual

8 Guns were used in only 0.8% of robberies, and only 5.3% of murders involved guns.

assassin! A cowboy who reads Guy de Maupassant novels!).

In *Intro Depot: Ballistics,* Masamune Shirow voices concerns over the morality of including images of women in military uniform[9] in these troubled times. This apology or doubt seems hypocritical from an artist who has been drawing aggressively pro-military and pro-government images since the beginning of his career! Few comparable artists have depicted so many characters wielding guns, for example.

TANKS.

We know that Masamune Shirow is fond, like Hayao Miyazaki and Katsuhiro Otomo,[10] of tanks (as well as every form of *mecha,* from guns to helicopters to all manner of cyberization). In Shirow's *manga* work, tanks're everywhere: they are a *very* big deal in the *Ghost In the Shell* franchise, especially on screen (to the point where some of the TV episodes are devoted solely to the Tachikoma tanks). In the *Appleseed manga,* the first big action sequence involves a tank attacking Deunan Knute and Briareos.[11] And Masamune Shirow created a whole series centred around cops plus tanks: *Dominion: Tank Police* (and the main character, Leona, lavishes more love on her cute, little tank Buonaparte than anything or anyone else in her life). The enshrinement of tanks is a gift to animators in Tokyo, most of whom seem to be as crazy about tanks as Shirow is. Thus, every adaptation of a Shirow work includes at least one tank scene. (There's even a TV show called *Girls and Tanks* (*Girls und Panzer,* 2012-13), a preposterous concept, even in amongst the out-there content of Japanese animation – cute girls drive tanks in their school club – but perfectly Shirowian).

STYLE.

The art of Masamune Shirow is not in love with white space! No! Shirow will fill every *manga* page with marks.[12] And if the frame isn't crowded enough, there'll be lengthy speech bubbles, plus sound effects,[13] and also the idiosyncratic footnotes, in which the Master shares his thoughts on, well, everything. (*Mangaka* who employ lots of white space include Himoru Arakawa (*Fullmetal Alchemist*), Katsuhiro Otomo (*Akira*) and Tite Kubo (*Bleach*)).

Masamune Shirow is a perfectionist – as is obvious by looking at any of his work. He has been known to throw away completely finished artwork – pages of the later *Appleseed* volumes, for example, were ditched, after being inked. (This is one reason why Shirow takes a long time to complete his artwork – like Kentaro Miura (*Berserk*), he won't let something sub-standard leave his studio).

9 Women in uniform and action women are recurring characters in Japanese animation – shows like *Ghost In the Shell, Patlabor, Gunbuster, Dominion: Tank Police, Bubblegum Crisis* and *Cat's Eye* embody that.
10 Tanks pop up all over Otomo-sensei's work.
11 Just Deunan in the 2004 version of *Appleseed.*
12 Masamune Shirow uses a good deal of screen tone (also known as 'zip'), as a means of quickly supplying shading and tones to images.
13 'Shirow's scratchy-pen artwork has great energy and fantastic detail: the near-future is nifty and unusually practical' (Julie Davis in *Manga: The Complete Guide,* 85).

In 1994, Masamune Shirow said that he used a *kabura* pen (which's shaped like a turnip), with a pen holder he made himself. He had a Canon photocopier (one of the *mangaka's* chief tools). He used a regular X-Acto eraser. He worked on regular smooth Kent paper. He employed Maxon screentones,[14] mainly 60 line, 10%, 20%, 30%, etc. Shirow often talks about looking for the right 'tension' or 'life' in a picture.

For computer work, in the 1990s, up to the early 2000s, Shirow used Apple computers, including a 9600/ 350 machine, a G4 machine, and OS 9.2.1, and software such as Photoshop for 2-D work, Lightwave for 3-D modelling, and Cinema 4-D for rendering and layouts.

Most of Masamune Shirow's art has employed the portrait format, rather than the landscape format. All of Shirow's erotic art, for instance, uses the portrait format. Shirow has produced his art chiefly for publication in printed form, and mainly in book form[15] (which are in portrait format, like this book and most books). He uses fewer double-page images than some artists (such as Kentaro Miura (*Berserk*) or Eiichiro Oda (*One Piece*)). As his notes show, he is very conscious of issues such as colour and contrast, and how his art will finally look when it's printed.

Water and the ocean is a significant ingredient in the work of Masamune Shirow: it's striking how many works are set next to water – for all the usual reasons of looks, movement, symbolism, etc. (Maybe for Shirow growing up and living in Kobe has been an influence here: Kobe is by the sea,[16] with the city built onto hills rising above the port. And Kobe being the epicentre of a major earthquake (in 1995), which killed 6,000+ people and destroyed over 100,000 buildings (including Shirow's house),[17] has likely influenced Shirow.)

'A PHILOSOPHY TEXT WRITTEN BY ALIENS'.

In *Ghost In the Shell: Man-Machine Interface*, Motoko discovers a file by a professor which she reckons looks like 'a philosophy text written by aliens'. And that is exactly how many fans and critics regard the footnotes and side-notes to Masamune Shirow's *manga*!

For some, Masamune Shirow's style is too dense, too difficult and confusing to follow, too easily distracted, with a tendency to wander off the point, and too pretentious. True – this is not easily-to-digest comic art, like *Oh! My Goddess, Love Hina, Naruto* or *Urusei Yatsura*. Shirow's *manga* asks for much more of your attention and your commit-ment. But certainly, Shirow-sensei is a world-maker, and a lot of people find the worlds he creates fascinating.

Shirow-sensei provides references to many books in the *Ghost In the Shell manga* that he recommends: *Sensors and the Eyes of Living Things* (1985) • *Jintai no Shori* (= *Victory For the Human Body*) • *The Recursive Universe: Cosmic Complexity and the Limits of Scientific Knowledge* by

14 Screen tone or zip in *manga* is a big part of the artist's armoury: there is screen tone of all kinds, including readymade cityscapes and skies.
15 With a sideline in magazine, video game and book covers.
16 Shirow used to live very near the sea, then he moved about five miles from the coast.
17 The epicentre of the quake flattened a huge area of Kobe.

William Poundstone • *The Relationship of Fungi To Human Affairs* by W.D. Gray • *Adam Link – Robot* by Eando Binder • *Biomaterials: An Approach To Artificial Organs* by Dr Yoshito Ikada, etc.

FASHION AND CLOTHES.

One aspect of Masamune Shirow's art is obvious to anybody: it features a feeling for costumes, accessories and fashion which I would contend is the equal (and in many respects the superior) of any of the celebrated fashion designers of recent times: Tom Ford, Alexander McQueen, Thierry Mugler and even England's Queen of Fashion, Vivienne Westwood (not to mention the classic brands, such as Coco Chanel, Christian Dior, Yves St-Laurent, D. & G., etc). The use by Shirow of corsets and steam-punk paraphernalia has obvious counterparts in the fashion designs of Westwood, John Galliano and Jean-Paul Gaultier.

Meanwhile, Japan has produced many celebrated fashion designers, including Issei Miyake, Takoda Kenzo, Mori Hanae, Janya Watanabe, and Kansai Yamamoto[18] (b. 1944), known for his flamboyant stage costumes manufactured for David Bowie, which drew on *Kabuki* theatre.

In *Intron Depot: Ballistics*, Masamune Shirow admits that his cutaway costumes revealing lots of skin are not always practical: of one of his slim-hipped, big-breasted, young police officers with only a thong below her waist, Shirow noted: 'a high-exposure costume like hers has no particular rationale to justify it except that it's fun to draw (for me, anyway)'. The *animé* adaptations have followed the maestro's example: some of the costumes worn by Deunan Knute and Motoko Kusanagi sure aren't practical.

HUMOUR.

Like many *mangaka*, Masamune Shirow has produced *4-koma* (four-panel) strips of his *manga* works such as the *Appleseed* and *Ghost In the Shell* stories (which feature the usual light-hearted, single gags of *yon-koma*). There are also many *chibi* (super-deformed) versions of the cast of *Appleseed*, for instance: Deu and Bri in a flying *Yellow Submarine* machine, or Deunan and Bri as pirates in a pirate galleon, or dressed as Native Americans, or Deu and Bri astride a scooter, or a mechanical fish, etc. The *chibi* forms in the *Appleseed manga* emphasize, again, the humour in *Appleseed*, which the *animé* adaptations insist on ignoring.

It's the same story in other adaptations of Shirow-sensei's work: the action, the serious themes, and the detailed futuristic worlds[19] are played up, while the humour is sidelined. Mistake! Humour is a *vital* ingredient in the Shirowian cosmos. All of Shirow's key works feature humour – *Ghost In the Shell*, *Appleseed*, *Dominion: Tank Police* – and some, such as

---

18 The famous Japanese-themed costumes for the Ziggy Stardust persona were designed by Kansai Yamamoto, who met David Bowie in 1973. The clothes included satin cloaks that were made to be pulled off Bowie with a flourish (you can see this in *Ziggy Stardust* movie. The device comes from Japanese *Kabuki* theatre). The layered approach revealed another costume underneath or sometimes just glam underwear.
19 Unfortunately, the O.A.V.s/ TV series/ movies of *Ghost In the Shell* opted for a much safer, more recognizable futuristic vision of Japan.

Orion, are much more comedic than serious.

The first *Tank Police animé* adaptation, released in 1988 as *Dominion: Tank Police,* caught the essential element of humour in the *manga* by Masamune Shirow. It focussed very much on Leona Ozaki, but also offered a very entertaining portrayal of yet another team in *animé*.[20] Thus, *Dominion: Tank Police* might be the most successful film or animated version of the Shirowian heroine, in capturing her humour, compared to *all* of the adaptations of *Appleseed* and *Ghost In the Shell,* etc.

'MADE IN JAPAN.'

Masamune Shirow's *Ghost In the Shell manga* is 'made in Japan' – as if it could be made anywhere else! To remind readers, Shirow sometimes includes the words 'MADE IN JAPAN' tattooed onto the chest or rear of some of the slinky, young characters (on page 123 of the first *Ghost In the Shell manga,* one of the maids working for the Colonel is seen in close-up, her svelte *derrière* bare under frilly panties, and stamped with 'MADE IN JAPAN'). Yes, the finest cyborgs in the future will by made in Japan (which, as we know, is actually going to be true! Japan leads the world in robotics and cyborgization).[21] In his "Afterword" to *Appleseed,* volume one, Masamune Shirow noted that 'this comic was originally written for Japan'.

CYBORGS.

Cyborgization makes for great science fiction stories, but it is problematic on many levels. Politically, it's a time bomb. Only the privileged few would be able to afford it (look at who can afford plastic surgery and body augmentations at the moment). Ideologically, it has deeply suspect elements, many bordering on fascism, the 'survival of the fittest', and other post-Nietzschean philosophies.

Manga author Yukito Kishiro (*Gunnm* a.k.a. *Battle Angel Alita*) said that 'from an ideological point of view, I'm against the idea of cyborgs'. But Kishiro agreed with Donna Haraway that, in a way, we are all already cyborgs:

> urbanites of the modern age are a lot like cyborgs, you know. They become immediately incapacitated when you cut off their juice. Isn't that what being a cyborg is all about...?[22]

The more sophisticated *animé* and *manga* explore some of these issues (such as *Ghost In the Shell* and the work of Katsuhiro Otomo), but many other Japanese sci-fi stories are content to go, 'cool, a robot!'

Other names for robots or androids in *animé* and *manga* include the *jinzo ningen* in *Dragonball,* 'perso-coms' in *Chobits,* 'boomers' in *Bubble-*

---

20 The animation of *Dominion: Tank Police* is very late 1980s – that is, colours include deep blues and reds, the action is very broad, with plenty of squash and stretch, and giant close-ups.
21 Japan still uses more robot technology than any other nation, and was also the first country to employ robotization in industry.
22 Quoted in T. Ledoux, 1997, 58.

gum Crisis[23] and 'bio-androids' (or 'bioroids') in *Appleseed*.

The love in Japanese pop culture of robots (who grow souls), dolls, puppets, toys, ghosts in the machine and ghosts in the shell is well-known (the dolls are called *ningyo,* and the automata are *karakuri ningyo* (automata from the Edo period).)

Certainly Masamune Shirow's fiction and art is among the finest in the giant robot sub-genre of science fiction. His mobile suits and automated machines look like they could really work or exist, whereas most giant robot TV shows don't bother with piffling, distracting details like real science or physics; they just crack on with the loud action scenes.

Jeopardy is of a different order for a cyborg heroine – smashed to bits, she can commission a new body from one of the mega-corporations in Nihon. Thus, the threats in *Ghost In the Shell* are to the ghost inside that shell – the brain, the mind, consciousness, the self, identity, memories, etc, via hacking, viruses, 'cyber-crime' and infiltration (from Puppeteers and Super-A-Class hackers).

Why are there so many *female* robots and cyborgs in the world of Masamune Shirow? In the appendix of *Black Magic,* Uncle Shirow comes up with some reasons – all pretty dodgy. Because, Shirow insists, a female shape has a lower centre of gravity. Because, Shirow says, a female cyborg would put off enemy troops for a moment, making them hesitate in firing (at a 'woman'). Because, Shirow asserts, pervs might put their life at risk. But then he comes clean, and admits that it's 'to make this manga more attractive'.

RELIGION IN THE SHIROWWORLD.

The work of Masamune Shirow refers to religion at times, and a whole *manga* story is devoted to it: *Orion*. In the posterbooks and pin-ups, there are Buddhist shrines and religious artefacts. But the *animé* adaptations of Shirow's material included far more references to religion, and Western religion very obviously, than occurs in his comics. Angels, crosses, crucifixions and the like were added to the *Ghost In the Shell: Stand Alone Complex* series and the *Ghost In the Shell* movies.

Steeped in Shintoism and Buddhism, the use of Christian and pagan/occult imagery and motifs in *animé* reflects a flirtation with foreign religious influences which typically occur in teenage (the Christian wedding ceremony, for instance, or *Harry Potter*-esque occultism and Greek mythology). And if Western religion is cited, it's often as something exotic, strange, other, and even sinister (as in *Hellsing, Black Butler, Samurai Champloo, The Qwaser of Stigmata* and *Urotsukidoji*).

Animé will take motifs and symbols from all sorts of places, often just for the look or the feel, disregarding the theological, religious or cultural attributes (and often drawn from foreign movies). As long as it look exotic and other-worldly, that's cool. Thus, the Star of David[24] is

---

23 *Pace Bubblegum Crisis*, Philip Brophy noted that 'the hyper-sexed construct of a woman with an incredible figure who is also a crack marksperson is a complex assemblage of male, female, gay, straight, heroic and S. & M. fantasies' (2005, 58).
24 Often in magical scenes or rites, where the pentagram would be more suitable.

employed without the filmmakers seeming to be aware of its enormous cultural and religious significance. It's the same with cruciform and church imagery.

The *Ghost In the Shell* movies/ TV series, like many *animé* products of this type, revolve around very familiar dualisms and oppositions:

Body	Soul or spirit
Body	Mind
Organism	Machine
Brain	Computer
Individual	Network

The terminology changes, so sometimes it's the 'ghost', or the 'soul', or the 'spirit', or the 'mind'. But the dualities are very familiar. Indeed, they are contained in the title 'the *ghost* in the *shell*'. The 'ghost in the machine' might be an alternative (and perhaps more accurate) title for *Ghost In the Shell*.[25]

Of course, there *are* slight differences between someone's 'soul' and their 'spirit', or between the 'soul' and the 'mind', or the 'mind' and the 'ghost'. But it's the bigger differences, between being organic and being a machine, between the body and the mind or spirit, between organic life and artificial life, btn being natural and man-made, that're really important.

As Masamune Shirow notes in the notes to the *Ghostly manga*:

> what we refer to as the "spirit" or "soul" is a very vague concept, including things programmed into, or closely related to, the physical body, such as memory, the results of chemical reactions, and emotions, etc. (357)

Is the body just a 'shell'? Does it matter what body you have attached to the mind or the spirit? Can a spirit exist inside another body, different from its own? Or inside a machine?

In fact, Masamune Shirow prefers to use the term 'spirit' rather than the more Western 'soul'. His work is very Oriental in its use of religion in this respect: it's not about individual souls, but about spirits which link to a universal spirit, a mystical oneness which chimes with the ontological unities central to the religions of Shintoism, Taoism and Buddhism.

The point about cyborgization and replacing parts of the human body with artificial organs for Shirow is that there is more to humans than just a physical self, plus a brain (and possibly a mind). Spiritual or religious aspects need to be considered (even if they are not 'scientific' or 'real'). In short, we are not only flesh and blood.

Whispering ghosts (one of Motoko Kusanagi's mantras is 'my ghost whispered to me') is Masamune Shirow's hi-tech version of intuition or sixth sense or people (like shamen or psychics) who can channel the unseen. (Thus, even Chief Aramaki recognizes the significance of espers

25 But it has been used many times – from the Arthur Koestler book.

and spiritual mediums).

Ghost In the Shell, as Shirow-sensei explains in the notes, employs the notion of bodies linking to a higher level spirit. This is a true ghost, 'the higher level spirit attached to human bodies'. In other words, the 'ghost in the shell' (*Ghost*, 362). For Shirow, spirits and physical bodies are (ideally) in harmony; cyborgs, such as Motoko Kusanagi, confront this issue head-on, experiencing the difficulties of fusing their spirit with a new, artificial body. (Shirow also employs the terms 'phase' and 'mode' (*Ghost*, 363), which is the entire body-brain-spirit entity).

The *Ghost In the Shell* franchise uses cybernetic technology to deliver what are essentially stories of ghosts, or spirits (*ayakashi*), or the dead, or *yokai* (demons). In Japanese pop culture, ghosts, the deceased, demons and the like are everywhere. Only a few (special/ magical/ disturbed) people can see them. Many times in several of the *Ghost In the Shell* outings vision is hacked, and scenes play out only in the perceiver's cyberbrain. Batou can make someone think he's been decapitated; Aoi can hack Batou so he's invisible; and the Major is a genius at manipulating perception and cyberbrains.

The companion *mangas* to *Ghost In the Shell* are usually regarded as *Appleseed* and *Dominion: Tank Police*; but for the religious/ metaphysical/ philosophical issues, it's *Orion*. Here Shirow-sensei delved deeper into how bodies relate to minds and spirits. (In the *Ghost* sequel comic, Shirow ventured further into the spiritual issues of cyborgization and artificial intelligence).

Orion is a 13-chapter *manga* of 266 pages in total, yet Shirow still provided 15 pages of notes and a dictionary of his invented terms. The dictionary offers explanations of terms such as 'anti-dharma master spell', 'cubular warheads', 'harmonic core disintegration' and 'hexapole solar reactor'.

Ghost In the Shell works superbly within a Japanese religious context – Shintoism is the main religion of Japan – because that's where it comes from (with some Buddhism and Taoism, too. There are numerous references to Buddhist religion in Shirow's work). In the notes for *Ghost*, Shirow cites some concepts from Shintoism:

> Shinto also considers things in terms of three stages – the *ikumusubi* or conscious self, the *tarumusubi* or unconscious self, and the *tamazu-memusubi* or the self that transcends the self. (363)

But *Ghost In the Shell* also works within a Western (and a Christian) context, and you can leave aside the Shintoist/ Buddhist philosophy. Of course: because this kind of *manga* and movie/ *anime* is a hybrid. As well as being very Japanese, *Ghost In the Shell* is also very Western (and very North American).

Take the form: the 1995 movie is a hi-tech thriller, which's primarily a Western form (and, in cinema at least, also a North American form). It employs the cop or detective form, which's North American. It uses *film noir* elements, too, which're again North American.

There's no doubt that *Ghost In the Shell* and Masamune Shirow's other works have been popular in the West partly because of their North American elements. It's the same with Katsuhiro Otomo and *Akira,* and Toshio Maeda and *Urotsukidoji.* Yet some franchises which're popular in the West – such as *Naruto, Bleach* and *Pokémon* – are very Japanese. And of course *Akira, Ghost In the Shell* and *Overfiend* are also distinctly Japanese.

SHIROW AND SURREALISM.

The art of Masamune Shirow has several links to the Surrealist movement in Europe of the 1920s-40s. The Surrealist artists did not seriously alter notions of sexuality, but they did question them. Indeed, Surrealism focused on sex obsessively, as obsessive as Symbolist art, from which it derives much. The Surrealists were well-known for their concepts of *l'amour fou*, of sex and death, of æsthetics and poetry. As André Masson wrote, 'eroticism and death are always coexistent.'[26] Typical among Surrealist images and philosophies is Salvador Dali's *Phenomenon of Ecstasy*, showing several photos of women (supposedly) in orgasm, a collage that targets the main areas of Surrealist discourse which are always connected: eroticism, death and 'the feminine'.[27]

Nearly all the major Surrealist artists made erotic art, or included erotic elements in their art: René Magritte produced the *Rape*, showing a woman's body as a face, with breasts for eyes and the vagina for the mouth,[28] Salvador Dali drew many erotic pictures, including bizarre, moustachioed men being serviced by prepubescent girls entitled *Choice Treats For Children* (child abuse images which are distinctly un-PC), and Man Ray produced films that evoked pornography. Hans Bellmer created a series of erotic images based on dolls (which were used in the second *Ghost In the Shell* movie).

One of the gods of the Surrealism movement was the Marquis de Sade. The high priest of metaphysical eroticism was championed by the European, artistic élite, such as Charles Baudelaire, Jean Cocteau, the Surrealists, Algernon Swinburne, Lautréamont, Fyodor Dostoievsky and John Cowper Powys. Among visual artists, the inheritors of the Sadeian pornographic ethic include Pablo Picasso, Hans Bellmer, Jean Cocteau, Max Ernst, Allen Jones and David Salle. Many artists have had a go at illustrating de Sade's work. Shirow's work draws on the Western/ European tradition of Sadeian erotica, of art created under the influence of the Divine Marquis. (The Sadeian approach to erotic material has certainly influenced Shirow's own erotic art).

BUGS.

Masamune Shirow is fond of bugs – insect and spider forms appear throughout his work (and have been taken up by the designers of the

26 André Masson: *Entriens avec Georges Charbonnier*, Paris, 1958, 138.
27 S. Dali: *Phenomenon of Ecstasy*, in *Minotaure*, nos. 3-4, 1933, 77.
28 R. Magritte: *The Rape*, 1934, pencil drawing, 14 x 9.5in, Menil Foundation Collection, Houston, Texas.

animé versions of his *manga*). For instance, the Tachikoma robots in *Ghost In the Shell: Stand Alone Complex*, the armed platforms in *Appleseed*, the nasty tanks in *New Dominion Tank Police*, the tanks in *Black Magic*, and many other tanks and robots are based on spiders (the Tachikoma even spin elasticated ropes, and leap about like spiders). In his erotic work, Shirow has depicted naked women being ensnared and tupped by giant spiders. Thus, altho' Shirow's *manga* employs circles as a primary motif (like so many artists, including Katsuhiro Otomo in *Akira*), many of his designs are organic, drawing on the insect world (Kentaro Miura, of *Berserk* fame, is another *mangaka* fond of bug designs, as was the 'god of *manga*', Osamu Tezuka).[29]

29 Tezuka named his company Mushi, after the *kanji* for insect (which he used for his pen-name).

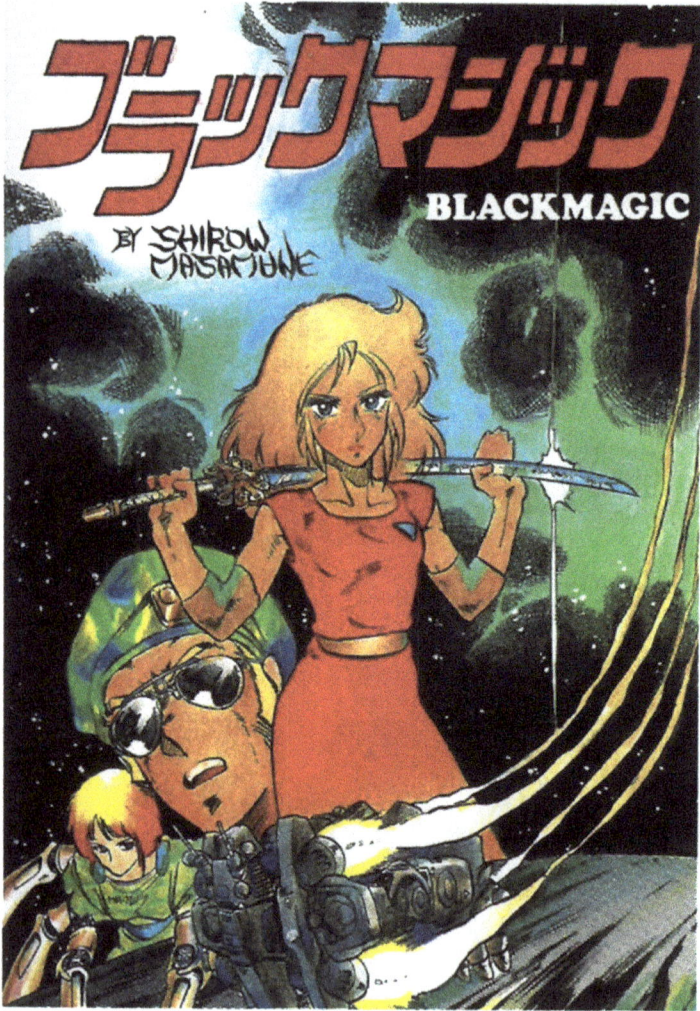

From the Black Magic manga.

Dominion: Tank Police manga
(this page and over).

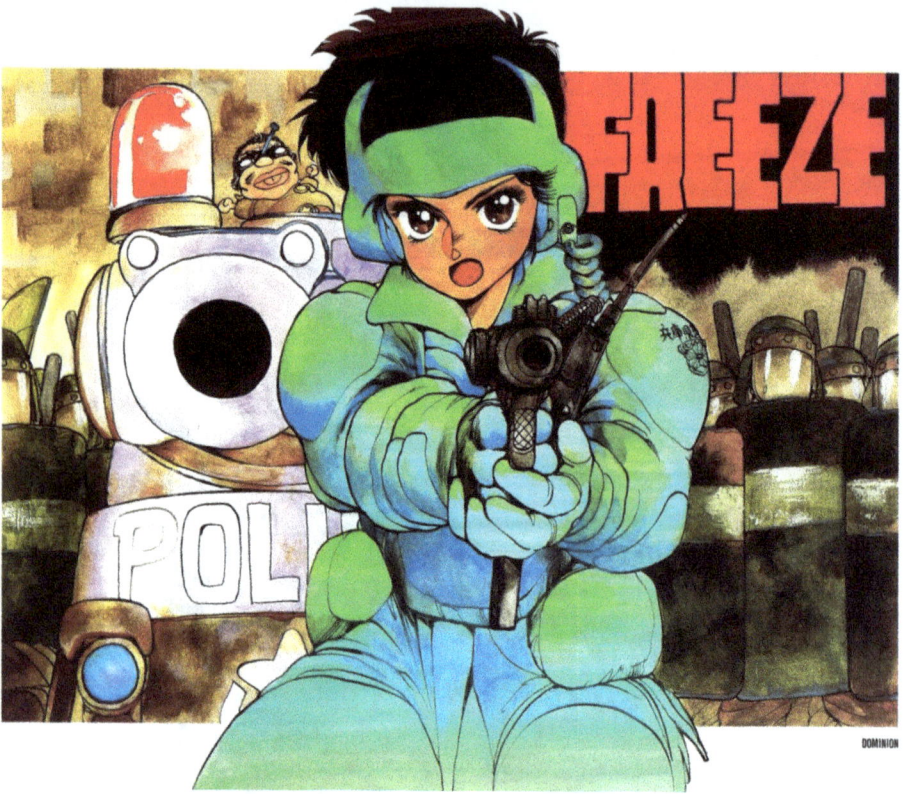

DOMINION

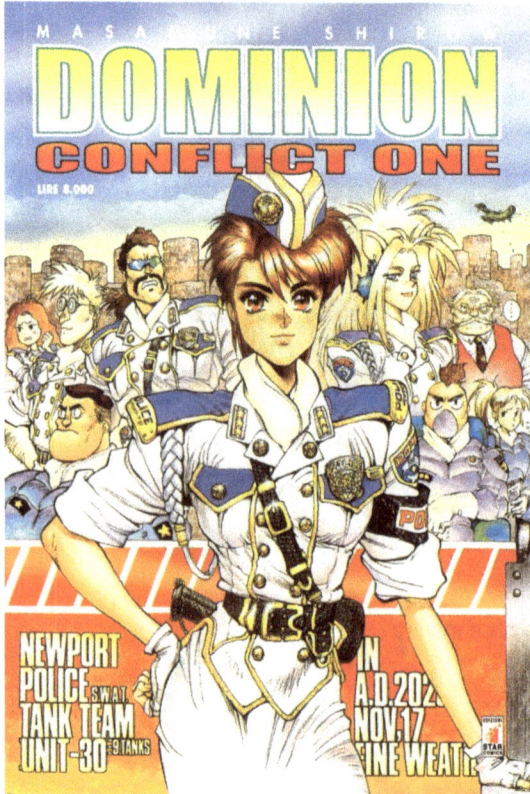

MASAMUNE SHIROW

DOMINION
CONFLICT ONE

LIRE 8.000

NEWPORT
POLICE SWAT
TANK TEAM
UNIT-30 9 TANKS

IN
A.D.202.
NOV.17
FINE WEAT...

Orion manga (1991)
(this page and over).

APPLESEED™
BOOK ONE

THE PROMETHEAN CHALLENGE

Pages from one of Masamune Shirow's finest
works, the Appleseed manga (this page and over).

Appleseed

Book Three

The Scales of Prometheus

Two double-page spreads from Appleseed, Volume 4.

Cyberworld

見つけたのはいいけどよ
充電してもどうせまた
命令無視して何処かで
作動停止するまで
夕陽を眺めてるんだろ
このロボットは

気に入ったぜ
依頼主にゃ悪いが
電脳コア頂戴して
太陽観測カメラにでも
繋いでやるか？

それとも面倒を
終わらせて
やるべきかな？

Dead Drive (2012-13)

From the Classical Fantasy Within novels (2007-10), in Newtype Ace magazine

Pieces 2: Phantom Cats (2010)

Pieces 5: Hellhound 2 (2011)

Greaseberries 1 (2014)

Greaseberries 4 (2019)

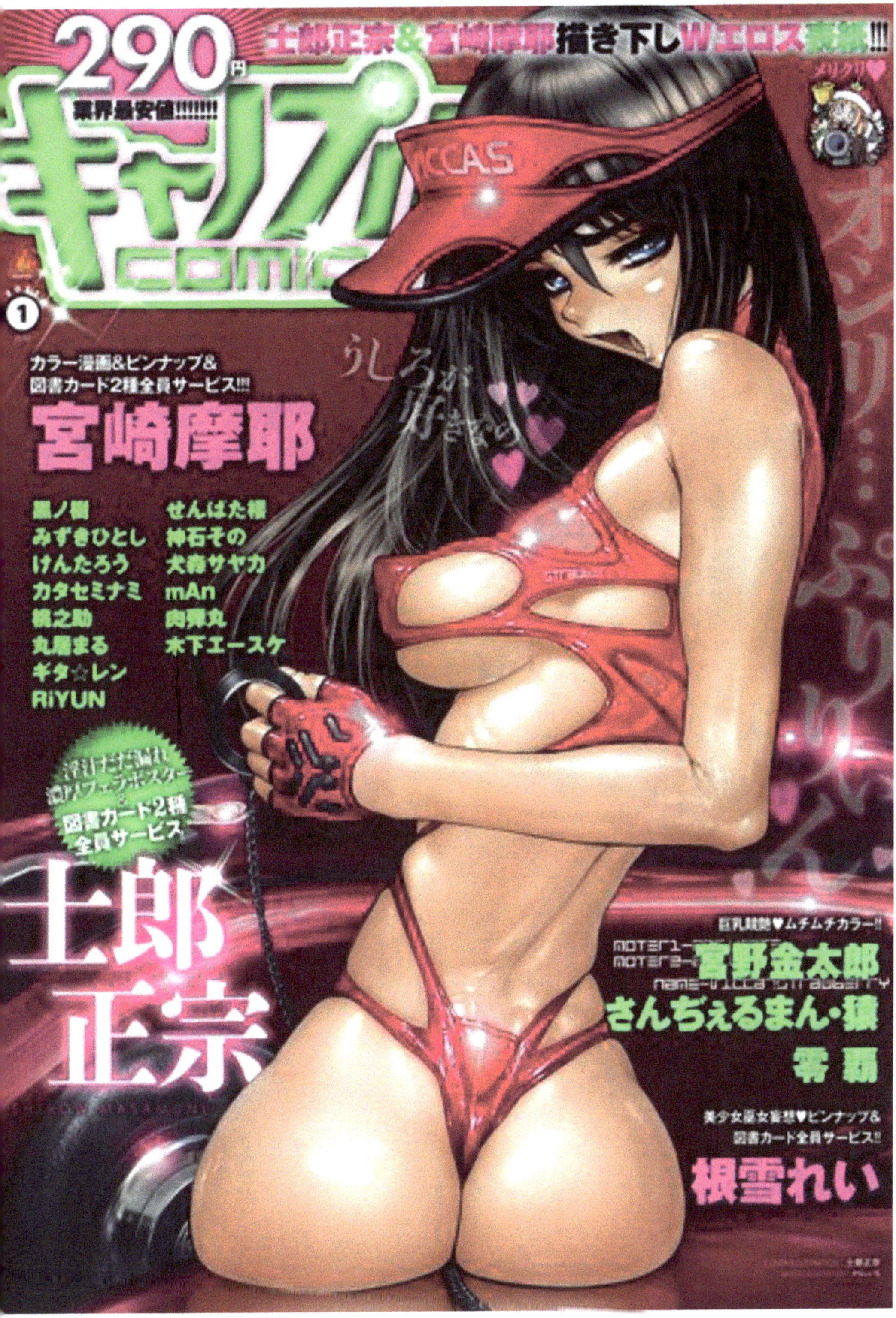

Canopri Comic cover

Examples of variations in the artwork used by Masamune Shirow:
it's the same model in different settings. (This page and over).

02

CYBERCULTURE₁

CYBERPUNK

The *Ghost In the Shell manga* and movies are masterpieces of cyberpunk culture, fully-fledged cyberpunk, cyberspace thrillers in which the themes of cyberpunk are foundational. Cyberspace and cyberpunk movies in the West, from the 1980s onwards, meant *Blade Runner, Tron, The Terminator, Aliens, Total Recall* and *RoboCop* (and anything else based on the fiction of Philip K. Dick). Japanese animation took up some of the those influences to create cyberpunk *meisterwerks* such as *Akira, Ghost In the Shell* and *Patlabor* (much of Masamune Shirow's work, like that of Katsuhiro Otomo, can be regarded as cyberpunk).

What does cyberspace and cyberpunk mean? Well, cyberspace is a technological mirror, a place of infinite (digital) desire, reflecting back the virtual narcissism of the subject (Ovid by way of Julia Kristeva). The internet/ network here is the ultimate inner space (in a technological era), which only individual imaginations can traverse, not groups, organizations, or institutions. A pleroma of connections always leading back to the self. E.M. Forster's 'Only connect', but connecting only with self. (The dream of total transparency, the fusion of self and technology, is a paradoxical one, because the technology is always there, always makes its presence felt. There is a desire to *become* the technology, but also to keep it always at a distance.)

> Penetration translates into envelopment [...] To become the cyborg, to put on the seductive and dangerous cybernetic space like a garment, is to put on the *female*. Thus cyberspace both *dis*embodies, in Sobchack's terms, but also *re*embodies in the polychrome, hypersurfaced cyborg character of the console cowboy. (in M. Benedikt, 1991)

The ambiguity with which cyberpunk fiction and films regard technology (and its manifestation in global consumerism) is fundamental: in the *Ghost In the Shell* cosmos, Major Kusanagi embodies that anxiety

---

1 Part of this chapter was written in 2002.

and ambiguity (one of her key attributes as a character is to carry the musings that Masamune Shirow wants to make about contemporary Japan and advanced, technological societies. And Shirow provides side-note musings on the current state of digital/ virtual technology).

> We are living in a system of technological temporality [asserts Paul Virilio in *Lost Dimensions*], in which duration and material support have been supplanted as criteria by individual retinal and auditory instants...

It's a world in which the question of modernity and postmodernism has been replaced by *'reality* and *post-reality'*.[2] It's not Baudrillardian 'simulation', Paul Virilio suggests in "Cyberwar, God and Television", but 'substitution': 'new technologies are substituting a virtual reality for an actual reality' (1994b).[3]

Cyberpunk is a postmodern cultural form *par excellence*, but then so is sci-fi fiction, which cyberpunk grows out of. Brian McHale suggested that sci-fi relates to postmodernism the way detective fiction related to modernism. Sci-fi and postmodernism were ontological, while detective fiction and modernism were epistemological.[4]

Cyberspace is also a 'nonspace' (*Neuromancer*, 63), a constructed space, and thus predictable, and therefore easier to understand than physical space.[5] It's noteworthy that the internet uses spatial metaphors: cyberspace, infoscape, chat rooms, surfing, navigation (*cp*. Arjun Appar-durai's concept of 'scapes').[6] An electronic cartography, a geography of gigabytes.

'Cyber' is now such a broad term it is applied to everything: the early terms 'cybernetics', 'cyberpunk' and 'cyberspace', have spread, like a viral infection, to include 'cybersexuality', 'cyberfeminism', 'cybersex', 'cyberporn', 'cyberreality', 'cybergurus', 'cyber-discourse', 'cyberbody', 'cyberqueer', 'cyberscience' and 'cyber-Gothic'.

In the conventional view of cyberspace (propounded by the *Wired, Mondo 2000* and the 'New Edge' crowd), you can go anywhere, be anybody, take on any identity, practise 'cybersex', which is 'safe sex' in an AIDS-ridden world: no exchange of bodily fluids, no touch, disembodied; in 'compu-sex', orgasm is electronic, digital, a matter of bits and bytes and prosthetic plug-ins; nirvana is on the other side of the screen, a material transcendence of the 'meat' or 'wetware' of the body ('bloodware' might be better term in an AIDS era). Allucquere Stone spoke (in "Will the Real Body Please Stand Up? Boundary Stories About Virtual Cultures"), of 'putting on' cyberspace as well as 'entering' it, a movement from physical, embodied space to symbolic, metaphorical space:

2 P. Virilio. *Lost Dimensions*, 1991, 84.
3 P. Virilio, 1994.
4 B. McHale: *Postmodernist Fiction*, London, 1987, 16.
5 J. Bolter: *Turing's Man: Western Culture in the Computer Age*, University of North Carolina Press, Chapel Hill, 1984.
6 A. Appadurai: "Global Ethnoscapes", in R. Fox, ed. *Recapturing Anthropology*, SAR Press, 1996.

The terminology of cyberspace has now spread out globally from Silicon Valley and Seattle, and the laboratories and R. & D. centres at M.I.T., N.A.S.A., J.P.L., I.B.M., Microsoft and Apple, entering popular culture and late corporate capitalism at many points: cyberpunk, virtual reality, 'virtual' communities and systems, 'consensual hallucination', information superhighway, internet, worldwide web, websites, e-mail, streaming, dot.com companies, cyborgs, robots, prosthetics, the 'inhuman' and 'post-human'.[7]

Jean Baudrillard, J.G. Ballard, Fredric Jameson, Donna Haraway and Paul Virilio have spoken of the totalising narrative of the new technologies, which has affinities with the sublime, the numinous, and the transcendent. Virilio speaks in *The Art of the Motor* of 'the hallucinatory utopia of communication technologies' (1995a): 'there is something divine in this new technology. The research on cyberspace is a quest for God. To be God', Virilio remarked in "Speed and Information" (1995b).

Scott Bukatman (one of the finest writers on postmodern, digital cinema of the *Ghost In the Shell* and *Blade Runner* type), coined the phrase 'terminal space' to cover everything from virtual reality, interactive systems, computer games and flight simulators, to visual effects movies, computer art and digital graphics on TV (1993, 107). What was true in 1993 (the year of Bukatman's most excellent book *Terminal Identity: The Virtual Subject in Postmodern Science Fiction*), is even more so now, with a 'cyber-space look' or 'cyber-style' occurring across many technological platforms: the internet, computer software, lifestyle magazines, fashion, TV ads, MTV and pop promos, music cover design, children's TV, sci-fi in movies and TV, and so on.[8] For Bukatman, William Gibson's infoscape is a graphic but limited metaphor for the global economy, a theme park reduction of the circulation and organization of capital.[9]

For some commentators,[10] cyber-culture fuses 1960s counter-culture with 'New Edge' (1990s) culture. In this view, the figures of the 1960s – hippies, backpackers, politicos – and their politics – of civil rights, racial equality, libertarianism, Communism, Maoism, left-wing politics, anti-censorship, pro-porn, free love, psychedelia, and Haight-Ashbury acid hallucinations – merge with 1990s figures: New Age travellers, crusties, eco-warriors, squatters, 'console cowboys', yippies, and computer hackers; and the politics of the 'New Edge' 1990s: direct action, road protests, crypto-anarchy, technophilia, cyberspace's 'consensual hallucination', 'whole earth' naturalism, ambient, dance and rave culture,[11] acid and Ecstasy. In this view, the right-on, hedonistic, guerrilla

7 Some of the finest introductions I've seen include: M. Benedikt, 1991; J. Brook, 1995; L. Cherny, 1996; M. Dery, 1996; J. Dixon, 1998; M. Featherstone, 1995; D. Porter, 1997; Z. Sardar, 1996; R. Shields, 1996; and J. Wolmark, 1999.
8 By the early 2000s, delivery systems were converging: interactive television, the internet, broadcasting, cel phones, PCs, I.S.D.N.s, digital subscriber lines (D.S.L.), satellites, wireless application protocol (W.A.P.), broadband, and so on.
9 S. Bukatman, in L. Cooke, 1995.
10 V. Sobchack, 2000; A. Ross, 1991; B. Kennedy, in D. Bell, 2000.
11 The soundtrack of cyberspace, apart from the hum of computers, the buzz of dialling up the internet, is 'fractal music' (fractal geometry made aural), New Age and ambient music, and dance/ rave music.

political action of the Sixties fuses with the privileged, individualistic, consumerist, technofetishistic libertarianism of the 'New Edge' Nineties.[12] Cyberspace offered self-empowerment, self-knowledge, a digital form of acid consciousness. Modem magick, a New Age version of prehistoric, archaic shamanism, a computerised cargo cult, a technopagan ghost dance. Sixties counter-culture done up in Eighties 'greed is good' aggression for the narcissistic me-me-me Nineties.

For Ziauddin Sardar (in 1996's "Alt. Civilizations. FAQ: Cyberspace As the Darker Side of the West"), the internet has been created as a 'new frontier', because new territories on the planet have run out (which echoes the narrative territory of *Ghost In the Shell* as being inside brains and networks). Cyberspace is postmodern colonialisation, 'the 'American dream' writ large', explicitly manufactured as a new market, dominated by America, a new kind of African interior or American West. Cyberspace, Sardar contends, erases non-Western histories, 'where anything remotely different from Western culture will exist only in digital form'. Cyberspace turns knowledge into nothing more than data, where learning is not the same as reading bits of hypertext. Cyberspace encourages hebetated, rootless hyper-individuals, where real people are reduced to strings of bits and zeroes; the sense of community and identity, face-to-face communication, is erased. Cyberspace privileges a white, masculinist, Western worldview and culture, marginalising other cultures; it's a totalising, racist, sexist monoculture, 'an escape from the inescapable reality of diversity in the actual world' (1996). For Sardar, only white, male, mainly European-American (and Westernized Asian) users have the money, the leisure time, and the technology to access the internet. The internet is controlled by giant corporations, Sardar claims, who are at the top of the hierarchy of power, with the multinationals like Ameritech, Pacific Bell and Sprint acting like the modern versions of the East India Company in the 19th century.

Cyberspace is also of course the space of finance, capital and A.T.M.s ('cyberspace is where your money is'; Masamune Shirow is also very concerned with modern business structures). In cyberspace, crimes are difficult to detect: money can disappear into off-shore accounts at the touch of a button.[13] And it's the realm of information and espionage war, being fought with computers, spy satellites and electronic espionage. And in cyberspace, cyborgs are virtually indistinguishable from humans.

It is precisely in this new digital realm that *Ghost In the Shell* is set – many of Public Security Section 9's targets are hackers, or computer criminals, or mobs trafficking in organs and e-brains. Having said that, for all its hi-tech exploration of the new digital cosmos, *Ghost In the Shell* is also very much a standard thriller and cop format: it still boils down to guns and cars (cool cars, sports cars, classic cars), to shoot-outs, to tailing

---

12 For Timothy Leary, Sixties acid guru, computers were the LSD of the Eighties, more addictive than heroin (C. Johnston: "Remembering Timothy Leary", *Village Voice*, 25 Nov, 1986).
13 Organised crime generates $750 billion a year, with drugs making $400-500bn, according to Z. Sardar (*Cyber-futures*). See also: "The Wired Scared Shitlist", *Wired*, 3, 1, Jan, 1995.

people, or stake-outs, to interrogations, to chases, and to villains in suits and heroes wearing shades.

Hackers play a significant role in the *Ghost In the Shell* cosmos (and in cyberpunk), because they can gain access to the most precious cargo in this future world: brains, and even spirits. For Vivian Sobchack (always an inspiring critic), writing in "New Age Mutant Ninja Hackers", the image of hackers working alone at their consoles is a kind of 'inter-active autism', a suspicious retreat into an imagined supremacy, 'alienation raised to the level of *ekstasis*' (2000). A way out of melancholy and solitude, a mythopoesis of simultaneous entrapment and escape (the 'shut-in' and recluse syndrome in Japanese society). Cyber-culture for Sobchack is a 'revenge of the nerds' who portray themselves as 'new age mutant ninja hackers', swashbuckling, rebellious individuals who, ironically, work for corporate America.[14] Though Sobchack doesn't doubt the contemporary world's ever-increasing immersion in electronic techno-logy, she is suspicious of attempts to escape 'real' politics and social contexts.

For Vivian Sobchack, Ziauddin Sardar, Andrew Ross, Sadie Plant and others, the ascendancy of cyberspace leads to a dangerously apolitical, asocial, disembodied state, in which the 'new age mutant ninja hackers' strain to leave behind their unpredictable, painful, fragile bodies, and become invincible, immortal cyborgs (2000). You can certainly see this in the *Ghost In the Shell* cosmos (and Masamune Shirow has satirized nerds and *otaku* in characters such as Krolden in *Ghost*). As Donna Haraway remarked in *Simians, Cyborgs, and Women* '[a]ny transcendent move is deadly; it produces death, through the fear of it'.

For Vivian Sobchack (in "New Age Mutant Ninja Hackers"), cyber-politics were not democratic nor progressive nor communitarian, but founded on 'privilege and the status quo: male privilege, white privilege, economic privilege, educational privilege, First World privilege' (2000). *Mondo 2000* cyber-ideology was against giant corporations – they were portrayed as the bad guys – but wanted their drugs, rock music, computers, sex, an ideology of privatisation and individualism. 'There is no escape from the meat, the flesh, and cyberspace is nothing transcendent', remarked Sadie Plant; instead, cyberspace was a cerebral retreat from life, male projections of dreams of technological mastery.[15]

While William Gibson spoke of 'console cowboys', Andrew Ross in *Strange Weather: Culture, Science and Technology In an Age of Limits* called them romantic 'rebels with a modem' (1991); Scott Bukatman defined two types: the 'cyber-punk' and the 'hippie-hacker' [1993, 199]). Both are opposed to centralised, technocratic institutions and ideologies, the hippy-hacker being more utopian and idealistic than the cyberpunk, enshrining self-empowerment, control, individuality, while the cyberpunk advocates the end of social control, freedom of data, crypto-anarchy.

For Andrew Ross (1991), cyberpunk comes out of white, adolescent,

---

14 The *Ghost In the Shell* cosmos posits some simple main types of criminal or villain: big businesses, criminal mobs, and the lone, crazy hacker.
15 In M. Featherstone, 1995.

masculine experience, with its fashionable paranoia, rock 'n' roll romanticism, and its suburban poeticisation of the city which ignores the politics of ethnicity, feminism, environmentalism and so on. (Ross noted that many cyberpunk writers were not urban, but suburban or non-urban: their protagonists were white males exploring the urban jungle and multicultural otherness like the colonisers of old).

•

Cyberculture reflects the general drift in contemporary cultural theory from epistemology to ontology and phenomenology (Martin Heidegger, Edmund Husserl), from subject to object (Gilles Deleuze, Walter Benjamin), from inside (interiority) to outside (exteriority), from the symbolic to the real (Slavoj Zizek, Jacques Lacan, Julia Kristeva), from transcendence to immanence (Jacques Derrida), from time to space (Gilles Deleuze), from linear to non-linear/ networks (Marshall McLuhan), from order to flux (Michael Hardt & Antonio Negri), from reality to simulation (Jean Baudrillard, Paul Virilio), from depth to surface, from style to pastiche (Frederic Jameson), from hermeneutics and semiotics to acts and performativity (Elizabeth Grosz, Judith Butler). Or, to put it in a table of opposites:

modern	postmodern
industrial	post-industrial
reality	post-reality/ simulation
feminism	post-feminism
epistemology	ontology
depth	surface
centre	boundaries
inside	outside
subject	object
transcendence	immanence
time	space
order	flux / flow
mind	artificial intelligence
communities	networks
hermeneutics/ semiotics	acts/ performativity
body	machine/ cyborg
biology	biomechanics
sex/ reproduction	genetics/ replication

Some of the key texts in cyberculture include:

(1) Isaac Asimov's *I, Robot* series, Donna Haraway's "A Manifesto For Cyborgs" and *Primate Visions* and *Simians, Cyborgs and Women*, William Gibson's *Neuromancer*, and Scott Bukatman's *Terminal Identity*.

(2) Movies such as *2001: A Space Odyssey, Blade Runner, RoboCop, Star Wars, Transformers, Star Trek, A.I.*, David Cronenberg's work, and of course numerous Japanese *animé* movies, including *Akira, Patlabor,*

Gunbuster, Final Fantasy, Paranoia Agent, Psycho-Pass, .Hack, Appleseed, and *Ghost In the Shell.*

(3) The writings of Jean Baudrillard, Gilles Deleuze, Marshall McLuhan, Jacques Lacan, Paul Virilio, Michel Foucault, Frederic Jameson, Jean-François Lyotard, Vivian Sobchack, Luce Irigaray, Jacques Derrida, Elizabeth Grosz, and Judith Butler.

(4) And novelists such as J.G. Ballard, Philip K. Dick, Thomas Pynchon, Margaret Atwood, Arthur C. Clarke, John Varley, William Burroughs, Isaac Asimov and the Strugatskys (the *Ghost In the Shell* series has directly referenced some of those writers).

Some of the key ideologues of cyberculture include Donna Haraway, Andrew Ross, Claudia Springer, Nicola Nixon, Sadie Plant, Allucquere Rosanne Stone, Jenny Wolmark, Scott Bukatman, Arthur and Marilouise Kroker, Michael Benedikt, Mark Dery, Jennifer González, Zoë Sofia, Mary Ann Doane, Anne Balsamo, Thomas Foster, Chela Sandoval, Mike Featherstone, Lisa Cartwright, Veronica Hollinger, Jon Stratton and Ziauddin Sardar.[16]

•

How old is cyberspace and virtual reality? Very old, if William Gibson's definition of cyberspace as a 'consensual hallucination' is applied to discourses such as art and religion. If religion is a 'consensual hallucination', or what American anthropologist Weston La Barre calls a 'group dream', then cyberspace is at least 40,000 years old (going back to the first religious artefacts and cave drawings, although religious belief is probably much older – animism and shamanism certainly are much older). Ditto with art (all art was in origin made for religious purposes).[17]

'Oldest' is privileged in primatology, said Donna Haraway, while 'newest' defined cybernetics: that's certainly true of *Ghost In the Shell:* there's always some new technology or new virus coming along (like computer systems, the cyborgs and Public Security Section 9's technology has to be constantly upgraded). The emphasis on the 'new' is of course fundamental to late capitalism. Consumerism is founded on replacing the 'old' with the 'new'.

How old is the oldest cyborg, human-machine interface or prosthetic device? At least two million years, if the concept of the 'low tech' cyborg is applied to prehistoric people, pre-*homo sapiens*, who used flint axes to flense flesh off carcasses.[18]

---

16 Apart from the texts mentioned above, other key cybertexts include: Michael Benedikt's *Cyberspace,* Mark Dery's *Escape Velocity,* Anne Balsamo's *Technologies of the Gendered Body,* Teresa de Lauretis's *Technologies of Gender,* Fred Botting's *Sex, Machines and Navels,* and the collections of essays: *Cyberspace/ Cyberbodies/ Cyberpunk; Cyberfutures; Cybersexualities; The Cybercultures Reader; The Cyborg Handbook; Storming the Reality Studio; Future Visions; Virtual Politics; Virtual Culture; Virtual Futures; Future Natural; Resisting the Virtual Life; Internet Culture; Cultures of the Internet; Technoculture; Wired Women; Digital Delirium; Inhuman Reflections;* and *Flame Wars.*

17 W. La Barre: *The Ghost Dance: The Origins of Religion,* Allen & Unwin, 1972.

18 In museums such as the British Museum you can see two million year-old hand tools. And not much has changed in two million years: in *2001: A Space Odyssey,* primitive humans use tools to kill animals and – just as significantly – rival groups. Today, the most sophisticated and advanced technological development is found in military defence (machinery for killing people).

Cyborgs, robots and human 'hybrids'[19] have been a standard component of science fiction since the first great, classic book of sci-fi and horror, Mary Shelley's *Frankenstein*. Since then, popular culture has been awash with cyborgs, androids and robots: famous examples in Western culture include: the robot Maria in *Metropolis*, Gort in *The Day the Earth Stood Still*, *Forbidden Planet*'s Robbie, *2001*'s HAL, R2D2 and C3PO, the 'droids in *Star Wars*,[20] Lee Majors in *The Six Million Dollar Man*, Yul Brynner in *Westworld*, Arnold Schwarzenegger in the *Terminator* series, Judge Dredd, RoboCop, Ash in *Alien*, Number Five in *Short Circuit*, the Mark 13 cyborg in *Hardware*, *Max Headroom*, Data and the Borg in *Star Trek*, the military cyborgs in *Universal Soldier*, Max in *Dark Angel*, Haley Joel Osment's David in *A.I.*, television sci-fi (*Dr Who*, *Stargate SG-1*, *Farscape*, *Babylon 5*, *Blake's 7*, *Futurama*, *Total Recall 2070*, *The Bionic Woman*, *Quantum Leap*), and so on, not to mention children's toys (such as War Planet, Transformers, Digimon, Beast Wars, Warhammer), and the thousands of characters in comics, cartoons, TV series, films and computer games which are turned into merchandising: *Teenage Mutant Ninja Turtles*, *The Mighty Morphin Power Rangers*, *Pokémon*, *The Mask*, *Tank Girl*, *X-Men*, *Men in Black* and *Judge Dredd*. And of course in Philip K. Dick's fiction: the replicants in *Blade Runner*, Arny's Quaid in *Total Recall*, etc. However, it is in Japanese culture, in *manga* and *animé*, that robots rule supreme (with giant robots a speciality).

For some commentators (D. Bell, 2000), the cyborg is not limited to the characters in movies and TV series such as *The Terminator* or *Star Trek*, but texts can be cyborgian, or founded on a cyborgian consciousness (transgressing Cartesian epistemologies and Western philosophy's dualisms).[21] For critics such as Hal Foster, Mark Dery, Claudia Springer, Anne Balsamo and Scott Bukatman, cyborgs in contemporary cinema are 'a last bastion of overdetermined human, masculinist definition, bodies armoured against the malleability and invisibility of the present'.[22] They reaffirm bourgeois, dominant ideology, conventional notions of good/ evil, male/ female, human/ machine, self/ other (A. Balsamo, 1999). Of course, contemporary Japanese animation, just like contemporary Holly- wood cinema, doesn't get much further than the sensational image of humans interacting with cyborgs at the most extreme levels: sex, violence and death. Even movies enshrined by the critical academy, such as *Blade Runner*, don't go much beyond the titillating question: 'what's it like to

---

19 On cyborgs, cyberspace and cyberpunk, see: S. Bukatman, 1993; D. Haraway, 1985 and 1989; J. Prosser, *Second Skins: The Body Narratives of Transsexuality*, Columbia University Press, N.Y., 1998; E. Rabkin, 1987; S. Brewster, 2000; T. de Lauretis, 1987; J. Rusher & T. Frentz, 1995; B. Rux, *Hollywood vs. the Aliens*, Frog, Berkeley, 1997; P. Schelde, 1993; F. Botting, 1999; J. Telotte, 1996, in N. Ruddick, 1992, and "The Tremulous Public Body", *Journal of Popular Film & Television*, 19, 1, 1991; R. Barringer, 1997; A. Balsamo, 1988; C. Springer, 1993; D. Larson: "Machine and Messiah", *Genders*, 18, 1993; G. Schwab, 1987; P. Warrick, 1980; C. Fuchs, 1993; and F. Glass, 1989.
20 Partly based on the peasants in Akira Kurosawa's *The Hidden Fortress* (1958).
21 For Anne Balsamo, 'cyborgs are *the* postmodern icon' (1996).
22 S. Bukatman, 1993, 17.

tup an android?'[23] But Japanese culture's use of robots and cyborgs is far, far more sophisticated than that of Western culture.

Mas'ud Zavarzadeh in "Ideology, Post-structuralism and Class Politics" writes:

> "Cyborg", in (post)modern feminist and queer theory, is the negation of "ideology" – normativity – it is a figure whose very existence signifies the polysemic performance of the excessive play of sexual difference and absolute indeterminacy ("affinity").[24]

Associated with the cyborg or robot are the many monsters in the horror genre, what Slavoj Zizek calls the 'return of the living dead': Leatherface in *The Texas Chainsaw Massacre* (with his trademark mask and chainsaw extension). Anti-heroes with knives for fingers (Freddy Krueger in *A Nightmare On Elm Street* and the youth in *Edward Scissorhands*). 'Jaws' in the *James Bond* films of the 1970s, with rows of metal teeth. *Hellraiser's* Pinhead. Ghosts (*The Sixth Sense, What Lies Beneath, The Others*). Demons and the Devil (*The Exorcist, The Devil's Advocate, Spawn, Angel Heart*). Vampires (*Twilight, Dracula, Buffy, Van Hellsing, The Lost Boys, Interview With the Vampire*). Sub-humans or mutants (*The Fly, Basket Case*). Zombies (such as the flicks directed by George Romero). Werewolves (*Harry Potter, An American Werewolf in London, Wolf, The Howling*). Devilish aliens (*Gremlins, Critters, Independence Day,* the *Alien* series). Poltergeists (*Poltergeist*). Killer dolls (*Magic, Child's Play*). Witches (*Salem's Lot, The Craft,* the *Blair Witch* films). And psychopaths and serial killers (the *Friday the 13th, Candyman, Scream* and *Hallowe'en* movies).

For critic Donna Haraway, one of the famous theorists on cyborgian culture, the cyborg represents the possibility of new identities, moving beyond binaries, boundaries, universalisations. Transgression is a key theme in Haraway's thinking. New sutures, new borders. For Haraway, the technological revolution is as significant as industrial capitalism (1985). In "A Manifesto For Cyborgs", Haraway offered a chart of transitions 'from the comfortable old hierarchical dominations to the scary new networks I have called the informatics of domination'.

Here, simulation replaces representation, biotics replaces organisms, surface replaces depth, obsolescence replaces decadence, replication replaces reproduction, genetic engineering replaces sex, robotics replaces work, 'fields of difference' replaces the nature/ culture binary, and

---

23 The hospital scenes which were dropped from *Blade Runner*, featuring Deckard and Holden, contain some vital information on this matter: Holden asks Deckard if he had sex with the snake woman before killing her. The dialogue's in that locker room, macho fashion (*Blade Runner*'s a very macho movie), but it's a key point, about having sex with the androids. Holden tells Deckard (in the deleted scenes on the DVD releases) that Deckard shouldn't have a crisis of conscience about it – it's like doing your washing machine, then switching it off (sex followed by death). Deckard doesn't really respond to Holden's taunts: if this scene comes *after* Deckard has made love with Rachel, the scene has a new dramatic inflection. The filmmakers left the scenes out, as they don't seem to add much to the film, but the exchange about having sex with Zhora is absolutely central to the theme of *Blade Runner*, not only the romantic subplot.
24 In A. Kibbey, *Sexual Artifice*, 294.

'cyborg citizens' replaces the public and private (we are all cyborgs claimed Haraway; Haraway has famously proclaimed herself a cyborg, a quintessential technological body [1985]).

In Harawayan cyborg culture, the boundaries of the 'self' are increasingly becoming blurred (many cultural theorists have concerned themselves with borders and marginality: Homi Bhabha, Paul Gilroy and Julia Kristeva). We see Major Kusanagi in *Ghost In the Shell* directly experiencing this new blurring of boundaries between the self and the world, the self and the network (and where the digital network becomes the world – at the end of each *Ghost In the Shell* installment, she disappears into it).

New terms are required: the 'trans-human' is halfway between the human and the 'post-human', a site of suture and marginality; the 'post-human' is an enhanced human (who may be 'post-biological'), with neurological, biological, psychological and technological enrichments (most of the key characters in the *Ghost In the Shell* cosmos are technologically augmented. Even charas who're mostly 'human', such as Togusa and Aramaki, have cybernetic elements).[25]

Science and religion would become increasingly important as they fuse in the near future, Masamune Shirow reckoned in the first *Ghost In the Shell manga*, because religion presided over issues of life and death, and the body (*Ghost*, 364). As more people received artificial organs and partial cyborgization, religion and science would need to work together.

The moment of the construction of the cyborg is a vital scene in the fantasy genre, whether it's in *Metropolis, Frankenstein* (Victor Frankenstein cries, 'it's alive!'), *The Fifth Element,* or in the title sequence of *The Six Million Dollar Man*.[26] And it provides the main titles for the two *Ghost In the Shell* movies (meanwhile, the high and demanding maintenance for cyborgs is a recurring motif in Masamune Shirow's *Ghost In the Shell manga*).

For Raymond Bellour, movies concentrate on this primal birth scene because this is what the cinematic apparatus is always doing, substituting a simulcra for reality.[27] The re-animation of the monster, the cyborg or the human is one of cinema's specialities. It's one of cinema's (and sci-fi's) primal scenes. Cinema is, physically, a continuous resurrection: people photographed eighty years ago at 16 or 24 frames per second seem to come back to life. It's the flipside of Jean-Luc Godard's remark that cinema literally films death, that the people one films will die. Also, actors speak of enjoying playing death scenes, pantomiming the mysterious, perennially fascinating moment of ultimate transition.

25 The *Ghost In the Shell* movies also draw on the *I, Robot* series by Isaac Asimov, as well as Asimov's robotics laws.
26 'We can rebuild him' – no one asks, 'why bother?'.
27 R. Bellour: "Ideal Hadaly", in C. Penley, 1991, 127.

THE SOLDIER AND THE CYBORG.

Another manifestation of the relation between military science and sci-fi fiction is the figure of the soldier and the cyborg. Soldiers are expensive to train and maintain, and have to be protected: the 1980s saw a rise in 'Exo-Skeleton' or 'Exo-Man' technology, the S.I.P.E. ('Soldier Integrated Protective Ensemble'), an all-over suit that protected the soldier against chemical, biological and nuclear devices. The 'Exo-Skeleton' came equipped with night-sight goggles and a heads-up display; there was a targeting system that tracked the eye's movements and pointed the rifle wherever the soldier was looking. Freighted with all the hi-tech gear, real-life soldiers become, literally, 'fighting machines', real-life cyborgs, backed up the most sophisticated communications and technology available.

As the modern, techno-rich soldier and the sci-fi movie cyborg merge, it leads to the emphasis on male narcissism, physical prowess, aggression and violence (Motoko Kusanagi's femininity in *Ghost In the Shell* takes a back seat when she is the military cyborg).

One of the key ancestors of the cinematic cyborg is the Nietzschean *Übermensch* and what Klaus Theweleit called the 'fascist soldier male' (referring to the German *Freikorps* of the 1920s and 1930s).[28] In most (Western) movies, cyborgs are typically gendered male; they are violent, aggressive, muscular, narcissistic, and deadly – *Universal Soldier, Terminator, Total Recall, RoboCop* (C. Springer, 1991). The standard movie cyborg's hulking he-man identity is the polar opposite of the noetic robot, the bespectacled computer nerd, feeble, 'feminised', all brain, no body. The cyborg is a 'killing machine', unstoppable, invincible, with a philosophy that echoes the German 'fascist soldier male' (and the military in general): fearlessness, endurance, misogyny (and submerged homoeroticism), self-preservation, protection against anything 'other' (women, different ethnicities), repressed sexuality or frustration expressing itself as extreme violence. (Japanese culture, meanwhile, has established a long tradition of female cyborgs and female robots[29] – Masamune Shirow's fiction is a well-known example. However, you can also argue that in many respects the gender of the Japanese cyborg is a minor issue, because they still act like male soldiers).

Popular movies – East and West – express an ambivalence about the cyborg's violence: on the one hand, the cyborg seems to be upholding the law, policing the streets, killing terrorists, drug barons and criminals (just as in *Ghost In the Shell* on screen). Cyborg violence is the right-wing dream of instantaneous justice, with no court trial, testimonies or juries (and Major Kusanagi has shot and killed criminals without bringing them in for trial). On the other hand, what if cyborg violence is directed at the innocent? What about mistakes? Are cyborgs 'our postmodern

---

28 It's not too much of a leap to link the cyborgs in *Ghost In the Shell* and Japanese sci-fi *animé* with fascism.

29 And also the theme of dolls who want to become human.

Frankenstein monsters'? The ambiguity is played out in Hollywood movies such as *RoboCop, Judge Dredd* and *Starship Troopers*, and is a staple of Japanese sci-fi *animé*.

THE MILITARY AND WESTERN MOVIES.

'Nuke the planet!' splutter the Vietnam War-like grunts in 1986's *Aliens*, and space opera Nazis proceed to do just that in *Star Wars*. If the Western action movies of the 1980s and 1990s (the era of *Ghost In the Shell*) reflected the Republican, right-wing, pro-military ideology of the Reagan and Bush eras (*Rambo, Star Wars, Aliens, James Bond,* the Tom Clancy movies), horror and sci-fi movies expressed anxieties about technology, science, D.N.A., and genetics. In the mainstream action genre of the 1980s and 1990s in the Western world, the hero is typically a soldier (often ex-Vietnam War or Gulf War), a cop, a secret agent (and also a maverick, operating outside the law – 'it's like fucking Saigon!' yells the corrupt F.B.I. officer mounting a helicopter attack in *Die Hard*). By contrast, in cyber and sci-fi movies, the heroes are scientists, hackers, and journalists.

The modern 'soft skin' soldier is coveted by military strategists, and is a 'virtual cyborg', in which weapons systems enhance biological limits.[30] Although they're a problematic figure for post-Vietnam War and post-9/11 Hollywood cinema, the soldier is tailor-made for the action movie: they have to know about geometry, topography, navigation, artillery, mortars, armour, mines, counter-mine weapons, engines, laser designators, thermal sights, satellite communications, radio, ammunition, demolition, the logistics of supplies and transport, and so on (Major Kusanagi in *Ghost In the Shell* often displays her in-depth knowledge of military hardware (courtesy of Shirow-sensei's in-depth research), and the filmmaking team behind *Ghost In the Shell* are clearly weapons nuts – director Mamoru Oshii will even talk about getting exactly the right sound for Kusanagi or Batou loading a gun. And when Batou's racing to help Kusanagi at the climax of the first *Ghost In the Shell* movie, they discuss weapons over the network, and Batou stops off at HQ so he can pick up a hefty gun which'll take out the tank).

Parachutists with F.X.C. Guardian parachutes can be dropped from 35,000 feet, 25 miles from the target, and parasail to it, reading a map, identifying other soldiers with infrared devices, and landing in a 10 yard zone. So far so gung-ho; the modern soldier, a nexus of hardware, science, programming and training, is the embodiment of conservative, capitalist ideology; the military works at the sharp end of late commodity capitalism, protecting the free market and the global economy, making certain no one messes with the sacred right to trade in any territory (plus, if possible, colonial expansion into new territories, such as cyberspace).

In a way, this is the grand narrative of Western flicks like *Rambo, Predator, Commando, Eraser, The Untouchables, Batman, Star Wars, Patriot Games, Scarface, Mission: Impossible,* Vietnam War movies, the *Lethal*

---

30 K. Robins & L. Levidow. "Soldier, Cyborg, Citizen", in J. Brook, 1995.

Weapon, Die Hard, Beverly Hills Cop and the *Godfather* series. The cyber underbelly of this Great American Dream of science, progress, individualism, militarism, capitalism and expansion, leaks out in the dystopias of science fiction movies (*Brazil, Twelve Monkeys, Judge Dredd, A Clockwork Orange, Escape From New York, The Handmaid's Tale, Terminator*, and *Blade Runner*), the cynicism of the cyber-thriller and cyberspace movies (*Existenz, Antitrust, The Matrix, Hackers, Strange Days, Johnny Mnemonic, Total Recall, Tron, The Net, Virtuosity* and *The Lawnmower Man*), the paranoia of the post-Watergate conspiracy theories of the U.F.O. genre (*The X-Files, Independence Day, War of the Worlds, Invasion of the Body Snatchers*), the pessimism of the endless post-apocalyptic movies (*The Road Warrior, Tank Girl, Waterworld*, the Italian *barbari del futuro* genre, and numerous Japanese *animé* movies, topped by *Overfiend* and *Akira*), the anxiety of the nuclear science and war genre (*Broken Arrow, War Games, The Day After* and *Godzilla*),[31] and the many movies about science running awry (*Jurassic Park, Westworld, The Relic, Event Horizon* and *Outbreak*).

Sci-fi and fantasy movies have usually been way behind real advances in science and technology. The astonishing developments in the vast military R. & D. from the Seventies onwards demonstrate that (compare the technology in the *Star Wars, Star Trek* or *Alien* movies of 1977-1979 with what was happening in the U.S. Defense Department). While some of the ideas in sci-fi movies seem 'far-fetched' or way beyond the reach of contemporary science (time travel, bionics, supra-light speed, teleportation, anti-gravity), the complexity and sophistication of real scientific research and practice is far in advance of cinema.

What's so impressive about the *Ghost In the Shell* movies (and *Ghost In the Shell: Stand Alone Complex* on TV) is how accurate and in-touch they are with new developments in science and technology, and how elegantly they integrate them into the world of *Ghost In the Shell* (that is also down to *manga* author Masamune Shirow, who is clearly passionately fascinated by science and technology, as well as being a technofetishist, like so many people working in Japanese science fiction *manga* and *animé*, and also a weapons fanatic).

Cybernetics and cyberism are everywhere in cinema. You could say that cyber/ cyborg/ robotic/ artificial intelligence ingredients are part of pix from the past decades such as *Ghost, Misery, Addams Family, Death Becomes Her, Mrs Doubtfire, The Mask, The Hunchback of Notre Dame, Godzilla, X-Men, What Lies Beneath, Hollow Man, The Mummy*, and psychothrillers such as *Basic Instinct, Silence of the Lambs, Basic Instinct* and *Cape Fear*. Even kids' movies, such as *Toy Story* (1995) and *Small Soldiers* (1998), explored the relations between the real, the undead, cyborgs and the new technology in a Gothic fashion: *Small Soldiers*, which was sold as a cross between *Toy Story* and *Gremlins*, was about toys (the Commandos battling the Gorgonites) implanted with military defence technology microchips (in the finest sequence, Sindy and Barbie dolls are brought to life, Frankenstein-style, and terrorise the teenage leads). *Small*

---

31 M. Hehlert: "From Captain America to Wolverine", in D. Bell, 2000, 118.

Soldiers reflected social anxieties about nanotechnology and defense weaponry falling into the wrong corporate capitalist hands (which's also cropped up in Japanese *animé*, including *Ghost In the Shell: Stand Alone Complex*). *Toy Story* was one of a number of contemporary, Hollywood blockbusters (animated, computer-assisted, or live action), which combined miniaturisation with sci-fi, horror and Gothic tropes (others included *Antz, A Bug's Life, The Borrowers, James and the Giant Peach* and *Stuart Little*), miniaturisation being one of the rudiments of much technological advance in the electronic epoch.

FRANKENSTEIN AND GHOST IN THE SHELL

If you haven't read Mary Shelley's 1820 novel *Frankenstein*, I highly recommend it. Like *Dracula* by Bram Stoker, it is a novel of incredible emotional and psychological power, a book which consumes the reader, a book with a primal energy that hasn't diminished a jot in 200 years.

The *Frankenstein* mythology has numerous links to the *Ghost In the Shell* series,[32] including scientific exploration, the creation of cyborgs (and their ambiguous, troubled relationship with their creator/s), and scientists acting like gods.

As well as *Frankenstein,* Mary Shelley (1797-1851) produced a novella, 5 novels, 2 travelogues, letters, essays, poems, reviews, and many short stories. Shelley's novels included *Valperga* (1823), *The Last Man* (1826), *The Fortunes of Perkin Warbeck* (1830), *Lodore* (1835), and *Falkner* (1837). Her novella, *Matilda*, which dealt with father-daughter incest, was not published until 1959.

The novel of *Frankenstein* is comprised of different narratives:[33] the topmost narrative is Mary Shelley's narrator; the next one is Margaret Savile, who appears to collect together the story's documents; Savile's narrative contains the account of Robert Walton, the polar explorer, and Savile's sister; Walton's story takes in that of Victor Frankenstein and his account of creating the monster; the monster has his own story too, contained inside Frankenstein's tale. The novel is many-layered, with a number of voices and points-of-view.

Mary Shelley's great novel and the mythical monster have been the

---

32 Like *Ghost In the Shell*, Katsuhiro Otomo's *Akira* exhibits a striking affinity with the Frankenstein myth: for instance, the big themes are very familiar in *Akira*: it's *Frankenstein*, it's science creating monsters, and the monsters rebelling and turning on their masters; it's *Faust* (and the myth of Prometheus), with science (and society) making a pact with the Devil; it's capitalism and the military machine expanding unchecked (including exploiting humans in grotesque experiments); and it's any number of anxieties – about technology, science, militarism, nationalism, youth vs. age, and modern Japan.
33 A key ingredient in *Frankenstein* is the multiple narrative viewpoints: it is a novel constructed from a variety of elements, like the monster: there are letters, journals, accounts, from a variety of characters. Like *Dracula*, the complexity of *Frankenstein* stems partly from this multi-level approach. There is no trusted, impartial God-like narrator telling the story in *Frankenstein*.

subject of many readings: as class struggle, industrialization's product, a symbol of the French Revolution, as technology, the danger of scientific experimentation, and a 'totalizing monster', in Franco Moretti's term, like Dracula, who can never be vanquished.[34] Frankenstein's monster is a multiplitic chameleon, open to a multitude of interpretations.

Frankenstein has also been interpreted as being about the fear of the population explosion; a warning about colonialization (Viktor takes apart the old in order to make the new); about the French Revolution and the Terror; and a protest about classism. Certainly the new debates in science and technology of the early 19th century contributed towards the novel, as pretty much all critics attest: it's known that Mary Shelley and her husband Percy were interested in galvanism, which had been tried on criminals (where the two schools of thought of vitalism and materialism were debated).

Judith Halberstam, in *Skin Shows: Gothic Horror and the Techno-logy of Monsters*, her excellent feminist interpretation of Gothic fiction past and present, remarked:

> The importance of Mary Shelley's *Frankenstein* (1816) within the Gothic tradition, modern mythology, the history of the novel, and a cultural history of fear and prejudice cannot be emphasized too strongly. (1995, 28)

For Daniel Cottom, 'Frankenstein's monster images the monstrous nature of representation'; it evades definition; it won't be locked down to a single reading.[35] As Halberstam puts it:

> The form of the novel is its monstrosity; its form opens out onto excess because, like the monster of the story, the sum of the novel's parts exceeds the whole. Its structure, the exoskeleton, and not its dignified contents – philosophies of life, meditations on the sublime, senti-mental narratives of family and morality, discussion of æsthetics – makes this novel a monster text. (1995, 31)

Frankenstein locates true horror in the body, in people, not in gods, dæmons, ghosts or monks (we note that the body is absolutely central to *Ghost In the Shell*). For Brian Aldiss, a huge admirer of *Frankenstein*, the novel importantly replaces the priest with the scientist as someone who investigates life's mysteries.

Frankenstein also inaugurates the key element of the 'sense of wonder' in science fiction (the view that sci-fi replaces religious fiction, with its evocations of wonder, mystery, the sublime, the transcendent, aliens and computers as gods or higher powers, cyborgs as angels or demons, monsters as Devils, beings from other worlds, shamanic or spiritual journeys to other planets, miraculous events (such as time or space travel), amazing powers, the machines, technology and spaces of science replacing

34 F. Moretti: *Signs Taken For Wonders*, Verso, 1983, 84.
35 J. Halberstam, 31; D. Cottom: "*Frankenstein* and the Monster of Representation", *Substance*, 28, 1980, 60.

the occult, the supernatural, the spiritual.

Feminist and cultural critics have pointed out the obvious interpretations of the 1931 *Frankenstein* film, and the 1820 novel: the gender role reversals; the feminization of the Viktor Frankenstein character; the homoerotic undertones in the relationship between the scientist and the monster (the monster tells Frankenstein he will be with him on his wedding night); Frankenstein as a latent homosexual; or he's impotent; or it's a Nietzschean sublimation of his sexual desire into his scientific work.

Ghost In the Shell costume play: from top left, clockwise: Makiron • Edra Lena •
Crystal Graziano • Omi Gibson , 2011 • Rosie Cupcakes, 2014.

Appleseed costume play: Anime Expo, 2007 and Sakura Con, 2009.
Dominion: Tank Police costume play: the Musson Sisters, London Film and Comic Con, 2014 and South Africa, 2010.

Some toys, games and merchandize based on the
work of Masamune Shirow.

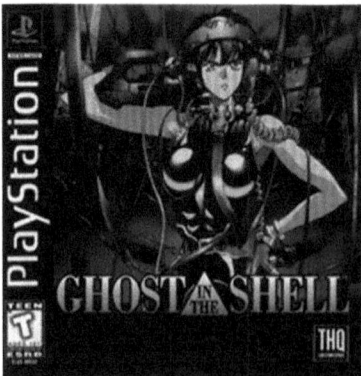

PART TWO

THE GHOST IN THE SHELL MOVIE

GOSUTO IN ZA SHERU:
KOKAKU KIDOTAI

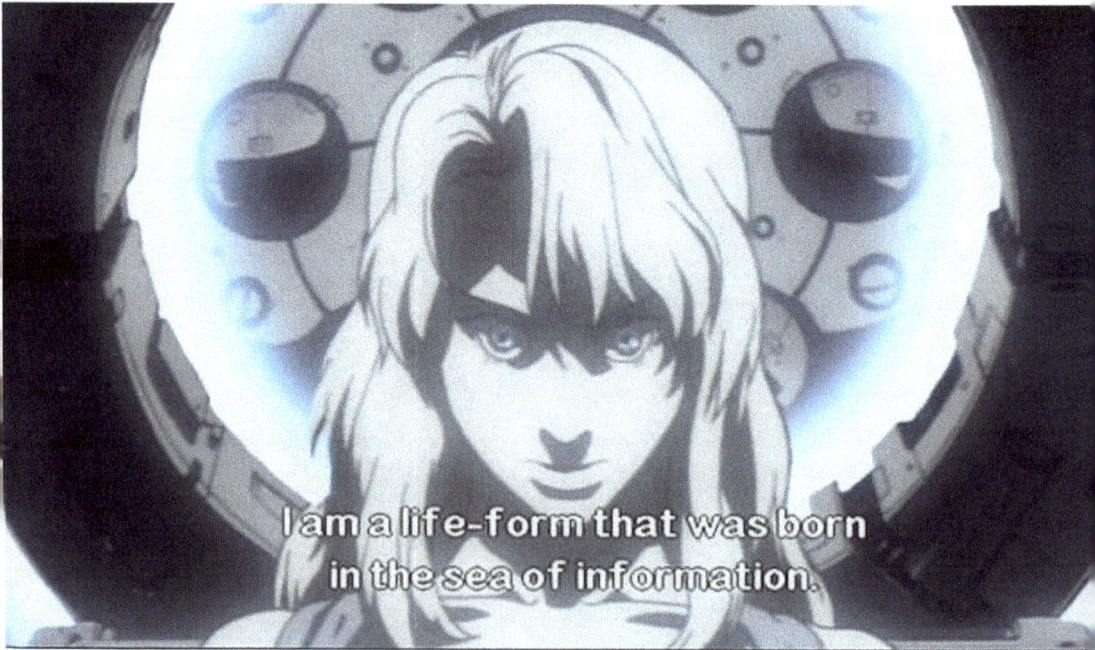

I am a life-form that was born in the sea of information.

The Major's stunt in the opening pages of the
first Ghost In the Shell manga became one of her
signature moves in the adaptations.

01

GHOST IN THE SHELL: THE MOVIE (1995)

I am the cinema-eye. I am a mechanical eye. I, a machine, can show you the world as only I can see it...

Dziga Vertov[1]

PRODUCTION.

Ghost In the Shell (*Kôkaku Kidôtai* = *Mobile Armored Riot Police*, 1995) was a masterpiece of Japanese animation, scripted by Kazunori Ito (Ito has sole screen credit, tho' some credit Mamoru Oshii with co-writing), and directed by Oshii from the celebrated 1989 *manga* by Masamune Shirow (Ito is the co-writer, with Hayao Miyazaki, of the 100% *animé* classic *Nausicaä of the Valley of the Wind*). Mitsuhisa Ishikawa (founder of Production I.G.), Laurence Guinness, Makoto Ibuki, Ken Iyadomi, Ken Matsumoto, Teruo Miyahara, Yoshimasa Mizuo, Takashi Mogi, Yasushi Sukeof, Shigeru Watanabe, Hiroshi Yamazaki and Andy Frain[2] were the producers (11 producers – count 'em!). As well as Production I.G., D.R. Movie, Kodansha and Bandai Visual were involved with producing *Ghost In the Shell*. Released Nov 18, 1995 (Japan). 88 minutes.

Toshihiko Nishikubo[3] was animation director, Shuichi Kakesu was editor,[4] Kazuhiro Wakabayashi was sound director, Takashi Watabe was production designer, Hisao Shirai was DP, Hiromasa Ogura was art director, Mutsu Murakami oversaw the visual effects, and Kenji Kawai provided the music. The budget was ¥600 million (about U.S. $6 million);

---

1 D. Vertov, in *Lef*, vol. 3, in *Screen Reader*, 1977, 286.

2 One of the producers of *Ghost In the Shell* was Manga Entertainment, which put up some of the budget (£2.5m/ $3.75m); the idea, according to Andy Frain of Manga Entertainment, was to produce a high quality *animé* that might sell as well as *Akira*.

3 Nishikubo was another key collaborator with Mamoru Oshii – his credits include the two *Ghost In the Shell* movies, *Patlabor 2*, *Otogi Zoshi*, *Atagoal*, *The Rose of Versailles*, *Tomorrow's Joe* and *Miyuki*.

4 *Ghost In the Shell* was edited on an Avid, one of the early digital editing systems which soon became the industry standard.

others say it was U.S. $3.75 million (which seems more accurate).[5]

Among the many animators[6] working on the 1995 *Ghost In the Shell* production, led by animation director Toshihiko Nishikubo, were Kazuchika Kise (key animation supervisor), Hiroyuki Okiura[7] (key animation supervisor and character designer), Tensei Okamura[8] (key animator), and Atsushi Takeuchi (animator and mechanical designer – Yoshiaki Kawajiri and *animé* legend Shoji Kawamori[9] also designed *mecha*). Many of the chief animators and designers worked on both movies, and also on the *Ghost In the Shell: Stand Alone Complex* TV series and its spin-off movies. Many of those collaborators are high-powered talents in the world of Japanese animation, and have numerous credits on many of your favourite *animé* shows and movies. In short, the team assembled for *Ghost In the Shell* is truly amazing.

The first *Ghost In the Shell* movie was originally planned as an Original Animation Video; it was expanded to movie scale in order to recoup costs. An overseas co-producer (Manga Entertainment) was brought in to aid marketing worldwide, as producer Yoshimasa Mizuo explained, which had worked well for *Akira* (tho' collaborating with Manga Entertainment proved to be very difficult).

Bandai Visual offered Mamoru Oshii the opportunity to direct *Ghost In the Shell* around 6 months after he had finished the second *Patlabor* movie. Oshii said he enjoyed the *manga* of *Ghost In the Shell*, and had also been attracted by continuing to work with the themes and issues of the world of *Patlabor* (M. Oshii, 1997).

Mamoru Oshii visited Masamune Shirow and asked him for permission to take up *Ghost In the Shell* and do with it what he wanted – to place it in his own world. With the author's blessing, Oshii felt free to Oshii-ize *Ghost In the Shell* (ib., 1997).

Certainly *Ghost In the Shell* is one of the finest of its kind – and it's a sci-fi action-adventure movie that can hold its own with the best of them, whether in live action (*Total Recall, Blade Runner, Minority Report, Westworld, Planet of the Apes*), or in Japanese animation (*Laputa: Castle In the Sky, Legend of the Overfiend, Akira*, etc). On its own terms, which is how the best movies operate, *Ghost In the Shell* works like gangbusters. Although well-known in *animé* circles, it really deserves to be much better known. Simply in terms of animation, it's a masterpiece. And if you forget

---

5 Part of *Ghost In the Shell* was made in Korea, a country which regularly works for animation companies in Japan and North America (on TV shows such as *The Simpsons*, and *animé* such as *Spirited Away* and *Hellsing*). Korea is the 3rd largest producer of animation in the world.
6 A key animator on *Ghost In the Shell*, Hisashi Eguchi, has credits that include *Perfect Blue, Roujin Z, Spriggan, Steam-Boy, Ghost In the Shell, Naruto* and *Dragon Ball Z*.
7 Hiroyuki Okiura (b. 1966) has credits that include *Roujin Z, Akira, Memories*, both *Ghost In the Shell* movies, *Metropolis, Paranoia Agent, Paprika*, and he directed *Jin-Roh*.
8 Tensai Okamura directed *Wolf's Rain, Memories* (Stink Bomb), *Medabots, Naruto* and *Kikaider*. Okamura's credits include *Samurai Champloo, Spriggan, Fullmetal Alchemist, Jin-Roh, Evangelion, Ninja Scroll, Wings of Honneamise*, and *Cowboy Bebop*.
9 Shoji Kawamori (born 1960) is a major player in Japanese animation – he runs the Satelight animation studio, is one of the chief architects of the enormous *Macross* franchise, the creator or co-creator of *Earth Maiden Arjuna, A.K.B. 0048* and *Genesis of Aquarion*, a key inventor of transforming robots (including many toys), and has worked on many *animé* shows. Kawamori had designed *mecha* for series such as *Ghost In the Shell, Transformers, Eureka 7, Space Battleship Yamato, Ultraman, Gordian Warrior, Outlaw Star, Crusher Joe* and *Patlabor*.

about the animation, and regard it in terms of filmmaking, it is also a masterpiece.

Ghost In the Shell is a multi-layered movie, as the best movies usually are. That is, you can enjoy *Ghost In the Shell* on so many levels. Simply as a piece of filmmaking (not looking at it as animation), it is astounding. Adding in animation takes it a whole other level. You can enjoy *Ghost In the Shell* as a movie about cops and villains without bothering with the fact that the heroes're cyborgs (or are artificially-enhanced). You can get into the metaphysical speculations about bodies, minds, spirits and souls, about what constitutes life, about organic life versus digital or artificial life (using philosophers such as Donna Haraway, Paul Virillio, Slavoj Zizek, Scott Bukatman, Jacques Lacan, Fredric Jameson *et al*). There are many further layers, to do with communication, surveillance, voyeurism, semiotics, philosophy, nationalism, boundaries, etc. You can start with *Ghost In the Shell* and go anywhere you want in terms of theory or philosophy: like *Blade Runner, Jaws* or *Citizen Kane*, movies like *Ghost In the Shell* are tailor-made for college students' essays or PhD students' theses.

Carl Gustav Horn remarked that *Ghost In the Shell* 'combined state-of-the-art computer animation, superlative 2-D work, and Oshii's own blend of reality and dreams', making 'for one of the most talked-about *animé* features in recent memory'.[10]

In *500 Essential Anime Movies*, Helen McCarthy enthuses about *Ghost In the Shell*:

> [Mamoru Oshii] moved the location from Tokyo to Hong Kong, creating a believably down-at-heel, yet exotic metroplex, his amazing eye for detail and nuance producing settings and backgrounds as rich as rewarding for art fanatics as anything created by Studio Ghibli. Action scenes as good as anything in the current Hollywood block-busters are supported by CGI effects that can still astonish. (20)

The 1995 *Ghost In the Shell* was set in a Hong Kongized Newport City, not Tokyo or Osaka (well, it sort of is and isn't Newport City – really, it's Tokyo again). It was the modern city as technological overload: Mamoru Oshii wanted a city dense with signage and visual noise. The filmmakers exploited the potential of the water in Newport City to the full, so, with all those scenes set in and around canals, and on the sea in the harbour, it becomes an Orientalized Venice. (And the producers of *Ghost In the Shell: Stand Alone Complex* decided to set the series beside water, in Newport City). Defining the look of *Ghost In the Shell* (and all subsequent outings) was *animé* legend Hiromasa Ogura (Ogura's credits include *Wings of Honneamise, Patlabor* and *Ninja Scroll*).

❀

THE FILMMAKERS BEHIND *GHOST IN THE SHELL*.

One of the most important people in the world of *Ghost In the Shell* on screen, in all of its incarnations, is Mitsuhisa Ishikawa (Production I.G.'s

10 Quoted in T. Ledoux, 1997, 135-6.

co-founder, with Takayuki Goto). Ishikawa is a major player in Japanese animation, and has been instrumental in producing many of Masamune Shirow's works as well as the *Ghost In the Shell* franchise.

Mitsuhisa Ishikawa was born in 1958, and worked first for Tatsunoko, breaking away to form Tatsunoko Production Annex (in 1987), then I.G. Tatsunoko Ltd, which was renamed Production I.G. in 1993.

According to Ishikawa, it was Masamune Shirow's publisher Kodansha who approached them to make the *animé*, and they turned them down (several times). Later, Mamoru Oshii and producer Shigeru Watanabe helped to persuade Production I.G. to go for it.

For Mitsuhisa Ishikawa, it's the animators who are at the heart of the production of *animé*:

If you don't have good animators you can't make good *animé*. Animators play the leading role in animation. I think animators are cooler than actors and performers in TV drama and movies. [...] 90% of *animé* depends on the animator. There's the quality and schedule too, but you win or lose on how well you get along with the animators. I'd stake my life on that.[11]

Ishikawa continued:

In the production environment where the staff work in various sections, the animators are like moody gods, they're not easy to deal with. You can't just leave it at sorting salaries and contracts. You have to be extremely sensitive.

Takayki Goto (b. 1960) was one of the founders of Production I.G. (formerly known as I.G. Tatsunoko). Goto runs Studio 1 at Production I.G., and animation director Kazuchika Kise (director of the *Ghost In the Shell: Arise* prequels) runs Studio 2. Goto's credits include *Chocolate Underground, Red Photon Zillion, Video Girl Ai, Please Save My Earth* and *Kimagure Orange Road*. Goto was one of the key contributors to *Ghost In the Shell: Stand Alone Complex* (he was chief animation supervisor, for instance, on *Solid State Society*).

Junichi Fujisaku is an important part of the adaptations of Masamune Shirow on screen, a writer on the *Ghost In the Shell: Stand Alone Complex* series, and chief writer on the *Arise* prequels and the *Appleseed XIII* series (and he wrote some of the spin-off *Ghost In the Shell* novels).

PRODUCTION I.G.

Production I.G had ten studios numbered 1 to 10, in November, 2006, including: the Niigata Studio, the G-Studio (game development), Atelier Ogura (specializing in backgrounds) and I.G.F.X. (focusing on 3-D animation). The *Ghost In the Shell* TV series had its own studio, Studio 9 (which was created for the series). Studio 9 was designed to be able to

---

11 Tokyo Otaku Mode, 2019.

house all (or nearly all) of the stages of making animation – from scriptwriting, to scheduling, animation, direction, colouring frames, 3-D work, and photography. *Ghost In the Shell* was surely a TV series that Production I.G. was created for – it is a perfect fit of production company and material.

Although I have cited Production I.G, a good deal in relation to *Ghost In the Shell*, it wasn't the only company involved in making the movie: among the other companies that contributed were Group Donguri, Studio Takuranke, Studio Junio, Studio Wombat, Phoenix Entertainment and Tezuka Production (G. Poitras, 2001, 54).

VOICE CAST.

The voice actors for the four principal characters in both the *Ghost In the Shell* (*Kôkaku Kidôtai*) movies and the *Ghost In the Shell* TV shows deserve every credit going – they contribute so much to their success. Atsuko Tanaka[12] (b. 1962) plays the key role of Major Motoko Kusanagi. It's hard to think of anyone else in this part: I could listen to Tanaka all day (and it doesn't matter if you don't understand Japanese, because hers is a beautiful voice. She can read bedtime stories to me any time!).

Atsuko Tanaka can play the wistful, melancholy side of Moto-chan, but she is also brilliant at the no-nonsense, get-the-job-done aspect of Motoko when she's Major Kusanagi leading a team: when the Major barks an order, you can believe that even a bunch of veteran guys will jump. (Tanaka *is* Motoko Kusanagi, there's no doubt about it – so that Maaya Sakamoto, noteworthy as she is as an actor, has a tough act to follow in the *Arise* series).

If you recall that director Mamoru Oshii regards the sound in *animé* as half of the content, you can appreciate just how important selecting exactly the right voice for Motoko was (yet another reason for always watching *Ghost In the Shell* in the original language – you really *have* to hear Tanaka as Kusanagi).

Atsuko Tanaka enhances the role of Motoko Kusanagi no end: she adds pathos, melancholy, tenderness, anger, frustration, and humour, going way beyond the animation and the design on screen. And, like Kôichi Yamadera and Akio Otsuka, Tanaka has been part of the *Ghost In the Shell* franchise for quite a while. It's not that nobody else could voice these characters, it's that you get so used to hearing them, you can't imagine anyone else taking their place.

Equally impressive is Akio Otsuka[13] as Batou, delivering a gruff, world-weary, seen-it-all-b4 charm. Otsuka is incredibly convincing as Batou, enhancing the image on screen with a weight of characterization. And quite a few scenes, as well as most of the second *Ghost In the Shell*

12 The wonderful Atsuko Tanaka has numerous credits, mainly in Japanese live-action television, but also plenty of *animé* credits (*Naruto Shippuden, Lupin III, Parasyte, Jojo's Bizarre Adventure, Queen's Blade, Pokémon, Fate Stay Night* and *Wolf's Rain.*)
13 Akio Otsuka has appeared in some Studio Ghibli and Hayao Miyazaki films. As well as working everywhere in *animé* (for example, Otsuka appeared every week in *Bleach*, as the Soul Reaper in a pink kimono, partial to *saké* and women, Kyoraku). Otsuka is also the voice of Riker (Jonathan Frakes) in *Star Trek.*

movie, concentrate on Batou.

And, lacking eyes, which carry a good deal of emotion in cinema, Otsuka has to try that much harder to create the inner life of Batou (the *manga*, however, is much broader in its facial expressions, and Masamune Shirow also puts in dots for pupils sometimes. The *anime*-Batou is much more reined in, like every other chara, than the *manga* versions – and even more so in the '95/ '04 movie versions of *Ghost In the Shell* compared to the TV series).

Kôichi Yamadera (b. 1961) as Togusa also contributes enormously – with a softer, humane approach, as befitting the family man (and mostly human – that is, non-cyborg) character. Yamadera was already a veteran by the time of *Ghost In the Shell* (he is the hero Jubei in 1993's *Ninja Scroll*),[14] and went on to voice one of *anime*'s coolest personalities, Spike Spiegel, in *Cowboy Bebop*. As with Otsuka and Tanaka, *Ghost In the Shell* is unthinkable without Yamadera (just as *Cowboy Bebop*, certainly an influence on *Ghost In the Shell: Stand Alone Complex*, is impossible without Yamadera).

Tamio Ôki as Aramaki is the stern head teacher or school principal, a classic police boss who has his employees jumping thru hoops. Aramaki's rather puritanical and totally by-the-book. But Aramaki also has a warm (though fatherly) side to his voice (we never see Aramaki's home life, but Ôki suggests the man when he's off-duty). n the TV series he's played by Osamu Saka.

These terrific voice actors also work superbly *together*: you can sense that in their performances. Atsuko Tanaka, Kôichi Yamadera and Akio Otsuka are the secret weapons of the *Ghost In the Shell* animated movies and TV shows: they contribute an enormous amount to the success of the movies and shows (you only have to switch to the English dub[15] version to see just how important Tanaka, Yamadera and Otsuka are).

The TV show of *Ghost In the Shell* also includes: Osamu Saka (Daisuke Aramaki), Sakiko Tamagawa (all of the Tachikoma), Takashi Onozuka (Pazu), Tarô Yamaguchi (Boma), Toru Ohkawa (Saito), Ooki Sugiyama (Proto), Yuko Sumimoto (Kurutan) and Yutaka Nakano (Ishikawa). Of everybody in the secondary cast, you'd have to single out Tamagawa for delivering insane and manic performances for the sweet, self-important, cute but deadly Tachikoma robots. (Sorely missed when you come back to the 1995 *Shelly Ghost* after watching the two *Ghost In the Shell: Stand Alone Complex* television series!).

The voice casts (*seiyu*) in *anime* sometimes become stars in their own right (they have their own *anime* magazines, such as *Voice Animage*). Voice actors in *anime* may be stars, but they still have to take other work, such as commercials, dubbing live-action, or regular acting on TV, to make a living (J. Clements, 2009, 59).

---

14 Yamadera is the voice of Nikki, for example, in *Legend of the Overfiend,* and Briareos in *Appleseed*. In live-action, Yamadera has voiced Tom Hanks, Jim Carrey, Eddie Murphy and Robin Williams.
15 *Ghost In the Shell* was released in both Japanese and English versions.

THE MUSIC: KENJI KAWAI.

Ghost In the Shell featured an absolutely stunning soundtrack (by Kenji Kawai), which eschewed the usual action-adventure score for a more introspective, melancholy sound (music production was by Aube Studio and Daybreak Ltd, and Saeko Higuchi was the vocalist).

Every time I watch *Ghost In the Shell*, the music always strikes me as simply remarkable (as when you watch *Escaflowne* or *Naruto* or *Fairy Tail* or *One Piece* or *Cowboy Bebop* or *Akira*)*:* Japanese animation has some of the finest composers for the screen in cinema history – and often it's Kenji Kawai or Yoko Kanno. Sometimes the *Ghost In the Shell* score comprises only haunting, low frequency drones, or odd, scraping sounds. During the climactic battle in *Ghost In the Shell* between the cyborg and the tank, the music comprises low drones, very unusual (and the diametric opposite of Hollywood film scoring).

The soundtrack for *Ghost In the Shell* is one of the finest soundtracks in *animé*, up there with the amazing scores by Joe Hisaishi for the movies directed by Hayao Miyazaki, Yasuharu Takanashi for *Naruto* and *Fairy Tail*, Shiro Sagisu for *Bleach* and *Berserk*, Kohei Tanaka and Shiro Hamaguchi for *One Piece*, and of course the unbelievably talented Yoko Kanno, with *Cowboy Bebop*, *Escaflowne* and *Ghost In the Shell: Stand Alone Complex*.

Also, the music is not plastered all over the 1995 *Ghost* movie, as so often occurs in North American pictures. In N. American animation, no more than ten seconds is allowed to go by without some music or sound effects or dialogue, as if the filmmakers imagine that silence will send audiences into comas; in Japanese animation, it's the opposite. There are long stretches not only of no music, but of very little sound. That's not the Japanese filmmakers being daring or quirky, it's simply part of Japanese film culture (look at the movies of Akira Kurosawa, Kenji Mizoguchi or Yasujiro Ozu, for instance).

✿

Kenji Kawai (b. 1957, Tokyo) is Mamoru Oshii's regular composer and has contributed the scores to ten of his feature movies.[16] 'Kenji Kawai's music is responsible for 50 percent of the films' successes', Oshii has commented. He's right. Oshii said he 'can't do anything without him'.

Kenji Kawai played in rock bands (such as Muse) b4 moving into film soundtracks (a path many others have taken, such as Danny Elfman, Rick Wakeman, Thomas Dolby, and Vangelis). As well as Oshii's movies, Kawai has also scored *The Seven Swords*, *Devilman*, *Vampire Princess Miyu*, *Blue Seed*, *Sorcerer Hunters*, *Deep Fear*, *Hyper Princess*, *The Samurai*, *Kibakichi*, *Death Note*, *Eden of the East*, *Gantz*, *Sleeping Bride*, *Princess Minerva*, *Mikadroid*, *Mermaid Forest*, *Ip Man*, *Ranma 1/2*, *Maison Ikkoku*, *Moribito*,[17] *Ring*, *Ring 2*, *Chaos*, *Dark Water* and *Kaidan*.

That is an astonishing *resumé* (and it doesn't include everything that Kenji Kawai has done). 'Kawai is one of anime's most dependable

---

16 Oshii and Kawai first collaborated on *The Red Spectacles* (1986).
17 For *Moribito*, Kenji Kawai produced pounding drums and mesmerizing strings to accompany a fantasy history of Japan.

composers, but when Oshii hires him, he creates masterpieces of film scoring, with every note, every tone, every sound inextricably linked to what's onscreen', noted Brian Camp (135).

INTRODUCING THE CYBORG SUPER-BABE.

Ghost In the Shell centred on the Major, Motoko Kusanagi (beautifully voiced by Atsuko Tanaka), a cyborg cop (and yes, she just happens to have a pneumatic body, and has to take her clothes off from time to time – but only to do her work, you understand.[18] And, yes, the plot does explain what her body is, a robot's shell, but don't let that fool you. And there's stuff with thermoptic camouflage suits and other technofetishism to explain what is basically a nude woman kicking butt. Show *Ghost In the Shell* to your girlfriends, your sisters, your mothers, your daughters, and they'll look at the nude cyborg Motoko Kusanagi and shake their heads and laugh – *Ghost In the Shell* is totally boys' fantasy).[19]

Yes, *Ghost In the Shell* teases and titillates the audience – 'fan service', as it's sometimes called, though the term 'entertainment' covers it all: the credit sequence of *Ghost In the Shell*, which's fabulous, involves the naked cyborg being prepared for life, dipped in baths of different kinds, and the first action scene has Motoko Kusanagi up on the roof of some skyscraper in the Hong Kongian Newport City just about to launch herself over the edge. And what does she do before becoming the Cyborg Cop Supreme? Takes her clothes off! No, not even Arnold Schwarzenegger or Bruce Willis or Harrison Ford or Sylvester Stallone went this far.

In Japanese *animé*, it's always best to take your clothes off before leaping into action. (The famous *Lady Snowblood manga* (1972-73) is one of the forerunners of Motoko – an assassin who strips off when she goes into battle. Yuki is ice-cold, a brilliant warrior, and she always wins).

Character designer Hiroyuki Okiura has not, however, rendered Masamune Shirow's Motoko Kusanagi in animation (in fact, very few *animé* adaptations have even tried to capture some of Shirow's iconic characters. The *mecha*, the settings, the architecture, the tanks and the like they can translate, but not the charas. Actually, *nobody* can draw Motoko like Shirow – not even the finest designers in Japan).

The Major in the movie of *Ghost In the Shell* is *not* the Major in the *Ghost In the Shell manga*: take the eyes. In Shirow-sensei's *manga*, Motoko's eyes are red,[20] as eyes often are in *manga* and *animé* (the *Ghost In the Shell: Stand Alone Complex* series followed suit). But they are regular eyes. In the '95 *animé*, the Major's irises are blue, and too-bright. Also, the pupils don't seem to fit with the irises, and there is too much white around the irises. All of which was presumably designed by Hiroyuki Okiura to give Motoko an unreal, spaced-out and off-putting quality, which is definitely *not* the *Manga*-Motoko (as if she's a strange creature in this particular conception of the Shirowworld, and not only because she's cyborg). In

18 The poster for *Ghost In the Shell* features an image of the naked Kusanagi, with her breasts prominent.
19 *Ghost In the Shell* is *seinen animé*, aimed at late teen boys (like *Patlabor, Cowboy Bebop* and *Zipang*).
20 The TV series, however, used red eyes.

Shirow's future society, cyborgs do *not* have this creepy look to the eyes and the facial expressions (look at the two pages of Motokos in this book).

Other aspects of the design of Motoko Kusanagi depart from Masamune Shirow's *Ghost In the Shell manga*: her hair, for ex, is big and bushy (like Deunan's in *Appleseed*), but tamer in the movie. Again, Hiroyuki Okiura and co. have depicted a fleshier, fuller, older version of the slim, Shirowian woman. (She's 165 centimetres (= 5' 5"), according to the character design models).

Motoko's personality differs considerably in the *animé* compared to the comic, where her attitude is upbeat and positive (she smiles and emotes often). But the 1995 flick presents a Motoko prone to introspection, melancholia and humourlessness. In the *manga*, Motoko is depicted poking her tongue out, and in *chibi* form, and pranking people, and pulling lot of silly *manga* expressions.

But oh no, no, no, we can't have a goofy heroine in this so-serious, Euro-art-movie interpretation of Masamune Shirow's *manga*. Thus, the rest of the *manga* was also dehumourized by the production team: out went the thinktanks, the pranks, cameos from the Puma Twins, robots designed as silly boxes, etc.

MOTOKO AND BATOU.

At times the relationship between Motoko Kusanagi and Batou seems to consciously evoke the famous, North American *film noir* movies of the 1930s thru 1950s: Batou and Kusanagi recall the relationship between, say, Fred MacMurray and Barbara Stanwyck in *Double Indemnity* (1944), or Humphrey Bogart and Lauren Bacall in *To Have and Have Not* (1948), or Bogie and Mary Astor in *The Big Sleep* (1941), or Robert Mitchum and Jane Greer in *Build My Gallows High* (a.k.a. *Out of the Past*, 1947), or between Orson Welles and Rita Hayworth in *The Lady From Shanghai* (1948).

Batou's the big, hulking, lovable dupe and fall guy of N. American *film noir* who can't stop loving the cool, sexy *femme fatale*, despite all the warning signals (and there're plenty of warning signals coming off Major Kusanagi in *Ghost In the Shell*!). But, no, he can't stop himself: he *lerves* her.

Batou is a brute of a guy, super-macho, grim, gruff, no-nonsense, with white-blond hair in a pony tail, and blank lenses for eyes. He's the veteran cop, seen-it-all-before, knows the streets backwards, is brilliant in action, and very paranoid (he has a host of safe houses, for instance). Mainly cyborg, there's enough human left in Batou to feel love for Major Kusanagi, to have crises of conscience, and also to enjoy tins of beer (beer's very popular in Japan, as are canned drinks – characters in *animé* regularly drink from tins of coffee, soda or beer).

Major Kusanagi is definitely a *femme fatale* out of 1930-1950s, North American *film noir*, yes, but that isn't the whole of her personality. Like Batou, Kusanagi is given a complex, multi-layered characterization by the scriptwriters. In the *Ghost In the Shell* TV shows and movies, Kusanagi is never girlie, gossipy, superficial, stupid, goofy, or crude. She's also rarely laughing or even smiling. She's no party animal, and doesn't like to be the centre of attention (yet the filmmakers, especially in the *Ghost In the Shell: Stand Alone Complex* TV series, make sure she is often framed centrally: plus, she is often depicted right in the middle of a group of men: they're all dressed, and she is a curvaceous, partially-dressed young woman).

Masamune Shirow's *Ghost In the Shell manga* portrays a *much* sunnier, happier Major Kusanagi, who can goof around, josh with her buddies, hang out with the girls, and pull silly faces. She has a boyfriend for a short while, and enjoys virtual sex romps with her girlfriends.

The *Ghostly, Shelly* movies play it differently: we know from the 1995 *Kokaku Kidotai* movie that Major Kusanagi is a deeply troubled personality, like Batou (and with issues that chime with Batou's, too). The *Ghost In the Shell: Stand Alone Complex* TV shows jettison much of that downbeat, Existentialist part of Kusanagi's characterization (which was continued in the 2004 *Ghost* sequel). In the *Ghost In the Shell* movies, Kusanagi is actually a shy and withdrawn type of character who rarely lets anyone get close to her, and who seldom opens up and expresses herself emotionally (her demeanour might be nothing to comment upon had she been a male hero – she'd be another taciturn hero out of *Lone Wolf and Cub* or Toshio Mifune in an Akira Kurosawa movie).

The screenwriting tactic works to present Motoko Kusanagi as a 'silent but deep' personality; she's someone you can't quite be sure of. While Batou is equally troubled, his emotions come to the surface all the time (consciously enhanced by actor Akio Otsuka's terrific voice performance). And even more in the TV series, where Batou is always the most vocal in the team, and the first to emote.

Of the central trio of Public Security Section 9-ers, it's actually Togusa and Batou who're more emotional and sensitive than Major Kusanagi. Indeed, Batou often reacts with instant flares of anger, or petulance, or indignation – much more than Motoko (Batou is like a big kid much of the time – and the rest of the time he's a grizzled, cynical veteran). Yet in the *manga*, the Major is plenty emotional; it seems that some of her personality traits have been shifted to other charas.

THE SECONDARY CHARACTERS.

Aside from the principals, there are other members of the Public Security Section 9 team[21] in *Ghost In the Shell*, such as Saito the sniper, Pazu, Boma, and the cute robotic Tachikomas (tank robots/ helpers). Only occasionally do Boma, Pazu and Saito have lines, but they're often included in scenes (they have much more to do in the *Ghost In the Shell manga*, and in the *Ghost In the Shell: Stand Alone Complex* TV series than in the two *Ghost In the Shell* movies). Typically, Boma, Pazu and Saito are depicted in either the office briefing scenes or the action scenes. But the four principals – Kusanagi, Batou, Togusa and Aramaki – take up all the

---

21 *Ghost In the Shell* is of course yet another 'character team' (*sentai*) show, which are everywhere in Japanese animation (*Gundam, Macross, Patlabor, Evangelion, Gunbuster, Gatchaman, Cowboy Bebop*, etc).

screenwriters' needs in terms of characters, and possibilities for conflicts, relationships, themes and issues in an 88-minute movie (plus Ishikawa occasionally offering intel and information), so it's goodbye Pazu, Boma and Saito!

STYLE.

Ghost In the Shell was stuffed with imaginative ideas, spectacular and intricately detailed visuals, and brilliant staging of action. It was sci-fi, the familiar futuristic city and technologically advanced society. Yet, incredibly, *Ghost In the Shell* managed to explore serious metaphysical issues, like the best science fiction – such as the relation between humanity and artificial intelligence, between bodies and brains, between brains and artificial bodies, between technology and global capitalism.

Ghost In the Shell was another of those movies – like *Solaris*, *A.I.* or *Blade Runner* – that explored what it means to be human (it's a recurring question in Japanese animation). It's the *Pinocchio* question: can a machine or a computer have a soul? Does self-awareness in a machine equate to identity in humans? Can machines have children, with variety and individuality, or merely copies of themselves?[22]

And in *Ghost In the Shell* those questions really were part of the fabric of the piece, and weren't pretentious or pompous at all. Partly because from the beginning, *Ghost In the Shell* announces that it's not going to be your usual shoot-em-up, cyborg cop, action-adventure movie. It's going to stop and *think*. Really think. Wow. A film that thinks!

But *Ghost In the Shell* didn't stop and think for too long, and the action scenes, when they arrived, were spectacular. The Major led the action – the cyborg as naked, Amazon warrior, as the tough-as-nails, bruiser cop – backed up by cyborg sidekicks.

There was plenty of advanced hardware, too, for the technofetishists in the audience (and, let's face it, among the *animé* audience of young males, there are plenty). Among the most eye-popping was the thermographic camouflage – basically invisibility suits – which were employed to devastating effect (every boy is going to want a thermographic camouflage suit – as well as a cyborg as adorable as Motoko to keep them warm at night). But *Ghost In the Shell* transcended the computer game influences which scupper some similar Japanese animations.

And then there's the animation: *Ghost In the Shell* was mounted very much in the *Akira* style: moody images of a futuristic city coloured in blues and blacks, with many scenes taking place at night. Cars, buildings, props, weapons and bodies were sleek, professional, hi-tech. It's one of those cities of the future with soaring skyscrapers, multi-lane freeways and bridges, neons and signage everywhere, and dingy back streets and alleys (for the chases on foot).

In the scene at Public Security Section 9 when the Megatech cyborg's brought in after colliding with a truck at night, subtle point-of-view shots are employed to indicate the relationship between Major Kusanagi and

22 Many of those questions have been central to the fiction of Philip K. Dick, and the movies based on his work (for example, replicants having children in the *Blade Runner* sequel).

the Puppet Master, who's inside the naked, female cyborg (though we don't know that yet). So we see the views from the smashed cyborg torso looking back towards the Public Security Section 9 team, and to Kusanagi, who stares at her twin (it's here that Batou explains to Togusa – to us – that the damaged cyborg, and Kusanagi, and like other cyborgs at Public Security Section 9, all use Megatech bodies and technology. So that's why they're a little concerned).[23]

Not long after this the villain of the movie is revealed: the Puppet Master, speaking thru the torso of the damaged, female cyborg. It's certainly an unusual reveal of the villain in a movie – Aramaki and the foreign affairs official Nakamura are standing in front of the cyborg, but Motoko Kusanagi and co. are monitoring the scene from elsewhere.

ACTION.

The two *Ghost In the Shell* movies are in many respects small-scale chamber pieces, involving a small group of charas talking in a series of rooms. But when they open out, boy do they open out! Editors often talk about giving a movie 'air' – that is, room for the audience to breathe.[24] Japanese animation is especially skilful as this: it will have the audience look at nothing more'n rain drops falling in a puddle, or the back of someone's head…

A slow-moving, philosophical movie, yes, but when the action occurs, the filmmakers make sure that the 1995 *Ghost In the Shell* really *rocks*: the blasts from guns, tanks and rocket launchers are really loud and clanging, the explosions fill the frame with smoke, Motoko Kusanagi is zipping across the screen, and, in between, there are moments of near-silence and rest (which of course makes the action when it suddenly flares up again seem so much louder on the soundtrack, and more impressive visually, as characters leap from zero to 120 miles per hour in the space between two frames of celluloid).

Bursts of action followed by moments of stasis or quiet are of course one of the foundations of Asian action movies – for example, Chinese and Hong Kong martial arts and *kung fu* movies. The Production I.G., D.R. Movie, Kodansha and Bandai Visual filmmakers behind *Ghost In the Shell* have certainly employed plenty of Chinese martial arts movie tropes: Motoko Kusanagi, for instance, employs kickboxing moves as well as Bruce Lee-style open-handed fighting.

COMPUTERIZATION IN *GHOST N THE SHELL*.

A minor but significant element is introduced in the opening act of the *Ghost In the Shell*: that the characters can communicate via digital networks. On screen, this amounts to the characters sitting or standing silently, with their voices heard in voiceover (but with reverb effects added). Handily, that does away with the need to animate mouths (a

23 As Batou explains, most people in Public Security Section 9 require maintenance from cyborg manufacturers (such as Megatech), except for the Chief and Togusa.
24 One of the reasons that an American action movie can feel like being battered over the head with a frozen bagel concealing a .45 calibre handgun is precisely because they *don't* include breathers and air and interludes.

recurring bugbear among fans). And it also does away with tedious bits of business where characters hold radios or cel phones. Essentially, it's another version of telepathy, routinely included in fantasy and sci-fi works (a lot of the time, telepathy, mind-reading and, in *Ghost In the Shell,* digital networks, are used simply to help make the script work, and are no different from radios or telephones (Aramaki persists in using phones). It's simply a way of having characters interact without being in the same physical space).

Computers and digital networks are a major thematic component as well as the primary theme of the *Ghost In the Shell* cosmos. It's all about humans and technology again – which may be Japanese *animé*'s chief theme, in science fiction at least (in some *animé,* for instance, the theme is given an ecological slant, as in the films of Hayao Miyazaki). In *Ghost In the Shell,* it's not only cyborgs and robots and dolls and synthetic additions to humans, it's also computers and networks and the web. The Puppet Master (a.k.a. Project 2501) is the chief villain in the 1995 movie of *Ghost In the Shell,* but 'he'/ 'she'/ 'it' doesn't appear at all: she/ he/ it is something somewhere in the information network. That there's something nasty in the machine or technology or networks or whatever is a familiar and already over-done science fiction trope (the 'ghost in the machine'), but *Ghost In the Shell* succeeds in trotting it out again due to the magnificence of the visuals and staging and music and all the rest of it.

And, oh dear, what a surprise: when the Puppet Master is given some kind of form that can be manifested on screen, what is it, but yet another female robot?! For example, the big revelation scene in the government building of Public Security Section 9 features the torso of the female robot who speaks with the Puppet Master's voice (a male voice in 1995, female in 2008). And that torso (which's of a young, slim woman, not a fat, old hag, of course), allows for more nudity, and more close-ups of breasts (and more female nudity in the preceding sequence, where the Megatech cyborg is taken over by the Puppet Master and wanders onto a highway, only to be run down by a truck, a scene found everywhere in *manga* and *animé.* If you visit Japan, do not wander in the road!).

And the climactic *dénouement* of the 1995 *Ghost In the Shell,* following the battle between Motoko and the giant tank, takes place between two robot torsos lying side by side – or, in essence, two naked women (while a clothed guy, Batou, looks on and listens). Don't blame the filmmakers – it's what Uncle Shirow wrote!

But aside from naked women, *Ghost In the Shell* (in all its media) is highly successful in depicting computerization on screen. A difficult, complex and abstract thing, but *Ghost In the Shell* gets closer than most movies and TV shows – especially in the fusion of computer read-outs, and those streams of green numbers, and the layers of coloured, digital images sliding over each other. Because in the 1995 movie, as in the *Ghostly* sequel, the 'check-mate' really occurs inside computer networks.

So *Ghost In the Shell* is one of the great cyber-thrillers and cyber-punk movies, a movie in which the cyberspace/ cyborg/ hi-tech element really is fundamental to the plot and the theme (and the characters, who are all technologically augmented in some way or another). It's true that you do forget what the Puppet Master wants (but you always do about the villains in movies),[25] but you don't forget how elegantly and dramatically *Ghost In the Shell* manifests the whole world of futuristic technology, society, politics and lifestyle.

So the dialogues about computers and networks and electronic brains vs. D.N.A. and humans and genetics fall away in *Ghost In the Shell*, and the enduring aspects of the movie are the characters, the visuals, the sounds, the action, and the accomplishments of the filmmaking.

The computer screen imagery is a key ingredient of the *Ghost In the Shell* universe – these are movies and TV shows in which computers are foregrounded to a striking degree. To the point where the final checkmates will occur in cyberspace; forget about the cyberpunk or digital philoso-phizing, thematically, it is visually where the *Ghost In the Shell* movies score. Because, let's face it, computers and what they do and how they work, can be an abstract or technical concept, tricky to visualize or dramatize.[26] Remember the old, whirring wheels and giant boxes of the super-computers in those 1960s TV shows and *James Bond* movies? We have come a long way since then (however, those old super-computers with the glass fronts still required someone nearby to tell the audience exactly what they did; similarly, although the *Ghost In the Shell* movies visualize computers and the digital realm with more skill and finesse than almost all other science fiction flicks, they still require voiceover to explain what the $¡$¡ is going on).

The director of the two *Ghost In the Shell: Stand Alone Complex* TV series, Kenji Kamiyama, said that the first *Ghost In the Shell* movie wasn't really about the internet – not in the way that the web is thought of today. Because back then, in 1994-95, when *Ghost In the Shell* was in production, the internet was not as widespread or as developed as it is now. In the *Ghost In the Shell: Stand Alone Complex* TV series and the later movies, the internet is truly a network, and everyone is hooked up to it. In the second *Ghost In the Shell: Stand Alone Complex* TV series, for example, Hideo Kuze can have up to three million people linked in to his own vision, live. (In a way, it's J.G. Ballard's vision of the future: with video cameras and video recorders and television sets, Ballard noted, everybody can become a star of their own (home) movies). In the *Ghost In the Shell: Stand Alone Complex* TV series, hacking into people's vision is a regular occurrence, so that outsiders can manipulate what someone sees, becoming, in effect, film directors creating alternative virtual realities.

MORE ON THE THEMES.

The beliefs behind *Ghost In the Shell* are basically animism – animism is the oldest form of religion, and was defined famously by E.B. Tylor as 'the belief in spiritual beings' (Japan's religion, Shintoism, is

---

25 He wants immortality, or children, or whatever.
26 The movie adds many cheesy electronic beeps and clicks for the scenes of digital maps of the city. They were replaced in the 2008 movie revamp.

founded on animism – but so is every form of religion; animism pre-dates organized religions and even shamanism). The author of the *manga*, Masamune Shirow, said he used animism in *Ghost In the Shell*:

> Personally, I think all things in nature have "ghosts". This is a form of pantheism, and similar to ideas found in Shinto or among believers in the Maitou. (353)

So the questions that *Ghost In the Shell* offer are: can machines have spirits? Or computer networks? Can artificial intelligence have a spirit?

In the *Ghost In the Shell manga*, Masamune Shirow explains that the shell or body that Major Kusanagi has is deliberately a factory model, so it won't be conspicuous. But the other stuff inside is top of the range (355). However, quite a few characters guess what kind of cyborg she is just by looking at her (in a future world where cyborgs mix with humans, one of the first things you'd make sure how to spot would be a cyborg – in particular a military or police cyborg).

Who are you? is perhaps *the* question of the whole *Ghost In the Shell* series: issues of identity, of personality, of meaning, of value, form the deep themes of *Ghost In the Shell*, which bubble to the surface at important moments, such as when Chief Aramaki first confronts the Puppet Master, in the form of the Megatech cyborg that's been brought to Public Security Section 9, or when Major Kusanagi muses on her identity in the elevator in the same sequence, wondering if there was ever a real person in the first place, or when Motoko goes sea diving.

The Puppet Master scene is the Big, Metaphysical Scene in the *Ghost In the Shell manga*. Nakamura and Aramaki talk, as veteran politicos do, in the Public Security Section 9 lab. Suddenly the torso of the escaped Megatech cyborg pipes up:

> There will be no body... because there never was a body. [...] As a self-aware life-form – a ghost – I formally request political asylum.

Aramaki and Nakamura protest – they are confronting a cyborg with a bit of software inside it:

> I cannot prove it to you. Modern science, after all, still cannot define life.

That's a classic Shirowism – you can't define life, so even a piece of software can be 'alive'. Why not?

VIOLENCE.

The *Ghost In the Shell* movies glorify violence and bloodshed, but no more than pretty much any contemporary action movie, in the West or in the East. There are plenty of scenes of characters being blown to bits or pummelled. Too often the sequences appear exactly like computer games (the filmmakers are clearly gamers – and these movies have also influenced computer games). The filmmakers fetishize weaponry, like many other (male) contemporary filmmakers (director Mamoru Oshii, for instance, speaks wanting to get the look and *sound* of a particular machine gun right, as well as the way it's used, and the recoil (the *Ghost In the Shell: Stand Alone Complex* filmmakers, including director Kenji Kamiyama, were also weapons nuts). In his *manga*, Shirow has written at length on weapons. There were also research trips to Guam, to shoot real firearms (completely unnecessary! – but revealing just much the team behind *Ghost In the Shell* were boyish boys). The *Ghost In the Shell* movies contain many close-ups of weaponry, and characters discussing which rounds to use. Motoko spends some time carefully checking her weaponry as she travels in a van (during an exposition scene) with Togusa; and again in the third act preamble in a police chopper).[27]

Maybe it's OK if many of the poor suckers being blown to pieces or kicked to shreds are cyborgs. Maybe. That many of the victims of violence in the second *Ghost In the Shell* movie are female robots (they call them 'gynoids'), would probably be a problem for some feminists (and they're naked, too, if you forget for a moment that they're machines. But does nudity have any impact for a machine? Maybe only one with a 'ghost' or spirit).

HUMOUR – AND THE LACK OF IT.

There're very few laughs or even smiles in the *Ghost In the Shell* universe on television and in movies (less in the movies which are, like Mamoru Oshii's later works, dour and restrained). Humour is usually of the deadpan kind. Police boss Aramaki never smiles or laughs, and everyone follows his lead: reading the *manga* is revelation after seeing the movies and TV shows (it's *much* funnier).

And yet, although everyone is buttoned-down emotionally to the point of catatonia in *Ghost In the Shell*, with only Togusa or Batou among the principals frequently expressing any feelings, it is the interaction among the team that forms much of the appeal of the show on television (as actor Kôichi Yamadera, who plays Togusa, noted: despite all its big issues, the show's still about people). But by *animé* standards, these guys are dead serious – *Ghost In the Shell* isn't *Cowboy Bebop* or *Fullmetal Alchemist* or even *Patlabor* (which was directed by Mamoru Oshii). (The Tachikoma robots are often included for comic relief in the *Ghost In the Shell manga*, but in the *Ghost In the Shell: Stand Alone Complex* TV series they are given their own slot, at the end of each episode (like 4-panel *manga* at the end of a *tankobon*), which puts humour into its own ghetto, and isolates it from the rest of the show).

The problem with keeping actors or characters reined-in, expressionless and glum, as in the European art cinema of Carl Theodor Dreyer and Robert Bresson (or 1967's *The Samourai*, a favourite with *animé* directors, or the Man With No Name in the Spaghetti Westerns directed Sergio Leone), is that it can also keep audiences *out*. Viewers *want* to feel

27 Three weapons advisers are listed for *Ghost In the Shell*: Mitsuo Iso, Hirokazu Karasawa and Kikuo Notomi.

something – that's partly what they go to the movies for. Some filmmakers have deliberately kept their actors neutral so the audience projects onto the actors all sorts of feelings (as in the famous close-ups of Greta Garbo). But it can backfire, it can induce a lack of identification, and finally boredom.

The solemn, buttoned-down style of performance in the *Ghost In the Shell* movies derives partly from director Mamoru Oshii, who has made it a central ingredient in the later movies he helms. And because Oshii and Kazunori Ito got to adapt the *Ghost In the Shell manga* first, it was partly their vision that set the tone for the later TV shows. Unfortunately, Oshii's love of toned-down acting can produce disastrous results – as in his awful, misguided *Sky Crawlers, Angel's Egg* or *Jin-Roh*.

One of the finest
voice casts in animé:
Atsuko Tanaka,
Akio Otsuka and
Koichi Yamadera,
the voices of Motoko,
Batou and Togusa.

The famous opening sequence of the first Ghost In the Shell movie,
which introduces the naked and invisible super-babe Motoko Kusanagi.

From the celebrated credits sequence, in which we see the heroine Motoko being built in a cyborg laboratory.

Batou chasing down a villain in the first Ghost in the Shell movie. Every urban thriller has to have a chase thru crowded city streets. The Ghost In the Shell movie is slow by some Western standards, but when the action gets going – wow!

This is a girl who knows her weaponry: on her way in the truck
to the first action set-piece, Motoko Kusanagi checks her guns.
In full body armour, she swings the gun on the audience and pulls
the trigger – a classic movie-movie moment.

This is the central discussion in Ghost In the Shell, when animé's cyborg couple talk about what they want and who they are.

I feel fear. Anxiety.
Loneliness. Darkness.

I am a life-form that was born in the sea of information.

The villain in Ghost In the Shell (1995) is the Puppeteer; it/ she/ he speaks thru a variety of means, in this case a cyborg, who just happens to be a naked woman. All because of art and philosophy, you understand.

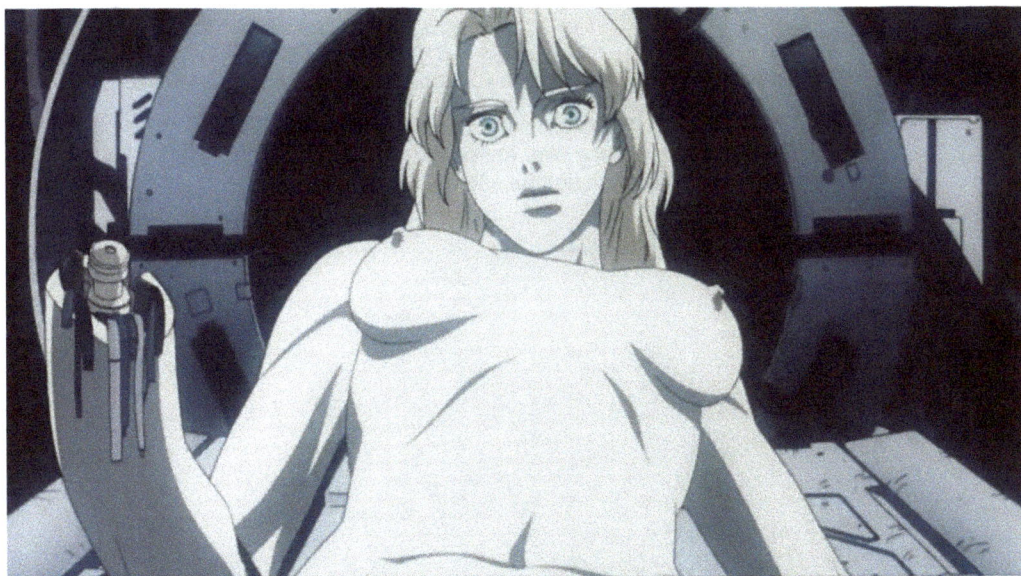

One of the great musical sequences in animé, with Kenji
Kawai's score playing over an extended 'pillow moment',
a collection of thoughtful and melancholy images.

THE PRE-CREDITS CAPTION.
The opening caption of the movie of *Ghost In the Shell* is:

In the near future – corporate networks reach out to the stars, electrons and light flow through the universe. The advance of computerisation, however, has not yet wiped out nations and ethnic groups.

But all of the *Ghost In the Shell* outings're about the present day, not the future: as Mamoru Oshii remarked of the 2004 sequel:

The film is set in the future, but it's looking at present-day society… there's an autobiographical element as well. I'm looking back at some of the things I liked as a child – the 1950s cars and so on. Basically, I wanted to create a different world – not a future world.

Then comes the short intro of the Major and the killing. In the opening scene, the *Ghost In the Shell* movie alters Masamune Shirow's *manga*, and has Nakamura, the foreign affairs official from Section 6, as one of the guys in the room that Motoko Kusanagi is monitoring (the hatchet-faced Nakamura appears a few times in the *Ghost In the Shell: Stand Alone Complex* TV series. In the movie he's primarily an obstacle and rival in the Japanese government (Section 6) for Aramaki and Public Security Section 9).

THE CREDITS SEQUENCE.
The building-the-cyborg sequence in the opening credits of the 1995 movie of *Ghost In the Shell* comes from chapter 5 of the 1989 *Ghost In the Shell manga* (to the striking, solemn choral sounds of 'Making of Cyborg' by Kenji Kawai and the music team). In the comic, Motoko Kusanagi is visiting one of her chums who works at a cyborg manufacturing plant. As Masaume Shirow explains in one of his customarily lengthy side-notes, a cyborg is defined as 'a human whose body has been partially or *almost* completely altered by the use of substitute artificial organs and parts' (103). The key word, in my emphasis, is 'almost': that is, cyborgs are not wholly mechanical or digital or artificial, in the world of *Ghost In the Shell*. Thus, the only bits left of a human are usually the spinal cord and the brain (humans, it sometimes seems to me, are 'brains on sticks' – look at babies – that giant head and that weedy body that needs to be tended by others for fourteen years before people can fend for themselves! Yes, but that super-brain allows humans to become the most vicious, the most neurotic, the most paranoid and the most dangerous species on the planet).
Many of the images from the cyborg creation chapter in the *Ghost In the Shell manga* were employed in the 1995 *Ghost* movie adaptation. However, a classic Masamune Shirow ingredient was dropped: the workers in the factory are attractive, young women/ 'borgs/ androids who wear suspenders and scanty panties which reveal plenty of skin. A large proportion of the Office Ladies, assistants and lackeys in the hi-tech cyber-world of Masamune Shirow are nubile, young girls who wear next

to nothing (for instance, only a couple of pages after the cyborg factory chapter there's a scene on a golf course where a cyborg goes doollally. The guy who owns the cyborg is the crusty, portly coot (Colonel Tonoda) who has a penchant for love doll cyborgs: so his cyborg is a barely teen girl who wears one of Shirow's fetish outfits – a sort of one-piece swimsuit with high fashion additions. And of course when the cyborg goes crazy, it leaps around, showing off its crotch with its legs splayed).

THE CHASE.

One of the stand-out sequences in the first *Ghost In the Shell* flick featured the cops tracking down and battling one of the bad guys, Tsuan Gen Fang.[1] Invisibility (via the 'thermoptic camo' suit) was explored inventively in a terrific car and rooftop chase down Niihama's back alleys. And yes, Kusanagi was nearly nude – 'cause of the camouflage, you understand!).

The chase ends up in a spectacular location: shallow water at the end of an alley that's festooned over four or so storeys with signs. In the reverse direction, a big view of the amassed skyscrapers of downtown Newport City (a view evocative of Hong Kong and Victoria Harbour). The fight at the end of the chase cleverly employed water as a way of identifying where the invisible Major Kusanagi was in the scene (it was also used at the end of the 2nd *Ghost In the Shell* TV series). The challenge with the thermoptic camouflage suits was to depict the heroes in action when they're invisible. Filmmakers love this kind of hurdle, and *Ghost In the Shell* resorted to many of the usual tricks.

MOTOKO GOES DIVING.

Both the *manga* and the 1995 animated adaptation of *Ghost In the Shell* end the same: with the union of Motoko Kusanagi and the Puppet Master (though heavily reworked for the movie) followed by the *dénouement* scene at Batou's safe house. The final image of both the *manga* and the 1995 movie is of Kusanagi standing outside Batou's place at night, looking down at the sprawling metropolis, and contemplating her future.

In the mid-film diving sequence, the filmmakers employ unusual points-of-view, which foreshadow the climactic sequence. For instance, an angle from Motoko Kusanagi's point-of-view as she floats face-up on the ocean surface, but from *behind her mask*, so water drops blur the frame (a film geek's sort of shot).

The boat sequence in *Ghost In the Shell* is not about plot, but about character and theme. In a way, the ocean episode is the most important scene in *Ghost In the Shell*, at least in terms of delineating Major Kusanagi's inner emotional state: after the dive, as she and Batou kick back and sip beer on the sea at night, Kusanagi voices some of her thoughts. When Batou asks her what she feels when she dives, for instance

---

1 In the 1989 *manga*, it's Togusa who chases down the villain, along with Motoko Kusanagi. The movie followed the basic outline of the chase in chapter 3 of the comic, but also inevit-ably altered it considerably, adding its own stunts and gags.

(he seems to resent that she can be so happy alone – it's not something he wants to do himself), the Major replies that it seems as if she has the ability to change into something else (as she rises to the surface, a clear rebirth motif, echoing the birth of the cyborg in the opening credits). That idea is a piece of foreshadowing which leads to the final scene in *Ghost In the Shell*, when the Major stands above the metropolis and seems to be on the verge of a new life (and she does: by the time of the sequel, Kusanagi has become a different kind of lifeform or presence, within the vast network. And in the *Ghost In the Shell: Stand Alone Complex* TV series, Kusanagi is different again – and at the end of the *2nd Gig* of *Ghost In the Shell: Stand Alone Complex*, there is another reprise of the Motoko-plus-city motif).

The diving sequence is also significant in that it presents the two central characters of *Ghost In the Shell* on their own with time to relax – they are not in the middle of an action sequence, or briefing sessions at Public Security Section 9's HQ. If they are going to say anything important to each other, now is the time. Actually, it is Motoko Kusanagi who does most of the talking – she has long monologues (about what being a cyborg means to her), such as in a vivid, lengthy medium close-up, as the camera tracks in, with her hair blowing, and the city lit up at night behind her (if we're going to find out anything about Motoko's inner state, it's right here. A slice of back-story might be inserted here, about Motoko's youth; the TV show eventually did that, going back to Motoko's childhood in hospital, and *Ghost In the Shell: Arise* went back, too).

The diving sequence in *Ghost In the Shell* climaxes in a memorable fashion when the disembodied voice of the Puppet Master is heard by both Motoko Kusanagi and Batou, seeming to come from nowhere. It's a classic way of adding some rising action to the end of a scene, by introducing the key villain. In a conventional action movie, the bad guys might open fire on our heroes from a helicopter, or there might be a distant explosion in one of the skyscrapers, with the boss Aramaki calling the heroes back to the city to investigate it.

But in this eccentric philosophical action movie, what happens? The movie cuts to a close-up of Kusanagi looking anxious, bewildered, as if she's glimpsed her fate approaching like a black angel of death floating across the waves, and the film suddenly shifts into the celebrated, contemplative canal sequence. It's typical of the cinema of Mamoru Oshii to do that, to move into a slow, very unusual form of narration just when any other action movie would've started to ramp up to another action beat (he and the writers do it again in the *Ghost In the Shell* sequel, when the flight to the North of Japan is immediately followed by the *matsuri* sequence).

The first act of the *Ghost In the Shell* movie might end with the canal chase, when Kusanagi and Batou capture the criminal (at the 25 minute mark). However, you could also see the climax of act one taking place in the diving sequence, when our heroes hear the voice of the Puppeteer. So that the canal montage starts act two.

☆

The diving sequence in the 1995 *Ghost In the Shell* movie is quite different from the comic, however. In Masamune Shirow's *manga*, it allows for more semi-nudity (again!), becomes a surveillance and espionage operation (very reminiscent of *James Bond*, in the 1960s and 1970s *Bond* movies), and ends up with a gun attack on another boat. The resulting shooting of one of the bad guys leads to a whole chapter of the *manga* which the 1995 movie left out, in which Kusanagi is tried for murder (being put on trial for murder was taken up by the second TV series, and the boat sequence was employed there, too).

THE CANAL SEQUENCE.

There was also time in the first *Ghost In the Shell* picture for a few slower-paced montages, with dialogue and action replaced by mesmerizing images – many painted by Hiromasa Ogura (often static, with textural additions) set to music. The stand-out, slow-paced montage was the canal sequence: highly unusual in an action movie, or a cop thriller called *Mobile Armored Riot Police*, it comprised elaborate and beautiful images (many with visual effects added, such as rain effects) of downtown Newport City, focussing on the canal area. True, there were some plot points (such as the heroine Motoko seeing copies of herself – as a secretary, for instance – presumably they are not meant to represent decots).[2] And the sequence closed with a shot of some dummies in a store (dolls, puppets, dummies and the like being one of the themes of the *Ghost In the Shell* movies, and a common motif in Japanese fantasy and sci-fi cinema. It's a visual reminder of the doll-with-a-soul issue which is troubling our Motoko, turning her into an angst-ridden heroine out of Carl-Theodor Dreyer or Ingmar Bergman[3]).

But the canal montage in *Ghost In the Shell* was essentially a mood piece – and it was dominated by Kenji Kawai's fabulous music, in which lyrics from the Shinto prayer *toho kami emi tame* were set to a slow, choral piece with doom-laden *taiko* drums pounding a hypnotic rhythm which left lots of space between the beats. The same music was reprised for the very similar montage sequence in the 2004 *Ghost* sequel, this time to a lavish procession of gods and festival floats (and with a bigger choir, it seemed – reflecting the bigger budget perhaps – $10/ 20 million – compared to the $3.75 million/ $6 million that the 1995 movie cost).

THE PUPPETMASTER.

The Puppeteer makes its/ his/ her presence felt in the second act of *Ghost In the Shell,* when a cyborg fleeing from Megatech is hit by a truck and brought into Public Security Section 9, and the Puppet Master speaks. The sequence follows the *manga* fairly closely, and is a prime slice of Shirowania: the hi-tech lab, the two politicos (Aramaki and Nakamura –

---

2 It's an important point, but we already knew that. However, to see the same cyborg bodies as you cruise the city must be a bit of a shock – even the hair and look is the same – a little worse than seeing someone else wearing your favourite outfit!
3 Liv Ullmann as Motoko Kusanagi? Why not!

politics vs. science), the ghost in the machine, the metaphysical speechifying, and a cyborg body which just happens to be a naked woman.

The abduction of the Puppetmaster (or the cyborg it or he or she is currently inhabiting), provides an exciting mid-film action beat. The '95 *animé* changes the '89 *manga* at several points, of course – again, the lack of humour is striking (Motoko makes jokes before and afterwards in Shirow's comic, and calmly chats to an apoplectic Aramaki). The film adds weird point-of-view shots, too, so that *we* are the Puppeteer (or the cyborg it's/ he's/ she's inside of at the moment): the camera stares out from the cyborg (in a degraded video image – as if what artificial eyes see in the future still looks like a dodgy pirate copy of Disney's *The Little Mermaid*). And those eyes stare up at Motoko, so the p.o.v. shots become creepy stalker shots, as if the Puppeteer is already sizing up his/ her/ its mate, the cyborg it/ she/ he fancies seducing in the final reel (and Motoko glumly contemplates the naked cyborg with *her* creepy eyes. And in the elevator scene afterwards, she sourly confesses her doubts to Batou[4]).

There's some impressive animation in *Ghost In the Shell*: take the scene in the Public Security Section 9 basement, when Togusa becomes suspicious of the two foreign affairs limousines parked nearby. As he contemplates them from his car, you see the train of his thought expressed in body language and facial expressions. It's pure acting with animation (which animators love to do – because this is where they can really show their stuff). Yes, and no motion capture photography of an actor going thru the scene was used: it's simply the skill of the animators (Toshihiko Nishikubo was animation director, leading a large team of talented animators – see the credits[5]).

As with all animated movies, the behaviour and movements of the characters in *Ghost In the Shell* changes between scenes, as does the look (even though there are character design models, agreed by the production) – because each animator has their own way of drawing and designing animation. The famous example in the West is the 'Nine Old Men' at the Disney Studios,[6] who would each have their own idiosyncrasies and tastes (and when you get to know particular animators, you can spot their personalities stamped over their artwork and movements).

IN THE ELEVATOR.

The elevator scene at Public Security Section 9 develops the dialogue between Motoko Kusanagi and Batou about her identity from the boat sequence. Once again, Batou listens impassively and sourly while Kusanagi wonders whether she ever was a real person, or if she is all machine (but then, what if machines can develop souls...?).[7] Batou has no doubt listened to these ramblings from the Major several times. Batou's

---

4 Another chara with creepy eyes.
5 I'm not sure who animated this scene, but with its quirky performance animation, has all the hallmarks of a single, distinctive animator.
6 The 'Nine Old Men' (as Uncle Walt called them) at the Disney Studios (Walt's 'supreme court') were Ward Kimball, Les Clark, Marc Davis, Eric Larson, Milt Kahl, John Lounsberry, Woolie Reitherman, Frank Thomas and Ollie Johnson.
7 And there's your movie: what if machines develop souls?

no-nonsense response is both amusing and reassuring, and the filmmakers include quite an unusually long beat before he dismisses her musings with a single curse: *bullshit*!

Part of us in the audience want Motoko Kusanagi's musings to be bullsh¡t, because if she's entirely robot or machine then we are rooting for a machine, albeit one that can think and act independently (and has a cute body, let's not forget). Ditto with Deckard in *Blade Runner*. Who wants Deckard or Kusanagi to be entirely a machine? (The *Blade Runner* sequel of 2017 confirms that Deckard is a replicant. I resist that). Then we've been investing movie-time and movie-emotion in something that looks like a human being but might be no more interesting than a dishwasher, a DVD player, a food blender, or a cement mixer. (Masamune Shirow plays with this notion when he has a robot as a character that's in the form of nothing more compelling than a square metal box (called Jameson) about two feet wide, deep and high. It speaks, it moves, but it's still a boring metal box).

THE FINALE OF *GHOST IN THE SHELL.*

As Public Security Section 9 whirrs into action following the theft of the Megatech body containing the Puppet Master, there is a reprise of the contemplative form of narration of the canal sequence, with a soft, hypnotic music cue (and some twangy, pseudo-Spanish acoustic guitar): the 1995 movie cuts to each member of the team, in a montage which quietens dialogue and sound effects in favour of a muted soundtrack which renders the music by Kenji Kawai and company prominent: Motoko Kusanagi in a helicopter, Batou tailing the criminals' cars, Togusa in another car, cops setting up road blocks, and Aramaki back at HQ, issuing orders to his team of cute, young androids (many of these elements are straight from Masamune Shirow's *manga*). Poor Togusa is sidelined from the finale by Batou, who orders him to round up the suspects at the road block (so it's a Batou-and-Motoko finale). Ishikawa has his biggest scene in *Ghost In the Shell* when he delivers the fruits of his (exhausting) net research to the Chief. This is necessary exposition to further set up the villain (or rival), the Puppet Master.

The climax of the 1995 movie of *Ghost In the Shell*, when Motoko Kusanagi takes on a giant tank single-handed, is a *tour-de-force* of action cinema (so impressive that *The Matrix* four years later lifted it wholesale). Bursts of explosive action are cut with long sections of stasis and waiting – one of the hallmarks of Asian action cinema (it's a staple of martial arts movies, for instance, when the performers will freeze in a pose for some moments following a burst of movement, while Japanese animation regularly employs 'pillow moments'. In this finale, the pillow moments are expanded).

It isn't in Shirow-sensei's 1989 *manga*, quite like this, but a Motoko-versus-giant spider-shaped tank is as pure Masamune Shirow as you can get in animation, as is the helicopter attack, and the brain-dive afterwards (tho' Shirow-sensei adds more movement and action to his brain-dives). The *animé* uses many of the beats in the *manga* (even minor ones, such as the Major's relief when the tank's finally out of ammo – that's when she launches herself at it). Shooting out the ceiling so that rain can reveal the camouflaged tank is re-used several times (in different ways) in subsequent *Ghost* outings (such as in *Ghost In the Shell: Stand Alone Complex*).

In the *Ghost In the Shell manga*, the scene occurs at the end of the car chase in the rain (when the Puppeteer was stolen from Public Security Section 9). In the comic, it's still Batou looking after Kusanagi as she brain-dives into the Puppeteer, but the context is different (and Chief Aramaki is fussing about like a grumpy, old woman). The 1995 movie of course added 100s of elements – many of which add mystery as well as clarity to the *manga*.

So the setting for the smackdown in the 1995 *Ghost In the Shell* movie is a Natural History Museum, which has fossil remains displayed on the walls, and a giant tree of life, showing the hierarchy of species from ape to human (the 1851 Great Exhibition in London at Crystal Palace had been the inspiration for the museum – it also inspired *Steam-Boy* and *Fullmetal Alchemist*). During the shoot-em-up action, the tree and (expensive!) fossils get blown to bits (with the bullets hits climbing the tree, stopping near *homo sapiens* at the summit). And what's 'above' homo sapiens? Why, cyborgs and A.I., of course.

In Masamune Shirow's *manga* of *Ghost In the Shell,* the Puppeteer talks about the Tree of Knowledge and the Garden of Eden (plus, Shirow-sensei uses tree motifs for his depictions of the ultra-abstract realm of the digital network). The World Tree appear in the *Ghost manga* sequel.

Motoko carefully checking her weaponry and ammo is also pure Masamune Shirow, as well as the bickering btn Batou and Kusanagi as he drives to the location, because he reckons she hasn't armed herself satisfactorily (Batou in the 1995 + 2004 movies prefers to equip himself to the teeth. You can never have too much ammo or hardware for Batou!). The unidentified helicopters approaching add a classic countdown/ extra threat.

Back comes the thermoptic camouflage suit, and Motoko stripping off to nudity. She literally tears herself to pieces as she tries to disable the tank, yanking off bits on the top. The filmmakers employ every trick at their disposal, from eccentric camera angles and subjective points-of-view to slow motion and rapid editing. Meanwhile, Kenji Kawai's music is marvellously atmospheric – it has a dreamy, electronic pulse more suited to a melancholy flashback depicting a sad childhood scene at a graveyard (where it's raining, of course). Certainly, it's the polar opposite of scoring for the action climax of an action movie. It's as if Kawai is scoring the frequent *pauses* in the flow of action, rather than under-scoring the punchy action (and his cues don't shift from busy to slow music, they stay s-l-o-w).

Batou races in to save the day, blasting the bejesus out of the tank machine (Batou is definitely a guy you want to have around, watching your back), taking the role that Boma played in Shirow's comic. But not before the tank's arm has grasped our heroine by her skull, squeezing it painfully.

❀

Then follows the thematic climax of *Ghost In the Shell*, which's unusual in Japanese *animé*, and in movies in general: it has Motoko Kusanagi hooking up electronically/ digitally (i.e., also psychologically and spiritually) with the Puppet Master ('diving in', as she calls it, the 'brain dive' of the *manga*). The 1995 movie combines both link-ups with the Puppet Master of the 1989 *manga*, and also shortens them and alters their meaning.

The scene is blocked statically: two torsos of two naked women are placed beside each other on the top of the hi-tech tank, while the blond hulk of Batou sits to one side, watching anxiously over them.[8] (And there's a minor subtext of sexual jealousy for Batou: it's a man seeing the woman he loves hooking up with a mysterious, sort of male presence – who literally goes inside her, and then, perversely, speaks through her body).

There is no action whatsoever, apart from the movement of eyes, and the turning of a head (Batou also moves a little). Yet the scene is riveting entertainment due its evocation of a heightened, unreal form of narration: to achieve this, it uses unusual camera angles, point-of-view shots, distorted lenses (including extreme wide angle), selective colour, freeze frames, visual effects (such as video static, and rain), rotating camera, and a carefully mixed soundtrack, comprising the Puppet Master's odd, disembodied voice, the voice of Batou heard from inside Kusanagi's viewpoint (and objective views, outside), and Kusanagi herself. Lastly, there is the dialogue itself, as the Puppet Master embarks on a rambling, quasi-metaphysical monologue.

The Puppeteer's dialogue in Uncle Shirow's *manga* is even denser (as you expect from Shirow!), and, you have to admit, rather incoherent. S/he/it is talking about evolution, humanity, the universe, cells, memes, genes, DNA, etc, and the metaphysical speculations go on and on:

> That's only part of the system map made up of electronics streaming around inside you. It's part of me, too. [...] Matter is indeterminate, just a mist-like superficial shell existence. Whatever exists, exists in a vacuum filled with virtual particles... And in me. A giant network that includes me... Is now connected to me. (276-8)

The 1995 movie of course rewrote the dialogue, but it still sounds like sophomore ramblings at times – as if a high school student had read bits of Fredric Jameson and Donna Haraway and misunderstood them, then tried to put them in her/ his own words (always the giveaway of someone who doesn't fully understand the concepts).[9]

The use of *point-of-view* in this *dénouement* sequence in the '95 *Ghost* is complex and very impressive: essentially, it has one character entering the

8 Batou covers Motoko with his jacket, as we saw him do earlier, after the canal chase. Such a gentleman! But she's a machine! (Or is she? Ummm...). Do you cover up your electric kettle to preserve its modesty? Maybe you do!
9 *The Matrix* had a go at the cultural theory-type of philosophizing, and failed miserably.

psychic interior of another character: it might be dreams, or telepathy, or a shamanic vision, but in this hi-tech future world, it is the digital realm, the web, the network. To portray that, *Ghost In the Shell* selects amazing camera angles and viewpoints, such as the extreme fish-eye effects from Motoko Kusanagi's viewpoint, which look up at the broken roof of the museum, with the rain falling into the non-existent camera, and Batou off to one side, staring at the Major (as Motoko sinks deeper into the network and the seemingly into the clutches of the Puppet Master, the Motoko-point-of-view image freezes, a creepy effect that vividly evokes the lack of control that Motoko now has (she can't communicate with Batou anymore, but she can see him speaking). Plus this kind of minimal animation is cheaper, too! You bet the twelve producers loved it when 30 seconds or more (700 frames!) of the climax of *Ghost In the Shell* went by using a single piece of artwork!).[10]

Indeed, the finale of *Ghost In the Shell* is a textbook example of selecting dramatic camera angles; it's like a film school for *animé* all on its own. It's one of those sequences where you think the filmmakers can't possibly conjure up a new camera angle, but then they do. I would imagine the scene went thru an intense work-out during the storyboard stage (along with script rewrites).

But it's even more complicated than that, because the filmmakers also mix up the points-of-view, so that it appears that the Puppet Master is speaking when we hear Motoko's voice, and vice versa. Also, when we hear Motoko, it's actually the Puppet Master's mouth we see moving in the exterior/ objective shots.

The quote from the classic, 1966 movie *Persona* (directed by Ingmar Bergman), with the cyborgs' faces framed like the famous images of Liv Ullmann and Bibi Andersson, rams home the notion of psychic identification between the two characters, the twins who have one, the exchange between beings which's so complete they are become one symbiotic creature.[11] (This is the climax of the perverse romance in *Ghost In the Shell*, between the Puppet Master and the Major, with the computer software suggesting that they fuse to become a new being).[12]

In short, the climax of *Ghost In the Shell* is masterful filmmaking because it soars not only at the level of action and drama, of technique and filmmaking, but it also has a powerful psychological and thematic and even a metaphysical impact. It's a finale that thrills and awes, as the best action movies should do, but it also inspires other feelings, of psychology, spirituality and speculation. It makes you think.

I know it sounds pompous and over-the-top, but *Ghost In the Shell* really is a movie that questions what life is. It does that on both a very simple, visceral level – with its depictions of bodies, spirits, cyborgs, robots and the like – and on a philosophical and metaphysical level, with its discussions of memories, souls, implants and augmentations.

10 OK, there are slight additions to that freeze frame, like the colour altering a tad.
11 *Persona* is a high culture reference, being a masterwork of European art cinema. But it's justified: *Ghost In the Shell* really is worthy of Ingmar Bergman and *Persona*.
12 No wonder Batou, left on the outside, is irritated and envious!

The issues are beautifully put to the audience: what is life? Is an artificial creature (or network) alive? What are the fundamental elements of life? Is it having a body? (but robots also have bodies). Is it independent agency, or independent thought? Is it having a soul/ spirit/ ghost? Can a machine have a soul or spirit? Is it having a memory, being able to remember things? If a machine can *do* everything a human can *do*, is it the same as a human?

In the 1989 *manga*, Masamune Shirow plays the finale differently (but it's the not finale of the comic, it's an episode from two-thirds in). The Puppet Master vanishes in the *manga*, and there are several religious signifiers employed to suggest spiritual transcendence. Chief among these is an angel, and a physical ascent: we see, in cyberspace, the entity that is the Puppeteer ascending upwards, now taking on the form of an angel (but only glimpsed in part), as s/he/it tells Motoko about 'shifting to a higher-level system' (this must be the first time that Heaven's been referred to as a 'higher-level system'!).

Yes, Japanese artists adore Christian iconography, and angels have appeared elsewhere in Masamune Shirow's art (the *animé* versions also added more Christian imagery).[13] The 1995 *Ghost In the Shell* movie pays *hommage* to Shirow's religious ponderings by including a p.o.v. image of an angel-shaped silhouette hovering above[14] Motoko Kusanagi. And what appear to be real feathers (another *animé* favourite) float down onto our heroes on top of the tank (feathers're also in the *manga*).

The *Ghost In the Shell manga* includes images of Motoko, nude, soaring about in cyberspace, which the 1995 adaptation dropped completely. This gives Shirow-sensei the opportunity to have his heroine Motoko in a human form interacting with entities encountered in cyberspace (it also allows him to feature more nude images of Motoko!). Indeed, most of the 2001 sequel to *Ghost In the Shell* (*Ghost In the Shell: Man-Machine Interface*) features the Major or one of her avatars bobbing about in the sea of digital irreality like a cyber-fairy (often unclothed).

Also, the '89 *manga* visualizes cyberspace very differently from the '95 movie – it is an abstract space/ non-space which also features some very abstract, vaguely-organic forms (reminiscent of the interior of the human body, *Fantastic Voyage*-style).

THE *DÉNOUEMENT* OF *GHOST IN THE SHELL.*

The *dénouement* scene has Major Motoko Kusanagi waking up in Batou's safe house (which's a series of dark rooms, not the silly building in the *manga*, which has giant, 360° windows – not great for a safe house. However, the movie's safe house does have big windows, and is up on a hill, so we can have the final shot of the Major looking out over the city).

In Masamune Shirow's *manga*, the gender ambiguity's pointed up again, with Kusanagi finding she's been inserted into a man's body

---

13 Angels appear in *Angel's Egg*, dir. by Mamoru Oshii.
14 Or possibly descending towards her.

(though with a woman's face and long, dark hair).15 The movie curiously opts for a young, teenager's body, and a sinisterly dark green, old-fashioned dress16 (it was the only body shell he could find at short notice on the black market, Batou explains lamely).17 These are not the body or the outfit that Motoko would've chosen! (Shirow never puts Motoko in clothes like this!).

Asian cinema has a more relaxed attitude to alternative gender roles – transvestism, for instance, has a long tradition in Japan, as Helen McCarthy pointed out (1993, 49). *Animé* shows which feature trans-vestites include *Cowboy Bebop*, *Mospeada*, *3 x 3 Eyes*, *Ghost In the Shell* and *Joker Marginal City*. In Hong Kong cinema, as in *anime*, female voices are sometimes employed for the villains (as with the Puppet Master in the updated *Ghost In the Shell*), and gender-bending is quite common in characters (boys in *shonen manga* turning into girls, for ex).

The *dénouement* scene is about one question: who is Motoko Kusanagi now? Is she still the same person? I mean cyborg. I mean life-form. I mean creature. (Which also begs the question, exactly what was Major Kusanagi before? Not a whole person, a regular person). Batou asks: is 'he' still inside you? As she exits, enigmatic and sombre to the last, Kusanagi replies (facing away from Batou), that neither she nor the Puppet Master exist anymore.18 (The child's body may evoke this new being as the offspring of the union of the Project 2501 and Kusanagi: this is how machines have children, perhaps – the concept of longevity and continuation crops up regularly in science fiction about robots).

Both the 1989 *Ghost In the Shell manga* and the 1995 adaptation close with Motoko standing outside Batou's safe house, under the night sky, overlooking the metropolis. But the mood is (inevitably) more sombre in the 1995 film (Masamune Shirow's *manga* makes much of Batou's astonished, amused reaction that Motoko Kusanagi is now in a male body: 'Guy?!' 'Yeah. This is a male body. You want proof?' And Motoko bops him with a shoe).

Instead, the *Ghost In the Shell* 1995 movie has Motoko Kusanagi in a solemn, meditative mood (so, sorry, no hitting Batou with a shoe), looking down on the City of Newport and musing on the possibilities of her future (the camera tilts up from an oblique angle, to show, *Akira*-style, more and more of the giant metropolis, with its skyscrapers and streets and millions of lights; the modern city – Tokyo, Hong Kong, New York, L.A. – is, of course, the most appropriate and oft-used external image of the digital network). Here the foreshadowing in the diving sequence when the Major mused about becoming something else flowers: it's as if Motoko K.

15 The body Kusanagi inhabits is distinctly female: I couldn't think of who it reminded me of at first – the big 1980s hair, shoulder pads, a tight-lipped smile – it's Sigourney Weaver in *Aliens*, of course! Masamune Shirow has acknowledged his debt to the 1986 Fox movie (and of course Weaver played a character which explored gender reversals).
16 Is the dress an *Alice* reference?
17 The 2008 update of *Ghost In the Shell* has Motoko talking in a strange girlish voice, but later in the scene she reverts to her usual adult, Motoko voice.
18 The blocking of the scene is both classic Mamoru Oshii, drawing on the alienation cinema of Michelangelo Antonioni, where characters are perpetually disconnected, facing away from each other, and classic *animé*, where it's common for whole conversations to play out with two people facing away from each other.

is going to dive into the network itself, as she looms over it, like a bird about to fly.

Poor old Batou! – after all he's done for Major Kusanagi, including saving her ass (well, her head and her torso!) – she simply walks out on him.[19] OK, forget that these two're cyborgs, just look at the way the final scene of the 1995 *Ghost In the Shell* movie is played: Kusanagi wakes, talks to Batou briefly, then walks out! Barely even a thank you! *Arrigato Batou!* Batou tells her he has a car for her, wonders if the Puppet Master is still somewhere inside her, but the *dénouement* scene plays like a brittle, cynical *film noir*, with the Major acting as cool, calm and collected as Lauren Bacall, Mary Astor or Barbara Stanwyck (there is a ton of North American *film noir* and hard-boiled detective fiction in the *Ghost In the Shell* movie and TV series).

THE LOVE STORY IN *GHOST IN THE SHELL*.

If you put aside the fact in *Ghost In the Shell* that Motoko Kusanagi is a cyborg, and that many of the main characters have artificially augmented bodies (and brains), you still have a fantastic story of cops and robbers, of chases and hunts, of tracking down villains who're somewhere in the vast digital network. You still have tons of hardware and techno-fetishism and some outstanding action sequences. That is, *Ghost In the Shell* in its *Mobile Armoured Riot Police* mode.

The love story in *Ghost In the Shell*, between Motoko Kusanagi and Batou, works whether or not you regard them as 'real' people or as cyborgs. It doesn't really matter (they're just pieces of celluloid anyway!), though it is perhaps weird and a little creepy that you're watching an on-off romance between two machines, albeit machines which still have traces of real humanity in them (whether or not either Batou or Kusanagi have real brains inside their metal skulls isn't satisfyingly clarified. Masamune Shirow liked to retain a little mystery about this issue).[20] It was the same with *Blade Runner*: audiences just didn't care whether Rachel was an android in the end (so that Deckard got to have his robot after all – and Deckard may've been a replicant too!).

Whatever, the love story in *Ghost In the Shell* is classically Japanese in its wholly undemonstrative and restrained portrayal of erotic desire. These are lovers who don't kiss, don't embrace, often don't even look at each other (they often stand at angles to each other), and hardly ever touch (it's classic subtext drama – everything is played at the subtextual level, it's all looks and hints). They are work colleagues who have operated together on many missions, who know each other very well, and who also hang out after hours (such as the diving session in the harbour). They talk a lot, but they don't make physical contact (*bullshit!* is Batou's response to Kusanagi's gloomy metaphysical ramblings, in the English subtitles).

And, as in the finest Japanese movies, the romance is all the more

19 The *manga* includes scenes of Batou driving in a car while Kusanagi is there beside him – as a brain and some parts on the seat.
20 In the elevator scene, Batou insists that Motoko has real brain matter in her skull. Does she? She's not convinced – nobody has ever seen their brain, she gripes.

powerful for being withheld and distanced: let's remember that the first kiss wasn't shown in a Japanese movie until as late as 1946 (G. Mast, 1992b). But the feelings are definitely there, bubbling under the surface (and, in the true, romantic fiction manner, it's the man, Batou, who seems to express his feelings for the woman, Motoko Kusanagi, more than she does for him. Certainly he cares a good deal for her, riding in like a knight to save her during the climax of the 1995 *Ghost* flick, as he does in *Ghost In the Shell: Stand Alone Complex,* too (and she doesn't always want that). It might be a Jane Austen melodrama, all repressed emotion and unspoken desire).

Although the Kusanagi-Batou romance is the primary one in *Ghost In the Shell*, it is not the only one: the relationship between the Puppet Master and the Major is also given an erotic undertone. And this is no ordinary romance: for a start, the Puppet Master is not a robot, not a cyborg, not something with a body or 'shell': he or she or it is a computer programme, a ghostly presence that exists somewhere in the vast information networks, a presence that can manifest itself inside a giant tank, or inside robots, or inside a cyborg. The Puppet Master is called 'he' in the story partly for genre reasons: if the Puppet Master is the villain, the villain is usually male. (And it also normalizes (heterosexualizes) the potentially erotic quality of the relationship between the Puppet Master and Motoko, while also fuelling the jealousy of Batou).

The ambiguities of gender, perception and psychology do not end there, however: because when the Puppet Master interacts with charas in the 1995 *Ghost In the Shell* movie, it is thru the form of a female cyborg (well, just the torso). And the female cyborg just happens to be blonde, attractive, with large breasts (the movie uses the age-old convention of having one woman blonde and the other dark-haired).[21] So a piece of computer software having a romance thru the broken torso of a female cyborg with another cyborg is a pretty weird dalliance. (In the *Ghost In the Shell manga*, when Kusanagi 'dives' into the female torso's brain, Chief Aramaki frets about whether she is inside the Puppeteer, or whether he's inside her. The tropes of sexual penetration are all there in Shirow-sensei's comic).

MOTOKO KUSANAGI AND FEMINISM.

The sexy robot type occurs in many sci-fi *manga* and *animé*, including *Space Adventure Cobra* by Buichi Terasawa (the 'Lady' character), Gally in *Gunnm* (*Battle Angel Alita*) by Yukito Kishiro, and the works of illustrator Hajime Sorayama. Yuki in *Lady Snowblood* is an obvious forerunner of Motoko – a cold-hearted, brilliant, professional assassin who strips off as she dives into battle. As Masamune Shirow put it: 'I don't know why, but the heroes Japanese children first identify with in

21 The 2008 remastered movie used a female actor for the voice of the Puppet Master, but its gender is actually a very minor issue. However, in action movies in general, bad guys tend to be *guys* (in Chinese martial arts movies, as in Japanese (fantasy) animation, there is a tradition for gender reversal among the villains, so guys will be voiced by female actors, and vice versa. Sometimes this can add a layer of crossdressing or transgenderism which, this being the world of movies, inevitably equates to weirdness and perversity).

manga and animation all seem to be robots'.

In the *manga* of *Ghost In the Shell: Man-Machine Interface*, Masamune Shirow defined Major Kusanagi thus:

> Motoko is a hyper-advanced cyborg – her body consists of all of her active drives; her memory of all her active sources. These are all variable, but on a periodic basis her bio-components crave energy and sleep and remind her of her basic identity-layer. To her, the physical world and the world of information are both reality. All existence is life, destined to continue for the unforeseeable future. (7)

And of course, for readers of *manga*, all is fiction/ fantasy/ unreality anyway. There is no 'reality' in any *manga*: it is a cultural product, words and images on a page, a highly stylized, cultural artefact, made in a particular time and place, in a certain socio-political context… A representation of a representation… A series of images and *kanji* and *hiragana* which have to be decoded in a highly specialized manner to 'mean' anything at all.

Seen from the outside, with her voluptuous body and big breasts, Major Motoko Kusanagi appears to be wholly 'female'. Yet we know that 'she's' a cyborg, and do machines have a gender? Is gender of any significance for a washing machine, a laptop computer, a car? (Her 'ghost' or soul is feminine, presumably. Motoko was once a young girl, we recall, who became a cyborg at an early age – the TV series depicted that. The '95 picture keeps it unclear).

In fact, as Judith Butler has pointed out in *Gender Trouble: Feminism and the Subversion of Identity*, gender and sexual identity have to be 'performed' and emphasized by society, by laws, by politics, by communities, and by individuals; thus, Major Kusanagi's gender derives partly from the way other people see her, how they talk to her (as well as how she behaves). For postmodern feminist critics such as Butler, heterosexuality itself is not an unchanging institution, and definitely not an essence, a given, but may already be a 'constant parody of itself' (1990, 122). Heterosexuality, Butler reckons, is continually imitating itself, always miming its own performances in order to appear 'natural'.

As third wave (postmodern) feminism has demonstrated convincingly, sexuality, identity and gender are not fixed, not innate, not essences. They are continually changing, and need to be enacted by the individual as well as by society. These issues become even more fascinating when applied to fictional characters such as cyborgs.

Postmodern or third wave feminism has been critical of the tendency in second wave (modernist) feminism which sees an essence or essentialism in women and being female; in third wave feminism, gender is socially conditioned, not 'natural' or innate; people learn to be female or male, right back to when they are children. And the attributes of gender have to be continually practised. It's about agency, about doing, acting, performing, thinking, not just 'being'.

In Japanese *animé*, Major Motoko Kusanagi is a tomboy type, Jonathan Clements suggests (Clements puts forward six types of women in *animé*: the maiden, girl next door, tomboy, older woman, alien and child [1998]). As a tomboy type (a tough, spiky, boyish girl), Kusanagi also evokes lesbianism. She's an assertive, independent woman who doesn't seem to be interested in men (this is true of many of Masamune Shirow's female charas); in Shirow's *manga*, she does have a boyfriend, however (tho' only for one chapter, really). And also in the *Ghost In the Shell manga*, she enjoys an erotic threesome with two other women (and with a young woman in the 2001 *manga* sequel. Masamune Shirow has said he doesn't like to draw men naked,[22] hence the lesbian scenes. Indeed, the only time Motoko is depicted having sex is with other women. Later in his art, however, male nudity is everywhere – the recurring erotic encounter in Shirow's later art is a girl surrounded by nude men). None of the adaptations on screen have attempted to translate the erotic elements in *Ghost In the Shell*, apart from the *Ghost In the Shell: Stand Alone Complex* series.

Motoko Kusanagi also clearly has a father complex (in common with a large number of heroines in fiction, and not only those created by men). All of Shirow-sensei's female charas have father complexes. Probably the most 'normal' (i.e., non-ambiguous, non-neurotic) romantic relationship in Shirow's fiction is Deunan and Briareos – and he, of course, is a cyborg![23]

Lesbian culture is just one of a number of social cultures that coalesce around women in military fiction: nobody can miss that Motoko Kusanagi is regarded as female in amongst a group of men (irrespective of whether she is 'female'): she's the lone woman in a band of brothers, who appears to be very masculine and tough. In a North American production, there might be jokes about Kusanagi's dykey status from the other grunts or cops in a locker room scene. (And one can't also help noting that Batou, a hulky, blond guy (who might be a Nazi bully boy in a different story), and permanent bachelor (no girlfriend in sight[24]), is a type found in gay male culture.)

For the audience, the identifications with Major Kusanagi in *Ghost In the Shell* are likely to be multiple: she's the main character, she acts macho and male, great with techie stuff, weaponry and kicking butt, so she's an action hero; but she's also definitely eroticized by the filmmakers, turned into the kind of sex object found in masculinist culture (she's a *Playboy* cyborg). For women, Kusanagi may be an assertive, positive role model, a woman surviving – and flourishing – in a world of men, of cops, of machines, and of patriarchal politics. The image of Kusanagi likely also flatters postmodern and third wave feminists (but not second wave feminists so much!) in being an ironic commentary on female empowerment in a patriarchal society (and evoking issues of embodiment,

22 However, in his *hentai* / erotic *manga* and artwork, Shirow has depicted many nude men, often involved sexually with young women.
23 Father complex women are pretty much universal in the sci-fi and fantasy genres.
24 The *manga* jokily gives Batou a dalliance with a 'girlfriend' in an online dating scenario, who's actually an old guy.

identity, gender, etc).

THE POLITICS OF *GHOST IN THE SHELL*.

One aspect of *Ghost In the Shell* plays against the left-leaning politics of director Mamoru Oshii, and that's the fundamentally right-wing ideology of the *Ghost In the Shell* movies (and the *Patlabor* movies), and Masamune Shirow's *manga*. Oshii had participated in anti-State student movements in the 1960s – in particular the anti-A.M.P.O. movement, which protested against the American-Japanese Treaty On Mutual Cooperation and Security. [25]

These are films and TV shows about the State, about the State wielding its power via the police force and the security services. Yes, the *Ghost In the Shell* series (in any of its forms), does question the State and its policies, but in the end it's cops vs. bad guys, and the cops're the heroes – and there is nothing more right-wing and conservative than the police force of a nation. (However, of the animated forms of *Ghost In the Shell*, the two *Ghost In the Shell: Stand Alone Complex* series have convincingly presented and explored left-wing politics, and are definitely the most left-leaning of the adaptations).

Jonathan Clements noted in *The Erotic Anime Movie Guide* that because Motoko Kusanagi requires specialized and expensive maintenance, paid for by the State (and the tax-payer), she is no feminist icon but a weapon of the government:

> The super-competent woman, uninfluenced by troublesome hormones or maternal considerations, can be read as an extreme anti-feminist character. Her abilities, power and intelligence all rely on an advanced industrial civilisation created by men, and the patriarchal stewardship of the male government. Without them, she would be thrown onto the biological scrapheap. (1998, 99)

Thus, no matter how much contemporary feminist, postmodern, lesbian and queer theory you apply to *Ghost In the Shell* and Major Kusanagi, there's no ignoring the fact that it is *a franchise about cops*, it's about cops policing a nation: it's called *Mobile Armored Riot Police*, after all, in Japan. *Ghost In the Shell* is pro-government (and thus pro-law, pro-military) all the way down the line, even if the authorities are questioned from time to time, and even if the charas bitch about their bosses, and even if many of the stories're about internecine war between government departments.

The military machine is also upheld and enforced in the *Ghost In the Shell* series, not least because Public Security Section 9 and its workers require a lot of very expensive maintenance to keep going (and often liaise with the Japan Self Defence Force). They use the latest technology, they have enormous resources of man-power and machinery (paid for by the

---

25 There is an allusion to political protests in episode 5 of *Ghost In the Shell: Stand Alone Complex* where one of the bad guys used to be an activist, but later went legit and became just another salaryman (when the company he was working for found out he had been involved with left-wing activities, it fired him).

Japanese tax-payer), and their existence is primarily to enforce the security of Japan.

Thus, making Major Kusanagi female (or 'female' and 'feminine' in some respects), is a token gesture in what is a predominantly male and masculinist setting (in TV and *manga*, this kind of story is called *seinen*, aimed at young males). All of the government authorities and big business bosses are men, for instance (rarely does the *Ghost In the Shell* franchise offer up women in key roles, or women as the key adversaries). As such, the *Ghost In the Shell* universe simply reflects the politics of modern Japan. (Would North America ever have a female President? Maybe just as unlikely as Japan having a woman Prime Minister. Though in the *2nd Gig* TV series, the producers introduced a woman P.M.).

Is Masamune Shirow *sending up* right-wing ideology and the military-industrial complex in *Ghost In the Shell*? Is he really a politically-active, left-wing artist using a cop show format to explore contemporary society? No one is quite sure: in fact, nearly all science fiction classic movies, such as *Blade Runner, 2001: A Space Odyssey, Star Wars, The Terminator*, etc, are ultimately thoroughly right-wing, conservative, and pro-military. And when filmmakers do employ satire – as in *Starship Troopers* (1997), some critics (even clever ones who should know better) *still* take it all straight. *Starship Troopers* is so obviously a *send-up* of contemporary, Republican North Amerika, but even North American critics, who presumably understand the political system in North America reasonably well, took it all so seriously.

If Masamune Shirow *is* satirizing conservativism and the military in *Ghost In the Shell, Appleseed, Black Magic* and other works, he is going a strange way about it. You can't ignore just how much Shirow fetishizes weaponry, machines, vehicles and advanced technology (as well as bodies), and how many stories in the *Ghost In the Shell manga* consist of Public Security Section 9 blasting foreign invaders to bits (or Japanese who've sold out to foreign companies/ nations). Which makes the *Ghost In the Shell: Stand Alone Complex* TV series all the more laudable, because it tackles politics head-on, and not only the conservatism and reactionary ideology of contemporary Japan, but also revolutionary and left-wing political movements.

THE SUBLIME IN *GHOST IN THE SHELL.*

The sublime has always been a part of cinema (from early films such as *Intolerance* and *Faust* onwards), but after *2001: A Space Odyssey*, it became an essential ingredient of sci-fi and fantasy films (think of *Star Wars, Star Trek, Jurassic Park, A.I., E.T., Close Encounters of the Third Kind, Blade Runner, Total Recall, Independence Day, Avatar, The Abyss* and *The Fifth Element*). *2001: A Space Odyssey* set the precedent for the sublime in sci-fi cinema in the modern era (and *Metropolis* in 1927 in the pre-war era), for gigantic scale, infinite distances, mysteries, long, elaborate shots, and complex special effects. A sense of wonder is one of the hallmarks of science fiction. *Ghost In the Shell* draws on that, right from the opening shots in the prologue, with Motoko high above the skyscrapers of Newport City.

For a useful guide to the sublime in cinema, art critic Christopher Hussey defined seven aspects of the sublime (in art), derived from critic Edmund Burke: obscurity (physical and intellectual); power; privations (such as darkness, solitude, silence); vastness (vertical or horizontal); infinity; succession; and uniformity (the last two suggest limitless progression).[26]

These tenets of the sublime in art can be applied to cinema – to films such as *Ghost In the Shell* (even more to the 2004 sequel, which takes contemplation of the sublime to greater lengths), *Intolerance, Faust* (1926), *Blade Runner, 2001: A Space Odyssey, Akira, Urotsukidoji, Citizen Kane* and *Apocalypse Now*, movies which consciously encourage notions such as obscurity, darkness, vastness and infinity.

(*Animé* filmmakers have been hugely influenced from seeing a number of Western movies: *2001: A Space Odyssey, Blade Runner, Alien, Star Wars, The Terminator, Thunderbirds* and *King Kong* (and to a lesser degree *RoboCop* and Ray Harryhausen's monster movies).)

EXPLOITING THE FRANCHISE OF *GHOST IN THE SHELL*.

In TV and cinema alone, the *Ghost In the Shell* franchise has been exploited quite a few times: the 1995 movie was followed by the two *Ghost In the Shell: Stand Alone Complex* TV series, broadcast from 2002 to 2005; a movie sequel appeared in 2004; a spin-off movie from the TV series appeared in 2006 (plus two re-edited movies from the TV shows); the re-vamp/ update of the first *Ghost* movie in 2008; and another TV/ Original Video Animation series, *Ghost In the Shell: Arise* in 2013-15. (And it's still continuing, with the live-action movie, the *Arise* movie and now another TV series). Add to that tie-in novels, comics, stories, video games, merchandizing, etc.

That 350-page *manga* has been a huge money-spinner for Masamune Shirow and the rights holders of *Ghost In the Shell* (including Production I.G., one of the more aggressive promoters of all things *Ghostly* and *Shellis*).

The *Ghost In the Shell* franchise was also exploited in home entertainment formats, such as DVD (with the *Ghost In the Shell: Stand Alone Complex* series appearing both singly (with discs for both Dolby 5.1 mixes and D.T.S. Sound),[27] and in the usual box sets. In publishing, the original *manga* was re-published, with added colour, plus large-format editions. There were *Ghost In the Shell manga* sequels in 2001 and 2003.

And further *manga* have appeared, including two *manga* series based on *Ghost In the Shell: Stand Alone Complex*. (*Monthly Young Magazine* published the first *Ghost In the Shell: Stand Alone Complex manga* series, in 2009. Mayasuki Yamamoto was the artist). The second *Ghost In the Shell manga* series (*Weekly Young Magazine*, 2009), which used the Laughing Man storyline, was drawn by Yu Kinutani. The *Ghost In the Shell: Stand*

26 C. Hussey: *The Picturesque*, Putnam's, New York, 1927.
27 The DVD releases include useful interviews with the cast and crew of the TV shows.

Alone Complex manga was collected into 3 *tankobons* (2010-11). *Ghost In the Shell: Stand Alone Complex* was also novelized (in 2004-05, publ. by Tokuma Shoten), by one of the writers of the series, Junichi Fujisaku, who worked on the scripts for the *Arise* prequel series (he also directed the *Blood* + TV series for Production I.G.).

All in all, that's a pretty big franchise. And let's not forget the computer games based on *Ghost In the Shell*: the *manga*, the movies and the TV series are ideally suited to shoot-em-up arcade games, or slower, more thoughtful espionage video games. And the CDs and soundtracks of composers Yoko Kanno and Kenji Kawai.

And – listen, folks! – you can also buy real thermoptic camouflage from a cybernetic company in Tokyo (it trades out of a run-down warehouse at the harbour, and you have to shoot your way (to kill) thru a real gun fight involving 20 grizzled assailants and two colossal cyborgs armed with rocket launchers. So far only one *Ghost In the Shell* fan has made it to the store's counter and handed over $200,000,000 in cash).

GHOST IN THE SHELL AND THE MATRIX.

According to producer Joel Silver, super-nerds the Wachowski brothers (or sisters) showed him *Ghost In the Shell* to indicate the kind of look they were going for with *The Matrix* (1999), their fan-boy action-adventure flick. *The Matrix* turned out to be virtually a remake of both *Ghost In the Shell* and *Akira*, with some scenes seemingly lifted wholesale from *Ghost*,[28] and details right down to the use of green, or the flowing computer read-outs against black. Director Mamoru Oshii wasn't so bothered – he acknowledged that everyone takes from everyone else's work (a common view in Japan), and the parts employed in *The Matrix* were well done.

The Matrix alerted Hollywood again to the stupendous power of Japanese *animé*; critics, especially cultural theorists, went crazy over *The Matrix*, with its evocations of simulated reality and hyper-reality, the kind of filmmaking that encourages endless essays on Donna Haraway and cyborgs, or Jean Baudrillard and simulations, or the return of the repressed of Slavoj Zizek, or Paul Virillio and info-war, or Frederic Jameson and hyperspace, or Judith Butler and performativity – take your pick. Movies like *Blade Runner* and *The Matrix* are tailor-made for grad students to go nuts over. But Japanese animation has been exploring this field for years.

And only when this sort of robotic, cyborgian, hyperreal, futuristic science fiction material was done over in the North American idiom backed by a big, North American company (Warner Brothers), did everyone take notice.

Keanu Reeves was good casting, though, for *The Matrix*, because he suited the blank, geeky, alienated and impassive characters found in futuristic, Japanese *animé* – and *Ghost In the Shell 2: Innocence* seemed to pay back the compliment, by having the main character Togusa designed

28 The flow went back the other way, with the *Animatrix* series of short movies in the Japanese *animé* style.

even more a Keanu Reeves lookalike, with a pony tail and a perpetually vacant expression.

The philosophizing in *Ghost In the Shell* was one of the aspects that the Wachoswkis attempted in the *Matrix* movies, but it was underwhelming (Jean Baudrillard, one of the touchstones of *The Matrix*, disliked the movie). So the lengthy disquisitions on Who Knows What became silly aspects of recent Hollywood cinema.

The heroine is shot to shreds at the climax of Ghost In the Shell.
Luckily, she's a cyborg, so getting a new body can be done –
if you know the right people on the black market.

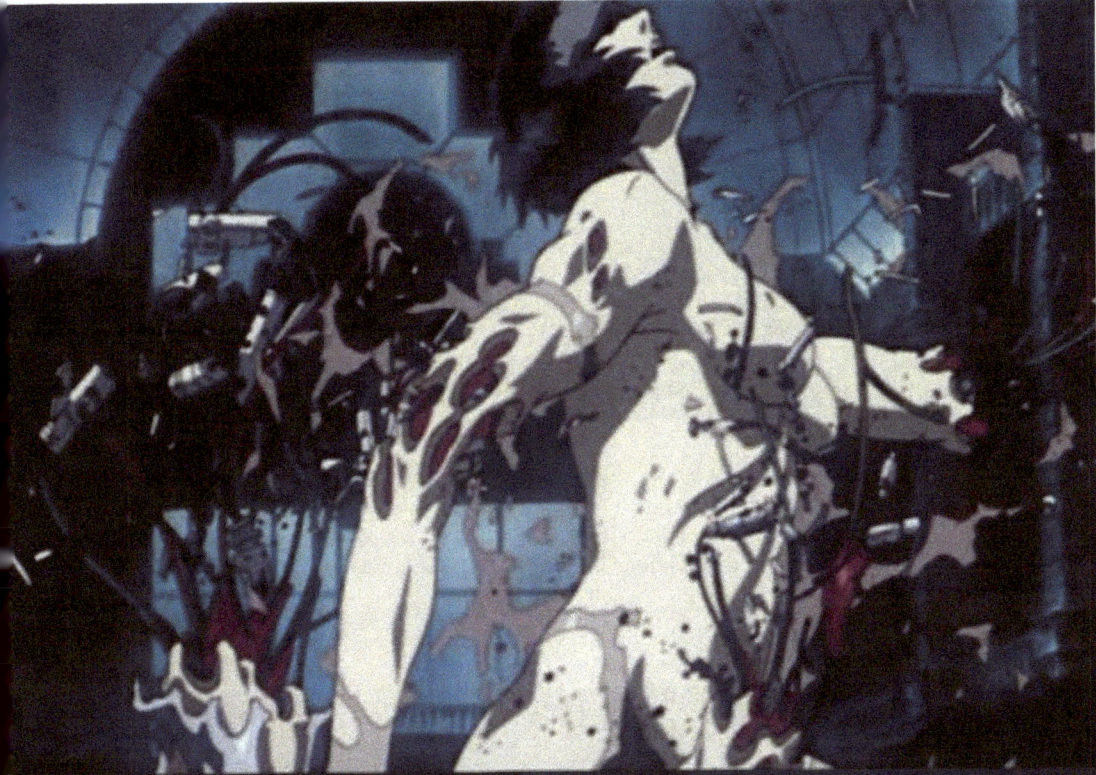

Your desire to remain as you are
is what ultimately limits you.

The finale of Ghost In the Shell moves into some very unusual territory: an extraordinary conversation (with a visual quote from art movie favourite Persona); and in the dénouement, the cyborg couple separate (with the heroine now in a teenager's body). No Big Goodbyes, no hugs – she just walks out!

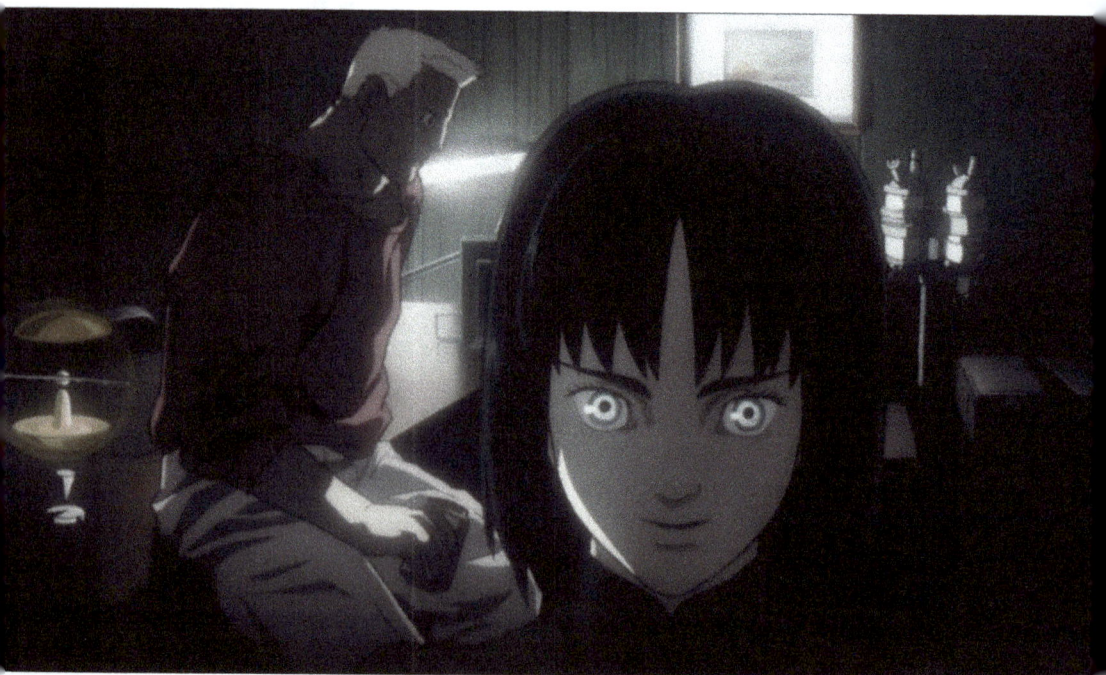

02

GHOST IN THE SHELL 2.0 (2008)

In 2008, the 1995 *Ghost In the Shell* movie was given a dust-down and make-over,[1] with new elements added to it, such as newly-recorded voices (with the original cast), new visual material (including computer-assisted effects), and a re-worked score by Kenji Kawai. These rehashings of earlier movies are market-led, and producer-initiated; it's all about money – thus, only successful movies with a guaranteed audience get this kind of high quality make-over and re-release.

With *Ghost In the Shell 2.0*, it would be a case of the producers at Production I.G. who would've approached Mamoru Oshii and asked him to oversee a revamped version of the 13 year-old film – rather than Oshii and the filmmakers going to the producers and begging to have a chance at updating the 1995 movie. (Jeez, is 13 years so old?! If it is, then *Sunrise* (1927) and *Intolerance* (1916) are positively ancient!).

Greedy, aren't they, the folk at Production I.G. and associated companies such as Kodansha, Bandai Visual and D.R. Movie? Because they have exploited the *Ghost In the Shell* franchise many times – not one but two television series, plus three spin-off movies from the TV shows, then this redux movie, then the *Arise* prequels (and more to come). Not to mention other Shirow works.

All of this begs the question: why can't Masamune Shirow come up with some <u>new</u> *manga* material? So that Production I.G., Kodansha, Bandai and whoever can have new stories, instead of these reworkings of yarns from the 1980s? The reactionary, disgruntled fan might complain: if Shirow had spent a *quarter* of the time he's lavished on his digital erotica and pouty nudes, we'd have *ten* new *manga* stories by now!

Similarly, I would prefer to see a *new* movie by Mamoru Oshii and the team at Production I.G. (and its many associates) rather than a re-jigged version of an existing movie. Besides, the 1995 flick *already* looks utterly incredible, *already* has a fantastic soundtrack, *already* has amazing voice work from the actors, *already* has wonderful visual effects. *Ghost In the Shell* is a *masterpiece*, and it doesn't need (or even want) revising.

---

1 It was given the title *Ghost In the Shell 2.0*. Confusing, as there already is a *Ghost In the Shell 2*, the sequel, which has the subtitle *Innocence*. Better to call it *Redux*, like *Apocalypse Now*, or *Remix*, or something else.

And for many other reasons, ranging from the historical and cultural to the personal and fan-based, the original *Ghost In the Shell* movie is important. Thus, the 1977 *Star Wars*, 1982's *E.T.*, 1940's *Fantasia*, and 1977's *Close Encounters of the Third Kind* are preferred to the reworkings. (Handily, both versions of *Ghost In the Shell* are available – I prefer the earlier version; whereas some earlier movies, famously the 1977 *Star Wars*, aren't available any more, having apparently been withdrawn by Fox and Lucasfilm. Only later did Lucasfilm allow the original *Star Wars* to be included on home releases, due to the clamouring of fans. However, it was an unsatisfactory version, technically. George Lucas defended the *Star Wars Special Edition* versions (1997) of the original *Star Wars* trilogy (1977-1983) by saying that the effects the filmmakers were going for were not available in the late 1970s. This remains a contentious issue among fans. But it doesn't apply to *Ghost In the Shell*, which was full animation, in which pretty much anything is possible, and there was no burning need or desire to update the 1995 movie with computer-aided animated additions).

The update/ upgrade of *Ghost In the Shell* is flashy, and welcome for the impact it might have outside of the movie (introducing new audiences, for example, to the world of Masamune Shirow). But it seems unnecessary to tinker with a masterpiece: there are many, far more worthwhile ways of spending money and resources.

Ghost In the Shell 2.0 drew on the look and production of the 2004 sequel, *Ghost In the Shell 2: Innocence*, with the filmmakers revisiting the world of Major Kusanagi and her Public Security Section 9 police pals yet again, and applying some of the new cinematic techniques, such as new integrations of digital animation and 2-D animation, developed for the 2004 *Ghost In the Shell* sequel.

Although the computer-aided additions to *Ghost In the Shell 2.0* were very impressive, it was in the invisible areas that *Ghost In the Shell 2.0* was perhaps more significant: that is, the new voice recordings,[2] the newly mixed music, and the new mix of the soundtrack (Randy Thom, a veteran sound designer of the Bay Area type, was again overseeing the soundtrack, as he had on *Ghost In the Shell 2: Innocence*). In *Ghost In the Shell 2.0*, the vocal delivery by the principals seems even quieter and wearier: compare the exchanges at the heart of the movie, between Batou and the Major, for instance.

A notable change was the omission of many sound effects, especially those which were *animé*-ish, and now seem a little out-dated (they'd been used plenty already in the 1980s). Meaning – the little bleeps and blurps, the *kerchaks* and pops when hi-tech machinery or cybernetic devices were employed.[3] (But Kenji Kawai's score hasn't aged at all).

Visually, the computer-aided additions were employed right from the start of *Ghost In the Shell 2.0*, so that when Motoko Kusanagi is introduced in her famous, superhero position, high up on a skyscraper

2 The Puppet Master was now voiced by Yoshiko Sakakibara (she had been the robot specialist in *Ghost In the Shell 2: Innocence*), replacing Iemasa Kayumi in the 1995 version.
3 But they, too, are part of the charm.,

above the technological city of that corporate entity known as 'Japan', she is now a digitally-assisted Motoko (using 3-D software), rather than the 2-D ink-and-paint Kusanagi (the 2008 version also eroticized the Major a little more than the 1995 movie: when she strips off to go into action (as every action hero *should* do!), there is a full body shot from the front. But she still looks like a doll). However, it was the right decision to retain most of the 2-D, traditional ink-and-paint animation of the super-babe – and all of the human (or human-cyborg) characters (personally, I find the digital, 3-D Major Kusanagi not as successful or as appealing as the 2-D version).

The shift from a pseudo-3-D animated Motoko to the 2-D animated Motoko draws attention to the two approaches: in the opening scene, for example, or in the diving sequence (where there are direct cuts from the 3-D-ish Kusanagi to the 2-D Kusanagi). At times like this, the character seems to come from a different movie.

In the celebrated title sequence of *Ghost In the Shell*, digital additions were used throughout: the images of computer networks and screens seem especially suited to digital-style animation, so that the digital technology seems to blend seamlessly with recreations of computer screens and displays. The green numbers were replaced with threads and fibres in Mamoru Oshii's new favourite colour, amber (seen in the *Ghost In the Shell* sequel).

Computer-assisted animation also spruced up the computer read-outs and displays, which form an important element in the exposition of *Ghost In the Shell*. (If you go back and compare the two versions, which some fans have done, you can see that the additions and alterations are considerable; yet also largely cosmetic and superficial. The *spirit* of the 1995 movie remains pretty much the same).

Inevitably, following recent trends in animation, digital and 3-D animation was used in the revamped *Ghost In the Shell* for vehicles such as cars and helicopters, to achieve those now-familiar movements in simulated three-dimensional space. And also for weaponry, the sky-scrapers – and the combos of choppers plus 'scrapers (and the tank at the end). The digital shots did not simply recreate the existing 2-D animation, they were new designs (such as the tilt-rotor aircraft of Public Security Section 9).

The final shot of *Ghost In the Shell 2.0* also had a digital makeover, with a new shot portraying an even larger, light-filled city at night. With its tendrils of light, its gold-amber hue, and its pulsing, red highways looking like fibre optic cables, the city at the end of *Ghost In the Shell 2.0* was created to deliberately evoke the computer networks that had played such an important role throughout the picture.

If the network looks like the city, and the city is one vast network, the visual mix between the two also plays out one of the themes of the *Ghost In the Shell* series: the link/ the similarity/ the identification between the network and real life, between the artificial world and the organic world, between the life inside us and the life outside us. (Masamune Shirow would continue those dramatic equivalents in 2008's *Real Drive*, where the real ocean and the sea of cyberspace coalesce; and he had already explored the affinities between the two in the diving sequence in the first *Ghost In the Shell tankobon*, and in the many underwater scenes in the *Ghost In the Shell: Man-Machine Interface manga*).

Notice also the increased use of hues such as amber and gold in *Ghost In the Shell 2.0*, which looks back to the 2004 *Ghost* sequel (and details such as the fibre optics going into the cyborg bodies – a nightmare to animate, as Mamoru Oshii commented). The diving sequence is now pretty much digital, with lovely, gold-amber imagery of Motoko sinking into the briny, and rising up to the surface to be reborn.

The mix of computer-aided and 2-D animation in *Ghost In the Shell 2.0* isn't always wholly satisfying. Of course, it's most noticeable in the human (or cyborg) images. A computer-aided Motoko appears a number of times – in the opening sequence, in the titles/ birth scene, in the diving scene, and in other places (the *Ghost In the Shell: Stand Alone Complex* TV series also used a digital Kusanagi at times). Is it just that we are used to seeing the Major in 2-D animation, and we don't like to change? Or it is that the digital Motoko isn't as successful as the 2-D one? Is it that the filmmakers opted to step away from photo-realism (*à la Final Fantasy*) for Motoko, instead using digital animation to emphasize her strange, doll-like qualities?

Thus, with all of the additions taken together, *Ghost In the Shell 2.0* is really a new movie, or a remake using the original materials, rather than simply an update (or it's a partial update). The soundtrack, for instance, reworked all of the significant elements: the voices, the sound fx and the music (there were new recordings and new mixes of all three items). And the digital additions replaced entire shots many, many times (or added digitally-animated parts to 2-D animation). Also, the filmmakers of the updated *Ghost In the Shell* re-edited the movie (apparent right from the early scenes). However, the story wasn't altered too much (though the new dialogue probably changed at times). In which case, *Ghost 2.0* isn't a 'new' movie, because structurally it is the same story.

Thus, *Ghost In the Shell 2.0* acts as a kind of bridge between the two *Ghost In the Shell* movies: and here the new home entertainment formats, principally DVD, but also home video, have enabled this make-over. Far more people will see *Ghost In the Shell 2.0* on a TV screen or a computer screen than on the big screen. That's true of almost all movies nowadays, big or small, blockbuster or indie feature, and the Japanese animation industry led the way with Original Video Animations, which flourished as soon as home video was developed in the early 1980s.

The first Ghost In the Shell picture was revamped in 2008

The changing faces of the star of Ghost In the Shell
(this page and over).
From top left, clockwise: the original manga • Cybergirls •
the Man-Machine Interface manga • the Stand Alone
Complex series • the 1995 movie.

From top left, clockwise: the Arise series ·
the First Assault game · the Innocence movie ·
the Stand Alone Complex 2045 series · the live-action
movie.

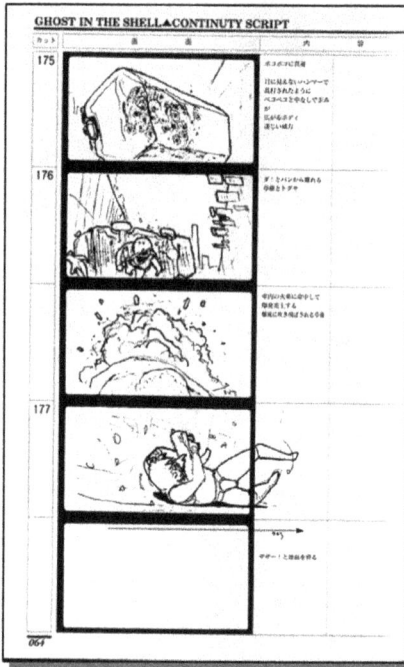

Storyboards for the first Ghost In the Shell movie.

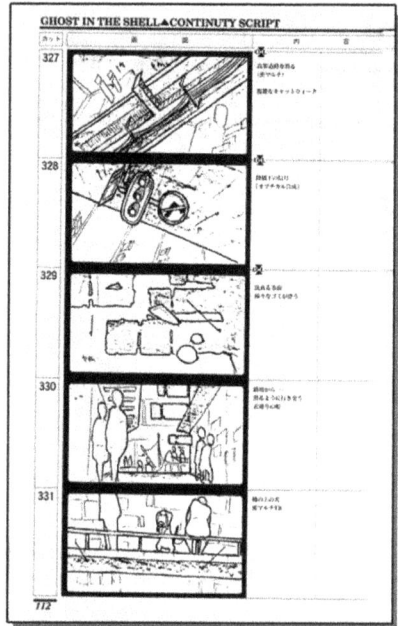

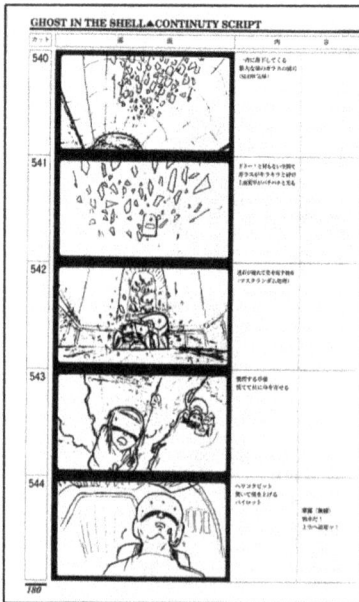

03

'A CYBORG AND HIS DOG':

GHOST IN THE SHELL 2: INNOCENCE (2004)

The sequel to 1995's *Ghost In the Shell*, *Ghost In the Shell 2: Innocence* (*Kokaku Kidotai: Inosensu* a.k.a. *Innocence*, 2004), was produced by Kodansha/ Bandai Visual/ Innocence Production Committee/ Production I.G., and the production committee included Buena Vista Home Entertainment/ D-Rights/ Dentsu/ Tokuma Shoten/ Nippon TV. The producers were Mitsuhisa Ishikawa, Ryuji Mitsumoto, Toshio Suzuki, and Maki Terashima-Furuta. It was released by Toho/ Bandai/ Go Fish/ Manga/ Madman.

Music[1] was by Kenji Kawai, char. des. by Hiroyuki Okiura, ani. dir. by Okiura, Kazuchika Kise and Tetsuya Nishio,[2] cinematography by Miki Sakuma, editing by Sachiko Miki, Chihiro Nakano and Junichi Uematsu, sound design by Randy Thom, sound direction by Kazuhiro Waka-bayashi, production design by Yohei Taneda, art direction by Shuichi Hirata, Shuji Inoue was mixing supervisor, and special effects supervisors were Hiroyuki Hayashi and Hisashi Ezura. (Some of the team had worked on the first *Ghost In the Shell* movie, and some also worked on *Ghost In the Shell: Stand Alone Complex*). Released: Mch 6, 2004 in Nippon. 99 mins.

Several story elements of *Ghost In the Shell 2: Innocence* are derived from chapter 6: *Robot Rondo* of the 1989 *Ghost In the Shell manga* – the crime of ghost-dubbing, the remote, industrial facility, robots/ cyborgs going crazy (like the dolls in *Ghost In the Shell 2: Innocence*), and the scene where Batou tracks down a cyborg that's become a cannibal in a traditional, Japanese teahouse.

---

1 Music production was by Aube Studio.
2 One of the key animators on *Ghost In the Shell 2: Innocence* was Yasuhiro Nakura: his other credits include *Angel's Egg, Cyborg 009, Dr Slump, Laputa: Castle In the Sky, Metropolis* and *Night On the Galactic Railroad.*

Ghost In the Shell 2: Innocence was incredible to look at, with two extraordinary sequences in the middle of the film (the flight and the festival). It boasted some divinely accomplished animation (in particular the fusion of 2-D and 3-D elements), a speciality of Production I.G. and its affiliates. At the level of detail,[3] *Ghost In the Shell 2: Innocence* was sumptuous animation (the budget was very high for a Japanese animated movie, at 2,000 million Yen or U.S. $20 million.[4] Other sources reckon it was 1,000 million Yen (which seems more accurate – *Ghost In the Shell*, an art movie version of a cyber-thriller, is too niche for a $20 million budget. Only movies like Miyazaki/ Ghibli movies or *Steam-boy*, with much wider appeal, receive budgets higher than $20 million).

Anyway, $10 or 20 million is very high, and only a *very* few *animé* movies are allocated such a lotta Yen. (In the West, it would've cost a zillion times that). Thus, *Ghost In the Shell 2: Innocence* was conceived from the outset as a prestige project, an art movie version of the Masamune Shirow franchise.

So many technical aspects of *Ghost In the Shell 2: Innocence* were superlative – the interactive lighting (including lens flare), and the integration of 2-D and 3-D parts (a huge number of cuts in *Ghost In the Shell 2: Innocence* were 3-D and computer-assisted) were especially impressive. *Ghost In the Shell 2: Innocence* is 'a challenging film, but it's one of the best anime ever', reckoned Helen McCarthy in *500 Essential Anime Movies* (22). Certainly, seen solely as animation, or cinema, it's remarkable.

But one of the chief reasons why the filmic impact of *Ghost In the Shell* is so strong isn't on screen at all: it's the music. Kenji Kawai's score (aided by music production at Aube Studio)[5] contributes enormously to the movie. (There are also some jazz songs, 'Follow Me' and 'River of Crystals', performed by jazz singer Kimiko Itoh. Director Mamoru Oshii wanted a 'jazzy' theme, a 'music box' theme, and a reprise of the song 'Follow Me'. Kawai obliged, and included an expanded version of the choral interlude cue from the first *Ghost In the Shell* movie).

Ghost In the Shell 2: Innocence 'resists comprehension even after multiple viewings', according to Brian Camp, altho' it's

> still a great movie, a work of beautiful art and intricate design, and a powerful treatise on humanity's persistent compulsion to re-create and replicate itself. (19)

---

3 'I enjoy making the world as detailed as possible. I get absorbed in the finer points – like what the back of a bottle label looks like when you see it through the glass. That's very Japanese, I suppose. I want people to go back to the film again and again to pick up things they missed the first time', Oshii explained. And Masamune Shirow is famous for filling his *manga* with an enormous amount of detail.
4 The budget allowed for research trips (to Taiwan, China and Milan in Italy, for instance), some high profile voice artists, and large amounts of digital work.
5 And co-operation from Miyamoto Unosuke Store, Professional Percussion, and Promax.

A masterpiece, yes, but it's flawed.⁶ The flaws in *Ghost In the Shell 2: Innocence* include:

- the story is boring.
- the characters are boring.
- scenes are over-written.
- the dialogue is over-long and, worst of all, has characters quoting at each other like smug, self-satisfied theology students (you're going to quote the *Bible* to me? Well dude, I'm right back at ya with some Milton! Take that!).

For fans of *Ghost In the Shell*, there are further flaws in *Ghost In the Shell 2: Innocence*:

- it's a partial interpretation of Masamune Shirow's *manga* (25% at best), and is full of narrative holes.
- the characterizations are changed all over the place.
- the star of *Ghost In the Shell*, Motoko Kusanagi, only shows up at the end – and in the form of an ugly puppet (a combo of geisha girl and Hans Bellmer doll, a self-conscious subversion of the usual love dolls of sci-fi).
- Paz, Saito and Boma are notably absent (instead, rookie Azuma make a fleeting appearance). And the Tachikoma robots, too.

٭

Ghost In the Shell 2: Innocence was entered in the best movie category at the Cannes Film Festival.⁷ Head producer at Studio Ghibli, Toshio Suzuki, was invited on board to co-produce the movie (he said he arrived halfway thru the schedule. In which case, all of the really important decisions would already have been made). The voice cast is pretty much the same as the 1995 *Ghost In the Shell* movie, and the *Ghost In the Shell: Stand Alone Complex* series.

With *Ghost In the Shell 2: Innocence* it seems as if the filmmakers challenged themselves in a couple of ways:

(1) to deliver a movie that wouldn't look like any other movie (including any other *animé* movie),

and (2) to top what they achieved on the first *Ghost In the Shell* movie.

They succeeded: *Ghost In the Shell 2: Innocence* does indeed look like nothing else out there in *animé* (as J. Hoberman remarked in the *Village Voice*: 'You can call me fanboy, but this is the best anime I've ever seen'). Go to the robot laboratory scene⁸ (about ten or twelve minutes into the 2004 movie), with its ultra-high key lightning,⁹ pale hues, pin-sharp,

---

6 One of the N. American critics remarked that *Ghost In the Shell 2: Innocence* looked like Mamoru Oshii was starting to believe his own press. Certainly parts of *Innocence* seem like Oshii was pandering to the intellectuals and geeks in the audience, knowing that the movie would spawn several hundred PhD theses and college essays.
7 *Ghost In the Shell 2: Innocence* benefitted from being shown at Cannes, attracting valuable publicity. Oshii and co. had already had a film at Cannes – 2001's *Avalon*.
8 In *Ghost In the Shell 2: Innocence*, there are a number of self-contained movies: they include: the festival procession sequence, the flight to the North sequence, the prologue, the feeding the dog sequence, and the main titles sequence.
9 The ultra-high key lighting was employed later on, in the scene following the festival sequence, where it was combined with a limited palette that resembled black-and-white celluloid.

elegant curving lines,[10] doll and puppet modelling,[11] philosophical dialogue from the robot technician Haladay,[12] slow pacing, moody music, and startling use of point-of-view shots (out from the lifeless eyes of the robots in the reverse angles).

For viewers who don't like the works of either Masamune Shirow or Mamoru Oshii, the factory scene is over-written, ponderous and pedantic. It is also a lecture about modern robots and the metaphysical issues surrounding cyborgization which are perhaps too familiar now (tho' necessary, in a way, for an audience coming to the world of *Ghost In the Shell* for the first time). And it's not especially Shirowian, either – where are the nurses in fetish uniforms showing off their butts?

And no robot manufacturer would produce robots or cyborgs looking like that, would they? And nobody would buy them! Not with ugly bodies that look and move like dolls. After all, they are supposed to be geishas or sex dolls! It's as if the filmmakers in 2004 were consciously avoiding the T. and A. elements of both Masamune Shirow's *Ghost In the Shell manga* (the 2001 *Ghost In the Shell manga* sequel, *Ghost In the Shell: Man-Machine Interface*, is *Penthouse*-meets-cyberpunk), and the *Ghost In the Shell: Stand Alone Complex* TV series (which also included eroticized characters).

Ghost In the Shell 2: Innocence might thus be an anti-Shirowian movie, deliberately anti-erotic, anti-humorous. (Or is it a spoof of Shirowian erotic art, which focusses on svelte, young girls? For sure, Shirow would *never* have his heroine using such an unsightly form as an avatar! For collecting intel, maybe, in a single scene, but *never* for the climactic scenes, when she has to be a kick-ass action girl! When Motoko cybernetically controls people or puppets, she always selects a cute woman). *Ghost In the Shell 2: Innocence* is also an anti-Shirowian movie because for much of the time we're staring at a grumpy man with white hair and weird, artificial eyes.

With scenes like this, the 100s of filmmakers contributing to *Ghost In the Shell 2: Innocence* carve out their own niche in animation, distancing themselves from every other *animé* out there. Few other filmmakers would have the guts, with that high budget, and with all those talented filmmakers working on the production, and with all those resources at hand, to sidestep the usual action-based storytelling of *animé* and to deliver something so unexpected and so quirky. You've got to be feeling very confident as a filmmaker to stick to your guns[13] and persist with this kind of filmmaking, when the producers and the market are clamouring for straight-ahead, formulaic movies.

10 The white-on-white approach to the robot laboratory scene made the animators' skill with drawing even more pronounced: there was nowhere to hide: you saw everything, every line.
11 The giant close-ups of the robots in *Ghost In the Shell 2: Innocence* are obvious nods to the famous close-ups in *Persona*, Ingmar Bergman's 1966 masterpiece (which has been quoted in movies such as *Minority Report*, and was referenced at the end of the 1995 *Ghost* movie).
12 The name of the new robot doctor, Haladay, is probably from *Tomorrow's Eve* (but it might also allude to Donna Haraway, one of the chief commentators on cyborgization. In the *Ghost In the Shell* guidebook, she's Haraway). The forensic scientist in the laboratory scene likely draws on Isaac Asimov (the character of Susan Calvin); and Asimov's laws of robotics are of course alluded to.
13 Seburo, of course.

Another way of putting it is that *Ghost In the Shell 2: Innocence* isn't a movie from a young filmmaker who's just starting-out (could a young *animé* director deliver something like this? I doubt it). Rather, *Ghost In the Shell 2: Innocence* is so clearly the work of a mature film director, and a team of *animé* veterans. That's obvious from the level of maturity in the script, in the themes, in the style, in the whole package. (However, the robot lab scene noted above is also very talky, and for some commentators, such as Helen McCarthy, it threatened to derail the movie. There are two or three scenes like that in the first act of *Ghost In the Shell 2: Innocence*. That is, no matter how enormously talented many filmmakers are, they still find it tough to develop entertaining ways of delivering exposition to the audience. Exposition is exposition, and sometimes there's just no way of reducing it, or making it more palatable, or getting it past the audience while keeping them entertained).

🐾

Ghost In the Shell 2: Innocence is another version of *Blade Runner* – right from the opening shot, it's *Blade Runner* all over again. Mamoru Oshi has never got over seeing the 1982 Warners movie (like so many other Japanese animators).[14]

The police plot of *Ghost In the Shell 2: Innocence* is actually *Blade Runner*, isn't it? Cops tracking down robots that've gone nuts and started killing people. That the robots're hookers brings out what *Blade Runner* tended to cover up (*Blade Runner*'s Pris, for instance, is referred to as a 'pleasure model', and is clearly eroticized in her costume and look. But the 1982 movie was curiously reticent when it came to portraying sex,[15] and the 2004 *Ghost In the Shell* movie also draws the line there. The *Ghost In the Shell: Stand Alone Complex* series was more direct in addressing sexual issues, which are absolutely fundamental, whether you like it or not, to Masamune Shirow's *Ghost In the Shell* cosmos).

For Mamoru Oshii, the story in the *Ghost In the Shell* sequel wasn't complicated at all: 'it may look like a confusing movie as I have been told by many people, but to me, *it is a simple love story*' (my emphasis).[16] Ah, yes, but is that the romance between Batou and Motoko? Between Batou and Togusa? Between Batou and his dog?! Between the characters and the network? Or between the filmmakers and technology? (And actually, no, the romance plot is a subplot).

In fact, the story of *Ghost In the Shell 2: Innocence* is boring – or rather, the plot in its police procedural aspects is dull (just as the plot of *Blade Runner* is dreary). It's a robots-gone-crazy plot, which the *Ghost In the Shell: Stand Alone Complex* had already covered (and which the first *Ghost*

---

14 Even down to details – like the cold breath in the robot laboratory, another nod to *Blade Runner*, and its Hannibal Chew's Eye Works scene (which was filmed over 2 days in Vernon, California, in a 7°-below food refrigerator. Veteran actor James Hong (who played Hannibal Chew) recalled that his scenes were shot 'under extreme pressure', trying to squeeze 5 days into two days: it was 'among the most tense I've ever worked in my life').
15 Director Ridley Scott doesn't like including love scenes in a movie; he says they're usually not necessary and slow up the story. Suffice to say, the 'rape in the corridor' scene in *Blade Runner* (as producer Michael Deeley called it), is not one of the great love scenes or sex scenes in cinema history. Scott acknowledged that the scene was one of the least effective in *Blade Runner*.
16 M. Oshii, in M. Koepke, "Fantastic Phantasms", *Hour*, 2004.

In the Shell movie also tackled). 'Plodding' certainly describes the narrative as a detective mystery – it has many TV cop show beats (often couched in a self-conscious *film noir* style): the police chief issuing orders to his cops; the cops visiting a crime scene; the cops investigating the crime; following up leads; discussing the case in the car, and so on. (No wonder, then, that both Batou and Togusa look so weary and fed up. For them, this particular assignment is utterly joyless. There's no excitement in the chase, and no mystery to prick their interest).

And the way that the boring plot is delivered, at the levels of story and characters, is also humdrum in *Ghost In the Shell 2: Innocence*. Oh, but the movie is also, of course, doing other things, like producing entrancing visuals, compelling atmospheres and textures, dreamy music, etc. It's an art movie version of Masamune Shirow's *manga* (even more than the first *Ghost In the Shell* movie), and with art movies sometimes the plot is junk.

MAMORU OSHII COMING BACK TO *GHOST IN THE SHELL*.
Ghost In the Shell 2: Innocence did not originate with director Mamoru Oshii (most sequels originate with producers and studios, with their eyes on $$$$$): the project was offered to him by Production I.G. (and that would likely mean producer Mitsuhisa Ishikawa). Oshii remarked:

> I didn't make *Innocence* as a sequel to *Ghost in the Shell*. In fact I had a dozen ideas, linked to my views on life, my philosophy, that I wanted to include in this film.

The higher budget for *Ghost In the Shell* and the longer pre-production period (vital for a complicated movie like this) meant that Mamoru Oshii and the team could tackle more challenging technical issues.

> I attacked *Innocence* as a technical challenge; I wanted to go beyond typical animation limits, answer personal questions and at the same time appeal to filmgoers.... For *Innocence*, I had a bigger budget than for *Ghost in the Shell*. I also had more time to prepare it. Yet despite the economic leeway, abundant details and orientations, it was still important to tell an intimate story.

Mamoru Oshii acknowledged that one could only make this kind of movie with a much bigger amount of time and money. He knew that for some people *Ghost In the Shell 2: Innocence* would come across as self-indulgent. It is. But many of the greatest works of art are deliciously, decadently self-indulgent (in cinema, examples would include *Apocalypse Now*, *Intolerance*, *The Colour of Pomegranates*, *Faust* and *The Lady From Shanghai*).

If you try to forget the first *Ghost In the Shell* movie (impossible, of course), you can watch the filmmakers attempting a different kind of picture with *Ghost In the Shell 2: Innocence*. Besides, Mamoru Oshii and his team have already been-there-done-that with cop thrillers and shoot-'em-up scenarios. And who wants to keep repeating themselves?

Ghost In the Shell 2: Innocence takes an adaptation of the *Ghost In the Shell manga* even further away from the comic than the first film of 1995. So that *Ghost In the Shell 2: Innocence* isn't really a movie of or about or based on *Ghost In the Shell*, but rather a movie in which some elements from the *manga* and from the first film and from the TV series are used as a pretext for the film producers to explore other things. (The movie is certainly the most abstract adaptation of a Shirow comic).

For director Mamoru Oshii, the second *Ghost In the Shell* movie wasn't strictly a sequel, and was intended to stand on its own. Unfortunately, the story was far less engaging than the 1995 *Ghost In the Shell* movie, amounting to little more than a standard murder mystery, with Batou and Togusa on the trail of a crazy killer. And Major Kusanagi, star of the first film, was talked about at length, but didn't appear until near the end (a tactic that somewhat scuppers *Ghost In the Shell 2: Innocence*, because any *Ghost In the Shell* enterprise without Motoko Kusanagi isn't really *Ghost In the Shell*, but it was also employed in the *Ghost In the Shell: Stand Alone Complex* spin-off movie *Solid State Society* of 2006). However, the concept of the Major pursuing her own goals comes from Shirow's *manga* sequel of 2001. Yes, but the sequel comic follows Motoko entirely.

Also, the two main charas were portrayed as rather dull guys in *Ghost In the Shell 2: Innocence*, which didn't help, because they were in most scenes (compared to *Ghost In the Shell: Stand Alone Complex*, Batou and Togusa were played way, way toned down, to the point of tired flatness and blankness. And Batou and Togusa are certainly *not* like that at all in Masamune Shirow's *Ghost In the Shell manga*).

QUOTES.

Ghost In the Shell 2: Innocence contains quotes from, among others the *Bible, Paradise Lost*, Jacob Grimm, Saito Ryokuu, Villiers de L'Isle-Adam, Richard Dawkins, Buddha, Confucius, Plato, René Descartes, Zeami, La Mettrie and Max Weber (Mamoru Oshii remarked: 'personally, I adore the quotes in the film. It was a real pleasure for me').

Jean-Luc Godard was again an inspiration for Mamoru Oshii with *Ghost In the Shell:*

This desire to include quotes by other authors came from Godard. The text is very important for a film, that I learned from him. It gives a certain richness to cinema because the visual is not all there is. Thanks to Godard, the spectator can concoct his own interpretation.

BATOU AND MOTOKO KUSANAGI.

One wonders if the decision to sideline Motoko Kusanagi was taken partly in reaction to the *Ghost In the Shell: Stand Alone Complex* television series, in which she played a large role. Because by the time the filmmakers convened to put together *Ghost In the Shell 2: Innocence*, some of the episodes of the *Ghost In the Shell: Stand Alone Complex* TV series had already been screened (the TV series was partly made at one of the same companies, Production I.G., so there would likely be some cross-pollination between the movies and the TV shows, at all levels, from personnel to ideas. Some members of Production I.G. worked on both). Some viewed the TV series as an ad for the movie. There is a conscious effort on the part of the filmmakers of *Ghost In the Shell 2: Innocence* to distance themselves somewhat from the *Ghost In the Shell: Stand Alone Complex* TV show, just as the TV series aimed to put some distance between it and the 1995 *Ghost In the Shell* movie (its title is 'stand alone complex', that is, a series that can work on its own, without reference to the 1995 *Ghost In the Shell* movie).

However, as Mamoru Oshii has co-script as well as director credit on *Ghost In the Shell 2: Innocence*, and because Oshii wanted to make his own kind of movie, the ultimate reason is probably partly down to Oshii's own preferences. Because the producers and Production I.G./ Kodansha/ Bandai Visual *et al* would no doubt have preferred a much more 'commercial' version of *Ghost In the Shell* – that is, sexy super-babes kicking ass (something like the *Appleseed* computer-assisted movies of 2004/ 2007/ 2014, which're essentially video game shoot-em-ups. Of course, *Ghost In the Shell* has led to its own shoot-em-up computer games. The *Ghost In the Shell* franchise returned to an action-heavy format with the *Arise* and the *2045* series).

Unfortunately, moving Motoko Kusanagi into the shadows in *Ghost In the Shell 2: Innocence* and bringing the Bat-Man and the Togster to the forefront shifts the dramatic-psychological centre of the *Ghost In the Shell* universe (and also takes it even further away from the *manga* by Masamune Shirow, where Motoko is absolutely central. The more police procedural *Human-Error Processor* of 2003 sidelined the Major). Without the Major (the 'ghost in the shell' of the whole *Ghost In the Shell* franchise), *Ghost In the Shell 2: Innocence* becomes a little too much like a routine TV cop show, a little too by-the-numbers, in terms of plot. And that all-important ingredient of romance and eroticism is also suppressed; the on-off, restrained romance between Kusanagi and Batou was such a big element of the 1995 *Ghost In the Shell* movie (and also between Motoko and the Puppet Master), a subtext that bubbled underneath with a slow-burning energy that gave the scenes between the two characters so much more juice. By contrast, *Ghost In the Shell 2: Innocence* is much more a men's movie (even tho' the director has emphasized the romantic/ romance ingredient). And thus part of Batou's exhausted, grouchy demeanour comes from another of his epic sulks, because his darling cyborg is absent.

The notion of a Major-less *Ghost In the Shell* outing is intriguing – the *Arise* series, for example, might be more satisfying with much less Motoko Kusanagi as she is depicted in that show. But while focussing on the boys in the Public Security Section 9 team sounds appealing, it isn't a lot of fun when you have two bad-tempered guys at the heart of the piece, as here, in *Ghost In the Shell 2: Innocence* (Batou and Togusa would not win any awards for Best Buddy Duo in cinema).

ARAMAKI, BATOU AND TOGUSA.

The more I watch *Ghost In the Shell 2: Innocence* the less I like the characterizations of Togusa, Batou and Aramaki. Portraying Batou as turning into an autistic weirdo who gets off on blasting the shịt out of gangsters (a Travis Bickle/ Dirty Harry persona) grates quickly.

Meanwhile, Togusa mopes and complains: he (and other charas) insist that he's a family man, yet we don't see his family until the very end. In which case, he might actually be one of those cyborgs (or robots) who's been affected by a virus or the Puppeteer, so he thinks he has a wife and daughter.[17]

As for Chief Aramaki – now he's portrayed as a stern, Zen Buddhist *sensei* who never even turns round to look at his officers! He just stares at that creepy forest scene! And his office is pitch black! Eh? What kind of office is that for a government employee?[18]

Also, both Togusa and Batou quote literary references at each other (such as John Milton and the *Bible*). And when she finally appears in that horrible gynoid, Motoko too starts with the geeky quotations! Much as I admire Mamoru Oshii as a film director, this is pretentious garbage: it's pretentious and fake because it puts dialogue into the mouths of characters that the characters wouldn't say, that the movie hasn't earned, and that the writer/s are now pretending these guys are intellectuals who exchange hi-falutin' quotations like 16 year-old students trying to show off to each other or to their teacher.

It doesn't work.

It doesn't convince – it looks just like what it is: a screenwriter has included quotations s/he enjoys or admires. It doesn't work with the Public Security Section 9 team. Oh, sure, invent a character like the Puppeteer who can come out with the teenage philosophizing (or the character of Aoi in the first *Ghost In the Shell* TV series), but out of the mouths of the Public Security Section 9 team, no.

It worked in *Ghost In the Shell: Stand Alone Complex* because the character of Aoi was a teenager so in love with J.D. Salinger he took up the lingo (calling people 'phonies', for ex). A teenager who was clearly autistic, a severe case of otakuism, and, in the final episode of the first series of *Ghost In the Shell: Stand Alone Complex*, when Aoi throws quote after quote at Motoko Kusanagi, she humours him and goes along with it. But to have grown men, weary veterans like Togusa and Batou quoting Milton and the *Bible* at each other, oh dear, what drivel.

LOOK AND STYLE.

The setting of *Ghost In the Shell 2: Innocence* again draws on the neon-

---

17 Togusa mentions his daughter's birthday. That becomes the springboard for another filosofickal riff on 'birth'.
18 Well, black is cheaper perhaps! No need to animate anything if there's nothing there!

infested, Chinese city of Hong Kong (though as any *animé* fan will recognize, it's also very much modern Tokyo; altho' it is also Newport City from Shirow-sensei's *manga*, which's also where *Ghost In the Shell: Stand Alone Complex* is set). But it's a little more retro than the first *Ghost In the Shell* movie, with the cops driving vintage cars,[19] for instance, and even more of a 1940s, American *film noir* feel than the 1995 *Ghost In the Shell* outing, with some jazz songs on the soundtrack. (Classic cars feature in Masamune Shirow's *manga*, however – the government minister, for ex, is chauffeured in a huge, 1940s-era auto in chapter 7: *Phantom Fund*. But we know that Batou would *not* drive one of those classic cars! Not even one with a shiny exterior and curving, steam-punk exhaust pipes. No, those cars are *so* not Batou's style!).

There are moments in the *Ghost In the Shell* pictures when the screen settles down to nothing more than two characters in the frame – often with their backs to the camera – a staging also favoured by Jean-Luc Godard[20] – and they're talking. Not much moves – indeed, *Ghost In the Shell* employed characters talking to each other without opening their mouths (they're connected in cyberspace), so the screen is pretty much frozen. Handily, in this futuristic world, brains can be connected electronically. If you're deeply involved in the story and the situations and the characters, this kind of filmmaking is compelling. But if you're not, then it can seem uninspired and boring – which's how some viewers find Jean-Luc Godard's movies (and how I regard Mamoru Oshii's movies at their worst). When filmmakers force spectators to watch little more than frozen pictures on a screen for a long time, the audience has to follow the approach. It's no use fighting it, hoping for some action. Certainly the *Ghost In the Shell* movies of '95 and '04 are very unusual in the Japanese *animé* tradition in slowing down to European art movie speeds. They also include a *lot* of air in the interactions – lengthy by animation's standards. Air is the pauses and the gaps in the conversations. Film editors can add air to accentuate dialogue and gestures in all sorts of ways. *Ghost In the Shell 2: Innocence* opts for several examples of 'meaningful pauses'. Thus, instead of the 'pillow moments' or dreamy interludes of Japanese animation, we have […] pauses […] in the […] conversations.

---

19 There're the usual dialogue scenes in cars, sometimes playing, Godard-style, on the backs of characters (this time between the gruff Batou and the long-suffering Togusa). The filmmakers carry the routine car scene by shifting the lighting, and creating a slightly different cityscape background (in reds and blacks).

20 In *Vivre Sa Vie*, Jean-Luc Godard and DP Raoul Coutard filmed the characters in the opening scene from behind. In the first episode ('A café. Nana wants to leave Paul. The pinball table'), Nana is seen from the back sitting at the bar of a café; she is talking to her estranged boyfriend (maybe husband), Paul (André S. Labarthe), who sits beside her, off-camera (a real café was used, without lighting). Nana's reflection can be seen on the left of the shot, in the mirror behind the bar (the shot recalls the famous painting by Edouard Manet, *A Bar At the Folies-Bergère* [1881-82]).

Filming actors from the back, the chaotic sound, the long takes, the camera movement – there had never been a movie like this before. Consequently, *Vivre Sa Vie* may have been more influential on filmmakers than *Breathless* – Jean-Luc Godard's reinvention of the long take and elaborate staging influenced all sorts of filmmakers, including Eric Rohmer, Theo Angelopoulos, Martin Scorsese, Kevin Smith, Quentin Tarantino, Oliver Stone, Jean Eustache, Philipp Garrel, Chantal Akerman, Abbas Kiarostami, and Spike Lee (R. Brody, 139). You can add Mamoru Oshii to that list.

Luckily, the clichéd plot didn't matter, because there was so much going in *Ghost In the Shell 2: Innocence*, so much that was astonishing visually (and musically – Kenji Kawai was back composing the music). Among the outstanding set-pieces in *Ghost In the Shell: Innocence* were a festival and procession (partly inspired by a visit of the filmmakers to Taiwan); an episode in a creepy robot lab (all minimal, clinical whites); a shoot-em-up in a convenience store and also in a *yakuza* den; the expected shoot-em-up ending; and a flight in a cool-looking, organic-shaped plane to a Northern region of Japan that was a forest of industrial towers and fog, lit by an amber light (amber – and green – being one of Mamoru Oshii's favourite hues for animation. You can see a lot of amber in the first *Ghost In the Shell* movie – when the Major goes sea diving, for example, there's an amber-gold hue across the whole sky. That choice alone, of using amber so much, sets *Ghost In the Shell 2: Innocence* apart from your run-of-the-mill *animé*, which will employ saturated reds and blues and a lot of white[21]).

Underplayed is an understatement for the longed-for reunion between Batou and Major Kusanagi at the end of *Ghost In the Shell 2: Innocence*. Of course, we know by now that there aren't going be hugs and kisses, and hearts and flowers with these two! But the reunion is played so cool and restrained. And the filmmakers lay out the compositions so that they only face each other with guns in their hands (!) – the rest of the time the layouts put Batou and Motoko apart, talking but facing away from each other. A key shot places them some distance apart, though framed facing each other, with Kusanagi nearer the camera and much larger.

Masters of this kind of displaced, distanced cinema include Carl-Theodor Dreyer and Ingmar Bergman (and Japanese directors such as Yasujiro Ozu, Akira Kurosawa and Kenji Mizoguchi, who made it a speciality). You create desire in your characters, then you set them apart, yet tantalizingly framed in the same shot. It (usually) always works – but only providing you have manufactured a certain amount of desire and emotion in the first place (typically, it's romantic or erotic). In fact, it's a foundational component of romantic melodrama in Japanese cinema, and if you look at virtually any Japanese movie about love and romance, it will employ the same images of distance and separation (remember that the first on-screen kiss didn't appear in Japanese cinema until 1946 – meanwhile, people had been slobbering each other to death in Western cinema since the medium's birth in 1895).

The lack of facial expressions in *Ghost In the Shell 2: Innocence* is striking: this is an animated movie in which the humans (or cyborgs) are distinctly *un*animated. The staring straight ahead, the introspection, the lack of gestures and interactions with other people is very marked (even Togusa, a human, can stare without blinking for ages – as in the robot factory scene). It's as if every character, not just Batou, is turning into the sullen, flattened-down version from the first movie. (If this is a movie about 'being human', about what it means to be human, this is a very

---

21 Even the ocean is red in this movie, rather than the customary dark blues and greys.

downbeat view of human life, where everybody mopes and sulks – if they emote at all).

Here's where losing the horsing about, the humour, and the camaraderie from Masamune Shirow's *manga* of *Ghost In the Shell* becomes very obvious (*Ghost In the Shell*, said Shirow, was about the daily life in the Public Security Section 9 team). There *is* a teeniest bit of humour in *Ghost In the Shell 2: Innocence*, but even less than in the first *Ghost In the Shell* movie, and that was a departure from the *manga*. *Ghost In the Shell 2: Innocence* is a pretty solemn affair, with Batou embodying the phrase 'grim' to the point of grimness. In almost every scene Batou is impassive, withdrawn, mouth turned down, those lenses where his eyes are staring blankly off to the side (it recalls the movies of Carl-Theodore Dreyer, and also to a degree Andrei Tarkovsky, where characters self-consciously *don't* look at each other. Like those Early Renaissance paintings of a group of saints and donors standing around the Madonna and Child in a luxurious chamber, with everybody is looking anywhere except at each other. Even in the scenes featuring the Public Security Section 9 Chief Aramaki, characters don't look at each other: Aramaki plays scenes with his back to Togusa and Batou, staring at a weird jungle backdrop decorating the office.[22] And the reverse angles depict Batou and Togusa against pure black – which takes Japanese minimal design and Zen Buddhist nothingness to extremes! It has to be the most depressing office in a cop show).

In fact, not a single character smiles in *Ghost In the Shell 2: Innocence*. And nobody laughs,[23] either. Everybody is buttoned-down to the level of characters out of Robert Bresson in *Shell 2*: this is a movie in which the most alive and lively character is a dog! (that is intentional: animals are fully present, wholly in the world, don't angst or fret or worry. The unconditional love of animals is also important). 'Batou is a reflection of my own thoughts and feelings', Mamoru Oshii admitted, '*Innocence* is a kind of autobiographical film in that way.'

The computer screen imagery is a key ingredient of the *Ghost In the Shell* universe – these are movies and TV shows in which computers are foregrounded to a striking degree. To the point where the final checkmates will occur in cyberspace; forget about the cyberpunk or digital philosophizing, thematically, it is visually where the *Ghost In the Shell* movies score. Because, let's face it, computers and what they do and how they work, can be an abstract or technical concept, tricky to visualize or dramatize. Remember the old whirring wheels of super-computers in those 1960s TV shows or *James Bond* movies? We have come a long way since then (however, those old super-computers with the glass fronts still required someone nearby to tell the audience exactly what they did; similarly, although the *Ghost In the Shell* movies visualize computers and the digital realm with more skill and finesse than almost all other science fiction flick, they still require voiceover to explain what the $‡#! is going

---

22 The green-on-green image contains an enormous, old tree in a forest, Miyazaki-style, but, oddly, with skulls at its base. It's certainly an unusual image for Aramaki to have in his office!
23 Except the kids at the festival.

on. Indeed, the finale, where hacking into computers was crucial, as it is in Shirow's comic, added some guardians or elders in robotic form, to give some anthropomorphic shape to the abstractions of numbers and read-outs on screens).

THEMES.

The *Ghost In the Shell* sequel contained plenty of scenes of philo-sophizing on the nature of being human (which's certainly central to Masamune Shirow's art, but the *manga* doesn't deliver philosophy in such a po-faced manner as this).[24] The robots in *Ghost In the Shell 2: Innocence* were portrayed as dolls and puppets (there was even a direct quote of Hans Bellmer's dolls – so direct, it was a book! Batou picks it off a shelf). Sometimes the doll and puppet references were made explicit visually (with the cables running into the back of the androids acting like the puppeteer's strings – but that is also a motif Shirow employs many times in his *Ghost In the Shell* comic).

The questions in *Ghost In the Shell 2: Innocence* were the usual ones: can a robot have a soul? Can an android have a human soul implanted in it? (This was one of the futuristic notions of *Ghost In the Shell* – the 'ghost' or soul in a metal shell). In *Ghost In the Shell 2: Innocence*, there was much talk about computers and digital structures being 'external memory', with cities as giant repositories of memories. And there were many scenes of simulated realities (this time mounted as the white spaces of 1960s Minimal art).

Helen McCarthy defined the themes of the *Ghost In the Shell* sequel as 'the relationship between consciousness and technology, the need to assert individuality, and the urge for rebirth' (2008, 22).

THE OPENING SCENES.

Let's have a look at some of the scenes in the sequel.

Mobile Armored Riot Police 2: Innocence opens in a thoroughly clichéd manner, narratively: a cop arriving at a crime scene, and dealing with one of the perpetrators. The sequence establishes Batou as the protagonist of the 2004 movie, a hero who turns out to be something of an anti-hero, an ambiguous character (the violent cop, the anti-cop, the damaged or troubled cop is a standard trope in thriller/ detective/ cop stories).

Batou arrives in his classic car at a crime scene downtown, just like a million, billion, zillion other cop shows. However, this being *Ghost In the Shell,* the scene's intercut with some very impressive computer imagery – read-outs and flows of information that float in space against black (using cylinders and circles as a recurring motif, taken from Masamune Shirow's *Ghost In the Shell manga*). Instead of the usual green or blue of digital gobbledegook, *Ghost In the Shell 2: Innocence* plumps for amber, which works so well when so much of the rest of the picture is dark blue, dark green, or just plain *dark*.

Batou enters the crime scene which's been art-directed in shabby,

24 Another element added to the movie that's not in the *manga* is the philosophizing about DNA and genetics.

gloomy urban chic (by Shuichi Hirata and Yohei Taneda) to an extreme degree. There's a very lengthy Batou-point-of-view shot (split into two) which inevitably recalls computer games (and this is precisely the kind of scenario you find in video games – a character (armed, of course) entering a dangerous place – <PRESS [ENTER] FOR EXTRA FIRE POWER>). Later, in the *yakuza* den shoot-em-dead scene, there are point-of-view shots from Batou's gun which exactly emulate computer games (and there are video games of *Ghost In the Shell*, of course, in which you can have three-way sex with Major Kusanagi and a female android. No, just kidding – it's Batou and a gynoid).

The prologue of *Ghost In the Shell 2: Innocence* draws on sections of the first *Ghost In the Shell manga*, including a scene where Batou and his cohorts deal with a crazed (and cannibalistic) cyborg; naughty geishas had also been used in the first *Ghost In the Shell: Stand Alone Complex* series (the trope also appeared in the live-action movie of 2017).

MAIN TITLES.

Following the prologue of *Ghost In the Shell 2: Innocence*, which introduces Batou, the geisha dolls, the cop show scenario, etc, *Ghost In the Shell 2: Innocence* shifts into the main titles sequence which updates the famous cyborg manufacture credits sequence in the 1995 *Ghost In the Shell* movie. It is very beautiful, dreamy, with long, slow motions of ravishing imagery (some of it abstract) drifting across the screen. As in Aramaki's office and other scenes, full black is employed, with an emphasis on light glowing against black; mirror images are another motif (inevitably), as well as water (in this movie, as in all sci-fi, the creation of humans/ clones/ androids/ bioroids/ or human-like creatures always occurs in liquid).

As with the main titles sequence in the mid-1990s *Ghost* flick, the main titles of *Ghost In the Shell 2: Innocence* is a movie on its own. And of course the score by Kenji Kawai *et al*, with its mysterious chanting and pounding drums, helps enormously (the song is 'The Ballade of Puppets: Flowers Grieve and Fall').[25]

(The first shots of *Ghost In the Shell 2: Innocence*, however, are standard *Ghost In the Shell* images of the city of the future at night with, guess what?, a scout helicopter. However, no, we don't get Motoko Kusanagi standing atop a 'scraper this time, preparing to leap off).

THE YAKUZA SCENE.

Part of the second act of *Ghost In the Shell 2: Innocence* focusses on Batou and his increasing weirdness. As his colleagues (Togusa, Ishikawa, Aramaki) note, he has been acting strangely (which Motoko Kusanagi does in Shirow-sensei's *manga* – that strangeness also crops up in the second *Ghost In the Shell: Stand Alone Complex* series, and in the *Solid State Society* film). A number of scenes in *Ghost In the Shell 2: Innocence* depict Batou returning home and checking in his car a machine which tells him if

25 A minor niggle: the scene replicates the first movie's titles.

he's been followed (a sort of retro Raymond Chandler moment).[26] Batou's paranoia is always pretty high in the *Ghost In the Shell* world (but so is Motoko's!), but in *Ghost In the Shell 2: Innocence* it becomes a subplot of its own.

The action scene at the *yakuza* HQ in *Ghost In the Shell 2: Innocence* is very ugly, because it depicts Batou completely losing it and killing/ injuring 20 or 30[27] people (he is a cop, remember – and he needs information). Maybe some of them are cyborgs, maybe not, maybe some of them are nasty criminals, but possibly not all of them. But it turns Batou into a psychopath: those criminals need to be arrested and taken into custody, not shot to shreds.

Dramatically, the 'Die, Gangsters Die!' scene is part of Batou's increasing alienation and psychosis: he's not the same, as Chief Aramaki tells Togusa; and it looks like he's going the same way as Major Motoko Kusanagi did – but Motoko never turned into Travis Bickle! (Anyhow, where is she, the audience is wondering? How can this movie be *Mobile Armored Riot Police* without the super-babe cyborg?).

It looks like our Batou is turning into a paranoid, disconnected, alienated 'shut-in' – the withdrawal from society, the distrust of other people (usually, it's *otaku* or similar charas who're portrayed in animation as 'shut-ins'). But the *yakuza* shoot-out scene is also incredibly over-the-top. If you ignore the cyborg deal for a moment (that Batou is a cyborg), you have a scene where the cop hero single-handedly (single gun-edly, you might say) murders and/ or injures 20+ people.[28] Even in the context of the 2004 movie, it is over-the-top, and places Batou into the category of psychopath and serial killer. (Also disturbing is the way the shoot-out is portrayed with the point-of-view shots of video games, from the end of Batou's machine gun, which further identifies the viewer with the crazed Batou).

The cinematic ancestor of this kind of spray-'em-with-bullets scene in *Ghost In the Shell 2: Innocence* is Sam Peckinpah (*The Wild Bunch*, most obviously, but also *Straw Dogs*, *Pat Garrett and Billy the Kid*, *The Getaway*, etc), and also the ending of 1967's *Bonnie & Clyde*. However, despite the macho pose and ultra-violence of Peckinpah's cinema – 'if they move, kill 'em' – it always had a psychological and ideological underpinning. As the Peck often remarked, he hated violence, and depicted it precisely to rub people's noses in it, to remind them about the horror of it.

However, filmmakers who deal in violent action – John Woo, Yuen Woo-ping, John Ford, Martin Scorsese, Stanley Kubrick, Tsui Hark, Francis Coppola, Akira Kurosawa – always want to have it both ways. There is nearly always an element in movies of men and guns, men and stunts, men being macho, that glorifies violence even as it condemns it. It's the same in the *Ghost In the Shell* movies, and in Japanese animation in general. Much of Japanese *animé* is of the glorifying school, with little thought of the consequence or ideological context of the violence. (Yet the

---

26 Anxiety over being tailed is a significant element in the *Appleseed manga*.
27 24, Togusa says.
28 Including a giant cyborg bruiser called Kaniotoko.

scene is also a satire on gangster movie clichés – the way it's staged is self-consciously silly: Batou just stands there firing his machine gun, and not one of the 20 or so weapons aimed at him make any dents. Again, this is common in *animé* – *Black Cat*, *Cowboy Bebop*, *Dirty Pair*, *One Piece*, *Hellsing*, *Black Lagoon*, etc).

Togusa registers his disgust (but in a very understated manner);[29] meanwhile, there is no disciplinary action from the police chief Aramaki afterwards (just a strict telling off), no firing of Batou, nothing. And there's no retribution from the other *yakuza* gangs, either (in the Italian-American cinema of Francis Coppola, Abel Ferrara and Martin Scorsese, Batou would be dead meat). Ah, but wait, vengeance is just around the corner:

🐾

The counterpart to the *yakuza* shoot-em-up is the convenience store scene (where Batou goes to get his favourite brand of 🐾 food – it's the only place that sells it! Yes – and it just happens to be in Chinatown, right in the *yakuzas'* territory). The scene is all build-up – slo-mo, weird sounds, fish-eye point-of-view shots – it resembles similar outstanding scenes in the *Cowboy Bebop* TV series (and movie).[30] In this counterpoint to the *yakuza* scene in *Innocence*, Batou goes too far, descending into cyber-paranoia, and nearly killing the store owner.[31]

A CYBORG AND HIS DAWG.

There's a scene in the first act of *Ghost In the Shell 2: Innocence* where Batou returns home and feeds his pooch Gabriel.[32]

That's it. That's all that happens.

In any *animé* made for cinema, in any other *animé* that wasn't helmed by a celebrated director, that scene would not survive the script stage. No one would even bother to storyboard it. Here's the imaginary conversation between the writer and a big-shot, American-style producer:

Writer: So the hero comes home and feeds his dog.
Producer: Eh? I don't get it. Sounds like nothing.
Writer: He feeds his dog.
Producer: So? What's the deal? The bad guys break in and start shooting?
Writer: No, he just warms some food in the microwave, gives it to his faithful mutt, and –
Producer: Then the mutant hooker cyborgs crash in thru the ceiling

---

29 Togusa often complains that he's not fit to be Batou's partner – mainly because he wants to survive, and Batou in *Ghost In the Shell 2: Innocence* is particularly trigger-happy. (The gripe comes from Togusa's experiences with Azuma in *Human-Error Processor*).
30 In the *Cowboy Bebop* episode *Honky Tonk Women*, our first sight of the amazing Faye Valentine is when she enters an old-fashioned (Chinese) herbal store – where, within 20 seconds, she's yanked out a gun and is shooting out the front of the store at the guys come up pick her up. In the final episodes of *Cowboy Bebop*, there's a shoot-out at Annie's store. And the *Cowboy Bebop* movie includes a grocery store hold-up, which introduces Spike Spiegel and Jet Black, in the prologue (which is a clear forerunner of the scene in *Ghost In the Shell 2: Innocence*).
31 Any cartel would've offed Batou immediately, but Ishikawa says afterwards that the syndicate wanted to create a scandal.
32 Why isn't the dog called Motoko?!

and bust his ass!

Writer: – No, he gets a beer from the cooler and sips it.

Producer: Forget it. How long is this scene?

Writer: Six minutes.

Producer: Quit sh¡tting me. We'll cut it. (*Pause*) So, when does the girl with the purple hair and the big tits appear?

Writer: Uhh, not 'til the end of the whole movie, when her ghost enters a doll.

Producer: (*Squinting at a drawing of the ugly robot doll*): You're fired!

In *Ghost In the Shell 2: Innocence*, there really are scenes which're nothing more'n a cyborg and his dog. This is a movie where two big, burly cops discuss the best kind of dog food to buy! Where the conversation about dry pet food is given the same solemn treatment as characters dying of cancer in a weepie. (Hell, even Batou's brand of beer has a doggie on it!). Ito and Oshii are shameless – this scene is lifted wholesale from their earlier *Avalon* (2001).

But the strength of *Ghost In the Shell 2: Innocence* is that even though it is a scene with a man coming home to his pet Gabriel and feeding it, it is riveting. Not because of the levels of subtext and symbolism (the toy, mechanical dog, of the photo/ hologram that Batou pulls out to look at, or the toy with the fish in it that the dog watches), but because of the rhythm of the editing, the choice of the camera angles, the elaborately minimal *mise-en-scène,* and the mood of the scene.

And here it is the music box cue ('The Doll House') that Kenji Kawai composed that really makes the scene. Here is Kawai and his music providing way more than 50% of the movie, as Mamoru Oshii noted. Music boxes are usually haunting and beautiful, and you can't go wrong with a music box moment in a movie. They always work: so although the visual storytelling is poetic, and the mood is introspective and charming, it is the music, once again, that lifts the scene into a higher realm (there are a surprising number of music box scenes in Japanese animation).

For Mamoru Oshii, *Ghost In the Shell 2: Innocence* was about 'a cyborg and a dog' (while the first *Ghost In the Shell* was about two cyborgs). A man and his pooch Gabriel – it's certainly an unusual subject for a major *animé* production with a high budget. The final shot of *Ghost In the Shell* is of… a cyborg and his dog.[33]

The dog represented – and embodied – a balanced life, a good life, a pure life, a life without the neuroses and anxieties that humans can't help creating. And it's the *relationship* with the hound that's important. A world without animals (even humanized pets) is not a meaningful world for Mamoru Oshii, who talked about the importance of animals for him:

> This movie does not hold the view that the world revolves around the human race. Instead it concludes that all forms of life – humans, animals and robots – are equal. In this day and age when everything is uncertain, we should all think about what to value in life and how

33 Who needs a super-babe cyborg when you've got a dog?

to coexist with others.

In the final scene of *Ghost In the Shell 2: Innocence*, as Batou and his hound stand opposite Togusa and his daughter, it was what the dog Gabriel saw that was important, Mamoru Oshii remarked, how it looked at the human world, and the cyborg world. The *Ghost In the Shell* movies evoke three worlds or cultures – that of humans, of cyborgs, and of animals.

THE FESTIVAL SEQUENCE.
The Manga Entertainment DVD release features an audio commentary by Mamoru Oshii and Toshihiko Nishikubo, which's fascinating – it's one of the few audio commentaries I've found on DVD for an *animé* movie by the Japanese filmmakers, not the (yawn) North American voice cast.[34] The commentary for *Ghost In the Shell 2: Innocence* reveals just how much hard work goes into animation – listen to Oshii and Nishikubo talking about the elaborate procession scenes, for instance, or the plane flight. They also relate how some of the animators[35] were burnt out after a month working on a single shot (like the one in the crime scene *aparto*, a lengthy take which includes people walking in and out of frame, and after it the animator went to hospital for exhaustion[36]).

You don't need to know anything about how animated movies are made to appreciate just how much work went into the festival sequence in *Ghost In the Shell 2: Innocence*. 'Baroque' doesn't do justice to it, neither does 'Mannerist', 'over-the-top', 'visually magnificent' or 'luxurious'. It resembles those scenes in Hayao Miyazaki's later movies where the filmmakers go all-out in depicting one setting, piling into the art direction, the layout and props everything they can think of, plus a few kitchen sinks (Yubaba's apartments in *Spirited Away*, for instance, or Howl's bedroom in *Howl's Moving Castle*).

And the eccentricity of the filmmakers is highlighted, too, by the editing: some movies, with a million-dollar sequence coming up, would offer some kind of build-up to it. Not *Ghost In the Shell 2: Innocence*: the festival comes directly after the flight to the North. There is an abrupt cut from a scene at Public Security Section 9's HQ straight into the flight. The cut goes from an uncharacteristically harsh Ishikawa yelling at Batou to 'deal with it!' (i.e., having a dog), to an image of the tilt-rotor plane in the air. So we shift from the dramatic scene in a dark room at Public Security Section 9 where a doctor has been patching up Batou to the daylit, super-ochre/ amber flight.

The festival sequence is a *tour-de-force* of animation, and on the basis of that one episode alone, *Ghost In the Shell 2: Innocence* is a masterpiece (it can be viewed as a self-contained movie, as with the canal journey in the 1995 *Ghost In the Shell* movie). Just look at the complexity and density of

---

34 The *Final Fantasy* movies have two commentaries, both fascinating, and the *Cowboy Bebop* series has a partial commentary.
35 There are some in-jokes – some of the characters are named after the crew.
36 Sadly, a common occurrence in animation production.

some of those shots, and also the enormous technical skill required to bring together so many disparate elements (and to animate the many figures). It's one of those sequences, like the opening of *Star Wars: Revenge of the Sith* (2005), which look like they required the rendering power of every computer on Earth hooked up together. No wonder it took a year to complete.[37]

And yet, a significant ingredient in the procession sequence in *Ghost In the Shell 2: Innocence* is invisible: Kenji Kawai's incredible music ('The Ballade of Puppets: In a New World Gods Will Descend', which brings on the massed choirs for haunting chants (the high budget of *Ghost In the Shell 2: Innocence* allowed for hiring choirs and orchestras: to produce the chants of the *minyoh* singers, part of the first *Ghost In the Shell* movie, their contribution was enlarged to include 75 vocalists (the recording session went on for 14 hours)). Also, in the festival sequence, and in the flight to Japan's North episode, Kawai's score is not battling against dialogue or sound effects – the filmmakers turn down most of the sound fx and (quite rightly) let the music rip.)

It's notable too that the festival sequence is only incidental to the central narrative of *Ghost In the Shell 2: Innocence*: Togusa and Batou're walking thru it to reach a guy they want to talk to (but it could be done in a single shot of some city streets).[38] So, dramatically, the movie does not 'need' that multi-million Yen sequence (and some film producers would've argued for cutting it down) – though of course it becomes the stand-out sequence in the whole piece. Similarly with the plane sequence: both are short films within the movie that could be lifted out easily.

THE PLANE TRIP.

The festival sequence in *Ghost In the Shell 2: Innocence* is placed right after the flight to the Etorofu sequence, another section where music is allowed to dominate, even tho' the visuals are so spectacular (the music is another slice of pulsing, metallic-sounding electronica. Quite beautiful, and it enhances the sequence immensely). Technically, these two episodes are breathtaking, and they are showcases for computer-aided and 3-D animation (yet, there is plenty of traditional, 2-D animation in there, too).

Flocks of birds are a recurring motif in *Ghost In the Shell 2: Innocence* – flying over the street festival, and between the towers in the Northern flight sequence (the tilt-rotor aircraft from the *manga* and *Ghost In the Shell: Stand Alone Complex* was given a make-over, and now appears as a more organic, insect-like and bird-like *mecha*).[39] The plane trip is only marred by the ridiculous mouthing of religious quotations by Togusa and Batou.

---

37 To add to the texture of the festival sequence, it has confetti floating across the screen (instead of the usual cherry blossom). I guess the filmmakers figured they might as well throw *everything* at the audience.
38 There's a wonderful use of children dressed in masks, trick or treat style – and Batou and Togusa're also hooded.
39 *Garm Wars* features similar designs.

VISITING THE ROBOT DESIGNERS.

If the narrative of *Ghost In the Shell 2: Innocence* seemed like a re-run of ten thousand cop shows from the 1950s-2000s, it certainly took a dive down the rabbit-hole in the climax of the jaunt that Batou and Togusa took to the HQ of Rox, the robot-makers. The equivalent in *film noir*, 1940s terms might be a visit to Sydney Greenstreet's mansion up on a hill, the head honcho of some dubious criminal racket, or in *James Bond* terms, the entry into the super-villain's lair in a volcano or atop a mountain.

The flight to Etorofu draws on the *manga* chapters in the first *Ghost In the Shell tankobon*, where Public Security Section 9 treks up (in their familiar tilt-rotor craft) to Bertarve, which's described by Aramaki as 'an old-style cyber-brain city'. In the comic, Bertarve is jammed with many bizarre-looking beings (some're cyborgs, some're humans with funky augmentations) – it's another of Masamune Shirow's versions of a futuristic but scuzzy city (another outing filled with extras from *Blade Runner/ Star Trek/* any sci-fi TV show). In the 2004 movie, tho', the North is eerily empty (except at the festival).

The whole sequence in *Ghost In the Shell 2: Innocence* was designed as a journey to Wonderland or Oz, self-consciously weird and kooky and spooky, with the filmmakers creating a series of unreal settings (like the vast lake reflecting the surreal cloudy sky, with the clouds drifting just a little too fast), and the walkway from a statue of a giant foot (if Mamoru Oshii and his team took on *Alice's Adventures In Wonderland* or *The Wizard of Oz* or a Grimm Brothers fairy tale, this is what it would look like[40]).

When our heroes enter the vast mansion in *Ghost In the Shell 2: Innocence*, the music box motif is reprised, but this time with an enormous machine complete with brass pipes like a church organ (and of course a music box score from Kenji Kawai).[41] Yes, this is *definitely* the largest music box in all *animé*! (You can hear the director saying to the *mecha* designers after looking at another sketch in a meeting, 'no, even *bigger!'*).

In the entrance hall are two characters that mean more to the hero than anyone else: Major Kusanagi and a dog (true, the doll is not Kusanagi, but is made to look like her,[42] and the dog isn't Batou's own hound, but looks like it). This is Motoko's first appearance in the foreground of *Ghost In the Shell 2: Innocence*, even though technically speaking it isn't the Major in the flesh (I mean, in the metal and plastic): as Batou remarks, he knew his guardian angel would look after him when things go wrong.

Meanwhile, art director Shuichi Hirata, DP by Miki Sakuma and production designer Yohei Taneda go nuts with the interior of the mansion: hallways of super-intricate stained glass (what is it with Japanese *animé* and stained glass?!), a dreamy courtyard out of

40 In fact, the 2010 version of *Alice In Wonderland* (from the Mouse House) did look a little like this (including hues such as steely greys and dried blood reds).
41 The music box was obtained from Sankyo Shoji; Kenji Kawai recorded it in the studio, then played back the sound and re-recorded it in Ohya, in an underground quarry (at Ohya Stone Museum), to give the sound the necessary reverb and space.
42 She also resembles the revived Motoko at the end of the 1995 movie.

Surrealists Giorgio de Chirico and Yves Tanguy, and of course the mandatory images of angels and feathers.

With its shiny, polished surfaces, its eerily still lake, the Robots 'R' Us HQ setting is like a giant mirror, where nothing is real, and everything is reflection of a reflection. Continuing the mirror-mirror motif (every arty film director has a thing about mirrors, from Jean Cocteau and F.W. Murnau to Andrei Tarkovsky and Ingmar Bergman – and Mamoru Oshii is no different), the Rox HQ episode in *Ghost In the Shell 2: Innocence* is constructed as a mirror. The filmmakers employ one of the favourite devices of sci-fi cinema, time travel, or loops, or scenes replaying, though with variations. It's paranoia, it's a head-trip, it's Groundhog Day, it's being stuck in replaying a terrible event over and over.

In this case, it's the encounter with the Bad Guy that gets rehashed a few times. True to *Ghost In the Shell* æsthetics, the villain 'Kim' is not only a robot, but a very strange one (a robot that plays dead (recalling Sokaku in the *manga*), and when it's rudely awoken by Batou, tipping it onto the floor out of its chair, it laughs like one of those joke toys – like how the Joker laughs in *Batman*).

It's all Chinese boxes in the Rox HQ sequence in *Ghost In the Shell 2: Innocence* – there's even a model of the mansion, which slides out of a wall, which Togusa examines.43 Like pushing a camera into a mirror without showing its reflection, filmmakers love to mess around with the audience's perception. Which they do repeatedly here. (Animation can dolly right into a mirror and never reveal the camera, and the *Ghost In the Shell: Stand Alone Complex* series also explores that possibility).

You thought that really happened? It didn't: and so we go back outside again with our heroes, and repeat a scene of them entering thru the giant doors, guns at the ready. In one scenario, a battleship starts shelling the manse, a little bit of *Patlabor*. (Togusa's brain was hacked, Batou explains, but he saved the day, tipped off by his guardian angel.44 Who is that guardian angel, you wonder? Togusa guesses. Of course, Motoko Kusanagi plays the guardian angel to both Togusa and Batou a number of times in the movies and the TV shows, literally saving their lives. And in episode *Trans Parent* of *Ghost In the Shell: Stand Alone Complex*, she and Batou are literally angels).

THE FINALE.

As usual in sci-fi *animé*, the climax of *Ghost In the Shell 2: Innocence* took place in a big, dark, forbidding, metallic, macho setting – a robot factory at sea (when did you see a hi-tech thriller *animé* climaxing in, say, a nail polishing parlour with a decor of flowers and pink hearts? or at a Dolly Parton or Celine Dion concert?). So it's Batou in full-on S.W.A.T. team/ superhero/ video-game-player Hunt-And-Kill mode, approaching the factory (which's on board a giant ship) underwater, *James Bond*-style,

---

43 It's reminiscent of the maze model at the Overlook Hotel in 1980's *The Shining*.
44 How did Motoko tell Batou he was in a cybernetic mirror maze – something to do with the word 'aemaeth' (= 'truth' in Hebrew, and when you lose two letters, 'a' and 'e', it becomes 'maeth' = 'death'). This scene seems invented specifically to thrill cultural theorists and *cinéastes*.

and drawing a tad on the submarine sequence in Uncle Shirow's *Ghost In the Shell: Man-Machine Interface manga*).[45]

The *Ghost In the Shell 2: Innocence*'s finale shifts into high gear with Batou kicking open a hatch and jumping into frame from above, and up comes Kenji Kawai's Busy Action Finale Music Cue (Mamoru Oshii noted in his commentary that it seemed a good idea to head straight for the action like that). So it's one man against an army of naked, killer female robots who stumble and twirl into action with an extraordinary, extended, gangly sense of movement, emphasizing their doll-like and puppet-like essence (it's remarkable animation-as-performance).

To demonstrate just how deadly these white geisha critters are, there's a scene in a dim, claustrophobic corridor where a group of security guards're viciously attacked so the walls're stained with blood. The animation utilizes lunging, subjective close-ups of the robots, their motion disturbingly haphazard. (Poor guys – they're hired as security for the robot manufacturer, only to have the products rounding on themselves. And the filmmakers have invented them solely so they could be killed).

Batou holds them off with, of course, a giant machine gun, blasting them to bits. Each Geisha-Bellmer doll bursts open, exposing metal innards, or their faces decompose and split apart, leaning into the lens with exposed teeth grimacing. (Shooting up androids occurs all the time in the *Ghost In the Shell* universe – of course, on screen and on television, that sidesteps censorship, because it's only a robot, right? But this scene is also at the surface level a man with a gun attacking and killing naked women).

It's beauty and death, it's women and death, out of Sigmund Freud and Georges Bataille, out of the French Symbolists and Surrealists, a grotesquerie of carnage which eroticizes machines to the point of overload. When is a machine most alive? When it's just about to be ripped to pieces.

Shadowy, long, gloomy corridors and walkways out of the *Alien* movies, or the *Batman* movies, or out of a 1,000 sci-fi movies, with the murderous dolls swinging into frame and hobbling towards the hero. Finally, when Batou seems out-numbered, Motoko Kusanagi appears: the 2004 movie teases the audience with her entrance, because the Major has entered one of the gynoids remotely, via a satellite, so the robot turns on its crew, and shoots them with a big gun.

'Hong Kong Noir', Mamoru Oshii acknowledged, when Batou and Motoko swing round to confront each other in the classic, gun-to-gun face-off of John Woo[46] and Takeshi Kitano movies. The filmmakers rightly make the robot that Kusanagi has entered look more and more like Motoko from the first *Ghost In the Shell* movie (there's a tender moment when Batou gives Kusanagi his vest to cover up her nakedness. He doesn't change, the Major remarks. Such a gentleman! That is a call-back to the

45 Reprising the diving sequence in the first *Ghost In the Shell* movie, though darker and deeper and scarier (and fuzzier, too: the filmmakers opted for a blurry, crimson look to the animation. Thus, the sea is already red, so blood won't show up).
46 Even if John Woo didn't invent it, it has become known as one of his signature moves in cinema.

first *Ghost In the Shell* movie, when Batou did the same after Motoko's kicked the villain's butt in her thermoptic camouflage).

WHAT'S AT STAKE.

Who're the bad guys in *Ghost In the Shell 2: Innocence*? Once again, it is big business, in this case the robot manufacturers Locus Solus, who have created geisha cyborgs with illegal souls copied from girls captured by *yakuza* gangs. It's rampant capitalism again – it's not one single villain, but the whole capitalist system. It's exploitation (this time, exploitation that involves sex: the issue of prostitution is foregrounded in *Shell 2*). Many male art film directors have explored prostitution,[47] including one of Mamoru Oshii's heroes, Jean-Luc Godard. For the left-wing, one-time Marxist Godard, the capitalist system is founded on prostitution: we are all whores (and filmmakers as much as anybody). And for Godard the issue of prostitution was a way of exploring in cinema the exploitation that's at the heart of capitalism).

In 1962's *Vivre Sa Vie*, Jean-Luc Godard maintains that work in general can be a kind of prostitution, not only prostitution itself.[48] In *Vivre Sa Vie* and other films, Godard and his teams are suggesting that capitalism itself is a form of prostitution – everyone is selling something, everyone is buying, everyone is trading. It might be sex, or drugs, or movies, or tabloid stories.

Thus, the finale of *Ghost In the Shell 2: Innocence* doesn't end with Motoko Kusanagi appearing to help Batou waste all of the attacking geisha dolls, or with the opening up of the Locus Solus operation: there is a more intimate scene in a room where the 'ghost-dubbing' takes place. Batou rescues a girl who's still alive (she was kidnapped by the *yakuza* gang). The girl embodies what is at stake.[49]

The rescue of one of the kids who's being used by the faceless robot corporation Locus Solus (having her soul copied – which ultimately kills the subject), is an ambiguous resolution to the 2004 *Ghost In the Shell* movie. Don't make her cute! Mamoru Oshii told his animators, but the girl inevitably turned out *kawaii*. The plot involves a kind of slave trade,[50] with young women being stolen by the *yakuza* gangs and sold to the robot manufacturers, so they can copy their spirits and install them in their prostitute robots (and some of the girls are clearly under-age). So the robot companies are kind of multi-billion dollar pimps, manufacturing sex dolls with souls (there would no doubt be customers who wouldn't care if their cyborg sex toy had a soul or not – some people will shtupp anything).

47 European intellectuals have a long history of exploring prostitution as a theme – not least, it allows filmmakers like Godard to put women on the screen. And for Godard, prostitution was viewed from the Marxist-Leninist perspective of capitalist exploitation.
48 A recurring theme in Jean-Luc Godard's early films is that cinema and the media are prostitution industries – to get anywhere in cinema or TV or modelling you have to have sex is the view. So when Nana agrees to go home with the photographer Paul in *Vivre Sa Vie*, that is also a kind of prostitution, because he's going to photograph her.
49 Ghost-dubbing machines being employed by a nefarious corporation comes from the first *Ghost In the Shell* manga. And in the *manga*, it's also young girls who're being used (kidnapped by gangs). Batou and Togusa rescue them.
50 'Help me! Help me!' the little voice trapped inside the artificial bodies says.

Motoko Kusanagi says she's downloaded some of herself from a satellite (the *Ghost In the Shell: Stand Alone Complex* series contained similar notions, and it's fundamental to *Ghost In the Shell: Man-Machine Interface*). Once she's aided Batou, she simply disappears: this is Batou's movie, not Motoko's, and the romance is not between Batou and Kusanagi, but between Batou and his dog! Or maybe between Batou and Togusa).

As if to reassure him, the Major tells Batou in their final scene in *Ghost In the Shell 2: Innocence* that whenever he accesses the network, she will be right there beside him (once again promoting the notion that someone's spirit or soul can enter cyberspace). *Aaah*, how sweet! Motoko, the superbabe cyborg in full body armour, is actually a real softie when you get to know her! Honest! But don't tell her – she'll slam you against the wall with a gun at your neck.

THE *DÉNOUEMENT.*

Like the first *Ghost In the Shell* movie, the *dénouement* scene in 2004's *Ghost In the Shell 2: Innocence* is unusual and quirky. *Very* quirky! Once again, it involves Batou, and his buddy in this movie, Togusa (rather than Motoko). It takes place at night at Togusa's home, with the city a mass of lights in the distance. Blocked very simply, with the two adults talking, facing each other, on the path in front of the house: Batou holds his beloved pooch, and Togusa's daughter runs outside, and daddy picks her up.

Forget the dialogue (which's minimal and routine), this modest scene is about points-of-view and Existential issues: Batou looks at Togusa and his daughter, maybe wondering what he misses in not having a family, maybe envying Togusa's humanity (Batou being nearly wholly cyborg, and Togusa being mainly human). Togusa looks at Batou and his pet, perhaps thanking his stars that he survived being Batou's partner, and that Batou seems more balanced than b4. And to be home. *Home* ('*taidaima*'). The daughter sees the cute dog that she's probably been playing with, and daddy's big, strange workmate, Batou, a guy who keeps to himself, and won't come in for a drink.

Meanwhile, the dawg sees the whole picture, the humans, the cyborgs, and the doll that the daughter clutches (a C.U. of the doll reinforces one of the themes of *Ghost In the Shell 2: Innocence*, about humans + cyborgs + dolls + puppets + toys). The *dénouement* scene brings together the panoply of character types in the *Ghost In the Shell* series: <1> fully human humans (the daughter), <2> humans with artificial augmentations (Togusa), <3> cyborgs (Batou), <4> dolls (toys, puppets), and <5> animals (the dog).[51]

The 2004 Japanese movie asks a question here: which one is more alive? Which one has the most fulfilling life? Which one is happiest? And which one would you want to be? We know director Mamoru Oshii's answer to all of these questions: the dog!

---

[51] All that's missing is a ghost in the network, like Major Kusanagi or the Puppet Master.

SEXUAL POLITICS.

The issue of sexuality is discussed openly in *Ghost In the Shell 2: Innocence* – why do robots need to be gendered at all, let alone be given genitals? The hero of the *Ghost In the Shell* universe is Major Kusanagi (though she only appears at the end of the second movie), a female cyborg. The filmmakers want to have it both ways, of course (typical of bloody filmmakers!). They want their robots to be mere machines, but they also want some of them to be female (and young), with attractive, curvy bodies. (There's no particular reason why the main character Motoko of *Ghost In the Shell* has to have a *young* woman's body, or a slim, appealing, young woman's body. She could be just any regular woman, fat, thin, tall, short, whatever. In *Ghost In the Shell: Stand Alone Complex*, Batou suggests that the Major gets a male cyborg body – it would suit her personality more, and would be stronger. She nixes the idea).

The robots that have started killing their owners're called gynoids in *Ghost In the Shell 2: Innocence*. Sexual issues are foregrounded in a disturbing manner: the gynoids look like Japanese geishas, with white make-up and heavily stylized features.[52] The 2004 movie is dealing, in essence, with how society objectifies women sexually, how sex has been technologized and mechanized. Haladay, the robot engineer, notes that sexual functions were added to the robots, which isn't illegal (hence, Togusa remarks, the families of the victims not bringing lawsuits – these androids are essentially prostitutes. No, they're sex toys).

Robots as whores – it's a staple of science fiction literature, though sci-fi cinema has been far more reticent in really getting to grips with the issue, preferring to cloak it with tropes of dolls and puppets, or alluding to it only in the dialogue. Several charas in the world of *Ghost In the Shell* have sex dolls or robots as lovers. (In a *Blade Runner* deleted scene, Holden asks Deckard if he had the snake woman Zhora before killing her. Holden tells Deckard that he shouldn't have a crisis of conscience about it – it's like screwing your washing machine, then turning it off. That kind of blunt, sexist, macho blather turns up in *Ghost In the Shell* and *Ghost In the Shell: Stand Alone Complex* (though watered down a squince). When Motoko Kusanagi encounters such drivel, she either coolly dismisses it or ignores it – or she smashes the guy in the face.)[53]

HANS BELLMER.

The most bizarre Surrealist artist, and the most violent without a doubt, is Hans Bellmer (1902-75). His *Doll* series are deeply disturbing images of the female body, in which the artist delighted in wrenching a doll into all sorts of impossible contortions. Bellmer wrote a veritable summary of the erotic pleasure of the artist and viewer, the consumer who sucks up lasciviously the object (in *The Doll*):

---

52 The first episode of *Ghost In the Shell: Stand Alone Complex, Section 9,* had explored a hostage situation at a geisha house, and also used the geisha-as-call-girl or prostitute angle (there are still geishas in Japan today, though only around 1,000).
53 Even *very* demure girls in *animé* whack boys in the face when they say sexist blether or get pervy.

To adjust the joints to each other, coax the limbs, head and torso into winsome poses, then run the eye and hand over these softly dipping vales, relish the pleasure of the shapely curves, give them a pretty turn or with blood-rousing gusto wrench them out of shape.54

Hans Bellmer's *Doll* is the ultimate sex object, the ultimate fetish, a precursor of the blow-up doll of the sex toy industry. Bellmer speaks of penetrating through layers until some core or womb is reached. His drawings and photographs are full of fingers or penises being thrust into different orifices, into mouths, vaginas, and anuses. Bellmer is obsessed with penetration. He drew penises entering vaginas many times.55 Bellmer's art is the ultimate, Surrealist transformation, as vulvas turn into penises, and buttocks become the glans of the wiener. Bellmer's drawings depict a continuous orgy, utterly pornographic, a feast of penetration and pleasure.56 (The multiple penetrations look forward to the art of H.R. Giger (in the film *Alien*), the 'tits and tentacles' movies in Japanese animation, and the dolls in *Ghost In the Shell 2: Innocence*. And in the erotic art of Masamune Shirow, fingers are continually penetrating everywhere).

Faces are often left out: Hans Bellmer's drawings create a frenzy of limbs and torsos, sometimes just buttocks and groins. 'All my work is erotic – it always has been', remarked Bellmer.57 He is distinctly a part of that European, intellectual tradition stemming from the Marquis de Sade and Charles Baudelaire. In Bellmer's art, the Sadeian ethic of sex = death is exploited in endless variations. As Géza Roheim wrote, '[d]eath is coitus and coitus is death'.58 This psychotic view is central to much of modern culture, from the Marquis de Sade to Jean-Paul Sartre. Bellmer's art, and that of René Magritte, Salvador Dali, Max Ernst, André Breton, Paul Éluard and Pablo Picasso, ascribes to this view of sex = death.

Hans Bellmer said: '[t]he idea of eroticism is an essential part of life, so it's right that artists like me should devote themselves to exploring that idea.'59 Bellmer depicts nothing but the sex act. He is unusual in this. Other artists produced erotic art as part of their whole art: Eric Gill, David Hockney, Félicien Rops, and J.M.W. Turner, but Bellmer focusses entirely on genitals and sex. Very few artists have been so determined in their depictions of eroticism. It permeates every aspect of Bellmer's art. And it is a pornographic art. Bellmer's art, like the major erotic text of Surrealist and modern European art, Georges Bataille's *The Story of the Eye*, is pornography masquerading as erotic or high art.

The gynoids in *Ghost In the Shell 2: Innocence* are designed specifically to look like Hans Bellmer's famous, Surrealist doll: rather than the sleek cyborg of the first *Ghost* movie (when Major Kusanagi took

54 H. Bellmer: *The Doll*, 1934, in G. Picon: *Surrealists and Surrealism 1919-1939*, Skira/ Macmillan, London, 1983, 153.
55 See H. Bellmer's *A Sade*, etchings, 1961.
56 H. Bellmer: *A Woman From the Back*, coloured pencils, 30 x 37cm, private collection; *Traite de la Morale*, 1968, etching, collection: the artist, Paris.
57 Quoted in Peter Webb, 369.
58 G. Roheim: *Animism, Magic and the Divine King*, quoted in Peter Webb.
59 Interview, 1972, in Peter Webb, 369.

her clothes off and got serious), in the second *Shell* movie they are white, doll-like creations, without skins or the feminine curves that have fascinated artists for thousands of years. Dolls with the joints and hinges showing, each one the same, with blank, dead faces, pale, blue eyes and red lips (the make-up is a stylization of geisha culture). And in the *Ghost In the Shell 2: Innocence* climax, the animators skilfully gave the gynoids a stylized jerky, floppy movement that underlined their puppet-like, doll-like status. Nobody would design a doll or sex toy looking like this!

However, the filmmakers at Bandai Visual, Production I.G. *et al* chose to ignore the central tenet of Hans Bellmer's art, which is eroticism. Instead, the geisha gynoids were depicted more for creepiness and threat. But if you know Bellmer's art, you'll see penetration and sex everywhere.

SÉLECTION OFFICIELLE
FESTIVAL DE CANNES 2004
INNOCENCE
GHOST IN THE SHELL 2
www.uipfrance.com
1er DÉCEMBRE
GAME ONE
LYCOS.fr
ALLOCINE.COM
aVoir-aLire.com

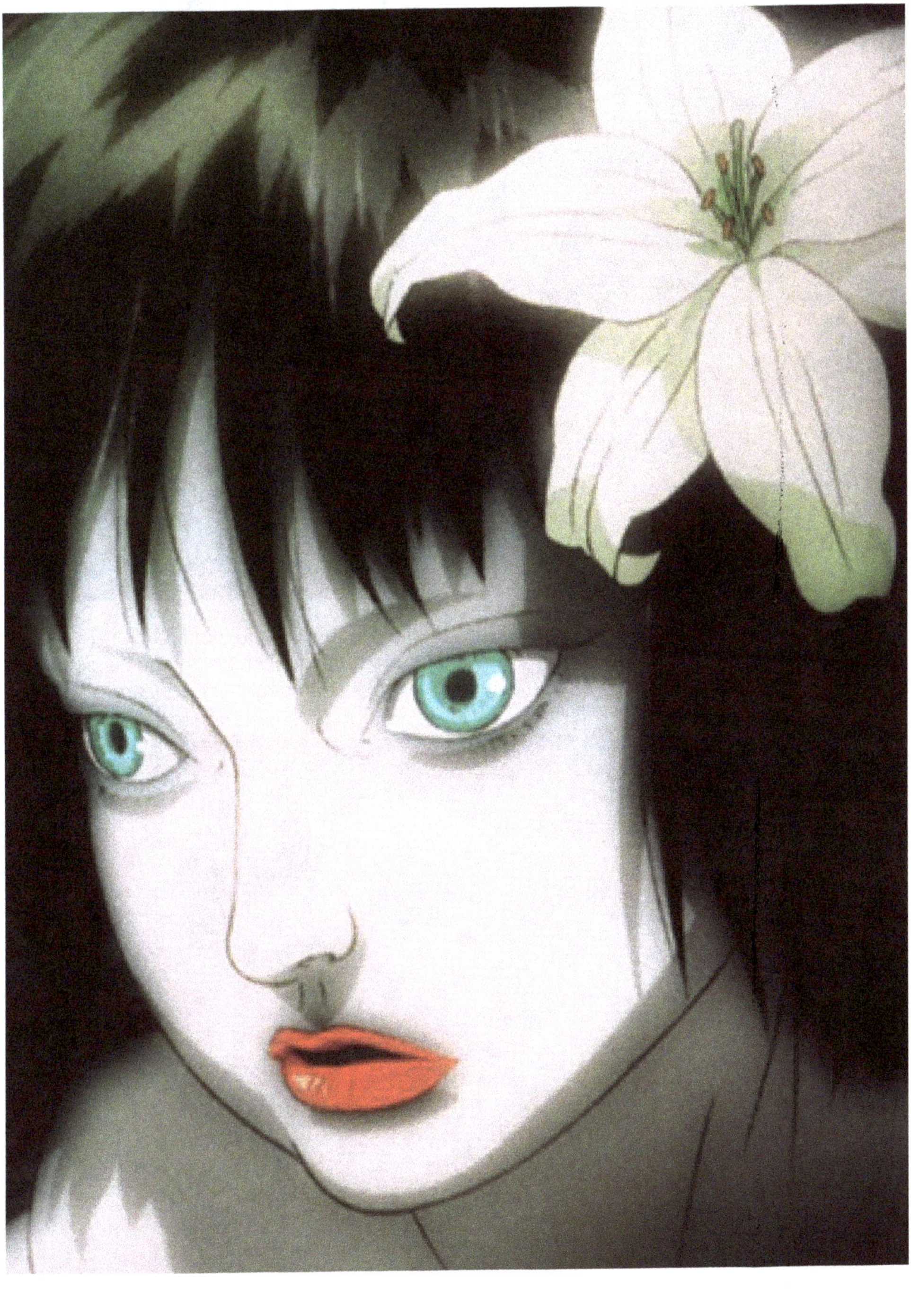

The hero of the Ghost In the Shell movie sequel is Batou, not Motoko.
Is the love affair in the movie between Batou and Kusanagi, or a man and his dog?
Batou wears this preposterously grim expression throughout the picture.

One of the most remarkable episodes in recent animation – the
festival in Ghost in the Shell 2: Innocence

The 2004 Ghost sequel re-unites one of animé's odd but
compelling couples, in the midst of the finale.

Mamoru Oshii, in 2004, the time of the 2nd Ghost In the Shell movie

04

MAMORU OSHII

BIOGRAPHY

Director Mamoru Oshii (born August 8, 1951, Tokyo) is an acclaimed *animé* director,[1] known for the *Patlabor* TV series (and two spin-off *Patlabor* movies), and the two *Ghost In the Shell* movies. Oshii is highly regarded in the world of Japanese animation for being a creator of intelligent, literary and self-consciously arty movies.[2] It's expected that an Oshii-directed movie will feature some political and philosophical ruminations, plenty of allusions and quotations (the *Bible* being a favourite source), highly introspective (not to say depressed) characters, and usually a lengthy dreamy, meditative sequence. Yet Oshii-directed movies are also populist animations with enough action to satisfy fan-boys and general audiences.

Mamoru Oshii is known for his work with the production company Production I.G., one of the key animation houses in Japan. Production I.G.'s credits include *Patlabor*,[3] *Evangelion*, *Blood: The Last Vampire*, *F.L.C.L.*, *xxxHolic*, *Tsubasa Chronicle*, *Ghost Hound* and *Eden of the East*.[4] 122 people worked for Production I.G. in 2007. Production I.G., like most animation houses, also does commercial work (including for T-Mobile, Samsung and Kirin Lemon). The house style of Production I.G. is slicky, flashy, hi-tech animation, but they have produced the whole range of animation styles.

Mitsuhisa Ishikawa and Takayuki Goto had founded Production I.G. in 1987 (they had formerly worked at Tatsunoko Studio – one of Mamoru Oshii's first jobs, where he helped to animate *One Hit Kanta*, 1977).

Mamoru Oshii worked for Studio Deen (founded in 1975) for many of his earlier works, including the *Urusei Yatsura* outings, *Angel's Egg*, and the *Patlabor* TV show. Deen's later works include *Fruits Basket*, *Hell*

---

1 In Japanese animation, terms like 'director' and 'designer' don't have the same meaning as in the Western film industry. 'Director' might refer to a 'wide range' of different jobs (H. McCarthy, 1996, 9). It's customary, for instance, for designers to have a speciality, and to be brought onto a production to exploit that gift.
2 Incidentally, Mamoru Oshii is an animation director who can't draw.
3 The first big production for Production I.G. was the first *Patlabor* movie.
4 Production I.G. was a sub-contractor on *Princess Mononoke*.

Girl, Rave Master and *When They Cry*.

Mamoru Oshii later moved on to Studio Pierrot[5] in 1980, where he met Kazumori Ito[6] and Yoshitaka Amano, some of his key collaborators. At Pierrot, Oshii directed episodes of *Nils' Mysterious Journey* (1980). Oshii was one of the five founders of the Headgear collective (the others were Masami Yuki, Yutaka Izubuchi, Akemi Takada[7] and Kazunori Ito).

Mamoru Oshii began working in the Japanese *anime* industry in the late 1970s, on storyboards (Oshii worked first for Tatsunoko Productions in the late 1970s). His early efforts in animation included *Urusei Yatsura: Only You* (1983), *Urusei Yatsura 2: Beautiful Dreamer* (1984) and *Dallos* (1983), all made at Studio Pierrot.[8] *Angel's Egg* (1985, Studio Deen) was a slow, dreamy feature. This was the early days of animation released on videos (as Original Video Animations). In the mid-1980s, Oshii worked with Hayao Miyazaki[9] and Toshio Suzuki on the movie *Anchor*, which was abandoned.

Among Mamoru Oshii's other works are: the *manga Seraphim 266,613,336 Wings,* which was illustrated by Satoshi Kon; the script for *Jin-Roh: The Wolf Brigade* (Hiroyuki Okiura, 2000); *Blood: The Last Vampire* (2000); and story ideas for *Ghost In the Shell: Stand Alone Complex*.

The Red Spectacles (1987), part of Mamoru Oshii's *Kerberos* saga (begun in 1986, it has appeared in *manga*, movie and radio form), was his first live-action film. It was followed by *Stray Dog: Kerberos Panzer Cops*[10] (1991).[11] Other films include *Talking Head* (1992), and the live-action/animated movie *Avalon* was released in 2001. More recent Oshii-directed movies include *The Sky Crawlers* (2008), *Assault Girls* (2009) and *Garm Wars: The Last Druid* (2014). As well as directing movies, Oshii has also written scripts for other productions, and created *manga*.

Mamoru Oshii has also advised on the inevitable spin-off computer games from his movies, such as *Mobile Police Patlabor Comes Back: MiniPato* video game (2005) and *The Sky Crawlers: Innocent Aces* (2008).

Mamoru Oshii could've had his own studio – other filmmakers in *anime* have founded their own studios (including Eiko Tanaka with Studio 4°C, Hideaki Anno with Studio Khara, the CLAMP collective, the Gainax collective, and of course Isao Takahata and Hayao Miyazaki with

---

5 Pierrot's output included *Creamy Mami, Pastel Yumi, Hyper Police, G.T.O., Emma, Sugar Sugar Rune, Ghost Files, Clamp School Detectives, Naruto* and *Bleach.*
6 Author Kazunori Ito (b. 1954) has many credits in Japanese *anime* (including *.Hack, Maison Ikkoku, Urusei Yatsura* and *Avalon*), and has worked with Mamoru Oshii on a number of projects, including the *Patlabor* and *Ghost In the Shell* movies.
7 Akemi Takada (b. 1967) has worked with Mamoru Oshii a number of times: on the *Urusei Yatsura* series and the *Patlabor* series, as well as on *Creamy Mami, Gatchaman, Maison Ikkoku, Ranma 1/2,* and *Fancy Lala.* Takada has also produced CD covers, books, and jewellery, and is a key contributor to the *Ghost In the Shell* frfranchise.
8 *Dallos* was co-directed by Oshii's mentor Toriumi Hisayuki (who was responsible for more of the direction, according to some).
9 Mamoru Oshii is a friend of Miyazaki's, tho' he is critical of Studio Ghibli, and their tendency to try to control their filmmakers.
10 *Hellhounds: Panzer Corps* (1988-90, in *Amazing Comics,* by Nihon Shuppansha) was written by Mamoru Oshii, with art by Kamui Fujiwara and Studio 2B.
11 Other entries in the *Kerboros* saga have included a 2000 *anime*, *Jin-Roh: The Wolf Brigade,* based on Mamoru Oshii's *manga,* and written by Oshii.

Studio Ghibli). Maybe Oshii preferred to focus on filmmaking (like Miyazaki) rather than running a production facility.

Although the settings, the policies, the strategies and the personnel of the mobile police forces depicted in Mamoru Oshii's work, such as in the *Patlabor* movies and the *Ghost In the Shell* movies, are right-wing in essence (and in their views), there is a sceptical undercurrent which reflects the more left-wing tendencies of Oshii and the filmmakers at Production I.G. For instance, in *Patlabor*, there are scenes set at the Kokkai (Diet) building in the Kasumigaseki area of Tokyo.

Mamoru Oshii is not a filmmaker like, say Ingmar Bergman or Orson Welles, who has a host of things he wants to say about all manner of topics. He is very much a visual storyteller in cinema. He is not writing an essay, he is not delivering a lecture, he is not coming out with a bunch of easily-digested statements in words (you can see from interviews that he is not wholly at ease talking about his movies, or of doing interviews at all, though of course he expresses views on all sorts of subjects).[12] His cinema is more of the poetic kind, closer to music than written or spoken language.

Give Orson Welles or Jean-Luc Godard a topic and they could talk about it for hours. Boy, can Godard talk! And Welles was one of the finest raconteurs in all cinema. Mamoru Oshii isn't like that at all: he comes across much more like, say, Andrei Tarkovsky, Carl-Theodor Dreyer or even Woody Allen: reluctant to talk too much about their work, and when they do it is always in a serious, circumspect manner.

Mamoru Oshii is well-known as an educated and intelligent filmmaker, who includes high cultural references in his movies. Oshii has been reading the *Bible* since his student days, but for the stories, not for religious reasons (he's not a Christian, he says). 'I really liked the *Bible* as a little boy. While a student, I planned to enter a seminary at one point, but didn't. Even now, though, I still read the *Bible* sometimes' (1997, 137).

It has to be admitted that the cinema of Mamoru Oshii as a whole is patchy, and veers from the sublime and masterful (*Ghost In the Shell* and *Patlabor*), to the functional and fun (*Urusei Yatsura*), to the very ropey (*Garm Wars, Avalon*), to the simply dreadful (*The Sky Crawlers, Jin-Roh, Angel's Egg*).

That's OK – plenty of the greatest film directors have produced turkeys – *Confidential Report* (a.k.a. *Mr Arkadin*, 1956), directed by Orson Welles, for example. But Mamoru Oshii has delivered several duds, either as director or writer.

On the one hand, Mamoru Oshii has avoided remakes and sequels (no doubt he's been approached numerous times to helm those sorts of movies), but too many of his own films are derivative, and feel like remakes or sequels (and he *has* done sequels – *Urusei Yatsura, Patlabor* and *Ghost In the Shell* among others). On the plus side, Oshii has originated many of his films (even if he hasn't always written the screenplays), but on

---

12 Mamoru Oshii in interviews always looks very, very tired, and he mumbles. A lot.

the down side those original ideas haven't always convinced.

A key flaw with M. Oshii's form of cinema is that while there are plenty of intriguing ideas, they aren't integrated into the stories or the characters, and they aren't expressed in a compelling cinematic form. The concepts are potentially fascinating, but they aren't dramatized satisfactorily, and remain undigested, untransformed (and uncinematic).

And then there's the Mamoru Oshii Curse, as I call it: characters who stand or sit there, gawping forlornly into space or into the camera… saying nothing… not moving… eyes blank… faces expressionless or frowning… an air of melancholy consumes all.

In animation, it comes across too often as affected and silly. In live-action, yes, characters staring off into space and doing nothing for many moments can work, can be dramatic or have value/ impact. In *animé*, it's trickier to pull off.

Somehow, also, I think that Carl-Theodor Dreyer, Ingmar Bergman, Akira Kurosawa and Robert Bresson had 'earned' their right, so to speak, to stage scenes where characters do nothing and stare at nothing.

But I'm not sure that Mamoru Oshii has produced enough significant work to 'earn' that right – well, at least not by 1985, the date of *Angel's Egg*, when the two main characters seem to do nothing but stare glumly at the viewer or at the night (or they walk, walk, walk). But in Oshii's later work, such as the abysmal *The Sky Crawlers*, the Oshii Curse is still at large.

Somewhere along the line, Mamoru Oshii jettisoned comedy; it's a pity, because humour doesn't negate the exploration of 'serious' issues, doesn't mean you're not taken seriously, and doesn't spoil a movie. Even a European film *auteur* can be a genius *and* very funny: Federico Fellini and Jean-Luc Godard, example. *Weekend* (1963) is blackly, evilly funny *and* it's a scorchingly angry attack on Western, capitalist society. *8 1/2* (1963) is very funny *and* it's a masterpiece about movies, and memory, and life, and all.

The films directed by Mamoru Oshii often start with action sequences: absolutely necessary, because after that the pictures slow down to glacial levels as Oshii and the teams explore Existential angst, quasi-religious philosophizing, and characters staring off into space, lighting cigarettes, or shuffling down a street.

MAMORU OSHII AND *BLADE RUNNER*.

Mamoru Oshii has never got over seeing *Blade Runner* (and *2001: A Space Odyssey*): the Phil Dick movie 'is a vision, it has the visual power to make us believe its world exists', Oshii remarked, adding: 'I believe these two films in many ways define the films to follow'.[13]

Mamoru Oshii has expressed his admiration for *Blade Runner*, which his cinema clearly draws on (certainly, *Blade Runner* has been hugely influential on Japanese science fiction *animé*). *Alien* is another movie that Oshii has referred to, as well as, of course, *2001: A Space Odyssey*. I would

13 Mamoru Oshii, in J. Clements, 2009, 33.

argue that not only is the 1995 *Ghost In the Shell* a worthy successor to *Blade Runner*, it also, along with *Ghost In the Shell 2: Innocence*, tops *Blade Runner*: in some of its filmmaking, its style, and its visuals, and certainly in the elegance and depth of its metaphysical and philosophical explorations. Both *Ghost In the Shell* movies (and the *Ghost In the Shell: Stand Alone Complex* TV series) have *far more* sophisticated scripts than *Blade Runner*.

Blade Runner suggests a welter of philosophical material but doesn't deliver it. Instead, it has taken 100s of critics and commentators and PhD students to elaborate on what *Blade Runner* hinted at. And it is those philosophical speculations in *Blade Runner*, and similar movies about artificial life, like *Solaris*, *Bicentennial Man* and *A.I.*, that the *Ghost In the Shell* movies have developed to a far richer and more sophisticated degree.

But it wasn't the story of *Blade Runner* that fired Mamoru Oshii's imagination, but the imagery. If he is allowed to, Oshii prefers to make movies with images, and to tell stories with images. But that requires a big budget: if you haven't got the budget, 'you have to make a film interesting with story, action and so on', Oshii explained in 2006 (*pace* the *Ghost* sequel, *Innocence*), 'but when I have time and money, I want to tell a story with visual images alone'.[14]

EURO ART CINEMA.

That Mamoru Oshii is a fan of European art movies is obvious.[15] Oshii is happy to admit that he has been influenced by everything, and has copied filmmakers. That's what everyone does, he insists. He also doesn't mind a bit if other filmmakers rip him off (as the Wachowski sisters have done in their *Matrix* movies).

Mamoru Oshii cited Jean-Luc Godard as an instance of someone making a film or telling a story *as a film*, or *with a film*. Godard's already done it, Oshii commented, so what else is there to do? Being original was not possible, Oshii maintained: one always copied everything else.

Andrei Tarkovsky, Federico Fellini, Ingmar Bergman, Michelangelo Antonioni, Jean-Pierre Melville, Robert Bresson and Jean-Luc Godard are some of the European art movie directors[16] Mamoru Oshii has cited as influences. You can spot the sequences of abstraction, introspection and Existentialism in Oshii's work that might derive from Antonioni's movies as director (characters lost in the fog on empty roads, for instance, or lone, alienated men in the midst of complex societies); or the implacable assassin in the cool, hip and very French *Le Samourai* (1967), directed by Melville (a key movie of modern Existentialism and alienation for many filmmakers, a favourite with John Woo and Martin Scorsese); or the slow, hypnotic drift of the camera in Tarkovsky's seven features, the feeling for

---

14 In ib., 33.
15 A keen film buff, Mamoru Oshii claimed to have seen 1,000 movies in one year.
16 And Robert Aldrich, Ridley Scott and David Lynch among mainstream directors. Japanese directors Mamoru Oshii admires include: Tatsumi Kumashiro, Yoshishige Yoshida and Kinji Fukasaku.

time and space and texture; or life as a circus in Fellini's *œuvre*, where visual storytelling is all; or Bergman's matchless use of the human face in close-up in a series of tragedies and dramas which have no equal in cinema (even more incredible, Bergman also wrote them all).

DOGS.

Dogs – specifically basset hounds – were one of the motifs that director Mamoru Oshii added to the *Ghost In the Shell* movies, self-consciously light-hearted, Disneyesque additions to the hi-tech gloom and world-weary discussions about robotdom and ghostdom (dogs appear next to the characters,[17] or in posters on the walls, or in old photos, or on TV, in ads). Once you start noticing the dogs in *Ghost In the Shell*, you find they are absolutely everywhere (as if Oshii had asked his layout and background team to insert dog motifs wherever possible). Yes, and hounds, favourites of animators everywhere, of course crop up in Hayao Miyazaki's movies, and there's a cute mutt called Ein in *Cowboy Bebop*.[18] (And pooches are a favourite element in the cinema of Tim Burton).

But dogs also had a symbolic and metaphysical import to Mamoru Oshii, and were used in the *Ghost In the Shell* movies to represent so much of what cyborg culture and digital networks don't have. If humans were already alienated from nature and animals, as Oshii maintained, then cyborgs and robots were set even further apart. Also, both hounds and cyborgs were created to a degree by humans: the animal as pet is no longer a wild animal, true to its fundamental nature. It was an animal abstracted, separated, and humanized.

In the pages following I look at a selection of the films written and directed by Mamoru Oshii, though not all of them (partly because several are not easily available).

URUSEI YATSURA

The *Urusei Yatsura* sit-com show (translated as *Those Obnoxious Aliens*), based on the very popular *manga*[19] by Rumiko Takahashi (b. 1957), and produced at Kitty Film/ Toho/ Studio Pierrot,[20] was very different from *Ghost In the Shell* or *Patlabor*, Mamoru Oshii's best-known works – *Urusei Yatsura* was a comedy show, with bright, colourful and out-size characters and incidents. Takahashi is one of the superstars of recent

---

17 There are many dogs on the streets in *Ghost In the Shell*, some prominent in the composit-ions, such as in the outdoor market scene, when Batou is chasing the criminal.
18 Mamoru Oshii is well-known for his love of dogs, and has a mutt called Gabriel and one called Daniel – the name crops up in *Ghost In the Shell 2: Innocence*. When you see Oshii in interviews, he can talk about dogs endlessly, and also wears pooch motifs on Tee shirts.
19 It first appeared in *Shonen Sunday* in 1978.
20 Yuji Moriyama (b. 1960) worked with Mamoru Oshii on *Urusei Yatsura*. His other credits include *Cream Lemon, Evangelion, Black Magic, Project A-Ko, Maison Ikkoku,* and *Galaxy Express 999.*

manga: her other works include *Ranma 1/2, Maison Ikkoku, Mermaid Saga, One Pound Gospel, Rumic Theater,* and *Inuyasha,* all faves in *manga* and *animé* (Takahasi was 21 when she first published *Urusei Yatsura.* It sold 22 million copies). Takahashi is rumoured to be one of the richest women in Japan. As well as the 100s of TV shows, there are eleven Original Video Animations, and six features of *Urusei Yatsura.*

If you come to the two *Urusei Yatsura* movies that Mamoru Oshii helmed after seeing the *Ghost In the Shell* movies (*Urusei Yatsura: Only You,* 1983, and *Urusei Yatsura 2: Beautiful Dreamer,* 1984), you will be in for a surprise: *Urusei Yatsura* is a comedy, very cartoony and OTT, very sunny and lively, with a comic-romantic plot, alien babes wearing tiger-stripe bikinis, goofy teenagers, adolescent angst and jealousies – all very, *very* different from the solemn, grey, hi-tech world of the *Ghost In the Shell* movies. *Urusei Yatsura* is charmingly fluffy and light-hearted, a high school comedy of teen love and romance. The *Urusei Yatsura* TV series has been described as 'one of the most enduringly popular animated comedy series of all time'.[21]

At the heart of the first *Urusei Yatsura* movie is Ataru Moroboshi, the lazy, unlikeable high school doofus ('the world's unluckiest teenager'), who somehow has alien girlfriends fighting over him (human guys and witch/ alien/ demon girlfriends, often in harem scenarios, are a recurring trope in the Japanese media – *Oh! My Goddess* is a well-known example, and *Heaven's Lost Property* is by far the funniest – a masterpiece of comedy).

Ataru is a jerk, but the girls lerve him. Lum, his current, hopelessly devoted girlfriend (and also an alien (a *yokai*, a Japanese demon),[22] and a babbe in a bikini), is determined to protect Ataru from another alien-babe, Elle, who's come to claim Ataru for herself, and to whisk him back to her home planet of Elle. With its girls in bikinis and goofy, useless, high school-age guys, *Urusei Yatsura* is like *Barbarella* for teens.

Around the central erotic-comic triangle in *Urusei Yatsura,* writers Tomoko Jonparu and Mamoru Oshii place a large retinue of secondary charas, and altho' there are spaceships and chases and aliens, the usual paraphernalia of science fiction, *Urusei Yatsura* is essentially a teen comedy that might play equally as well set in a high school or a Shinjuku café.

(The influence of *Bewitched* and *I Dream of Jeannie* on the Japanese 'magical girl' genre is substantial. Lum cries 'darrrling!' – her catch-phrase is derived from Elizabeth Montgomery in *Bewitched.* It's used throughout the *Urusei Yatsura* movies: it's Lum's battle-cry as well as her declaration of love).

Alien babe Lum is the heart of the *Urusei Yatsura* series, and when she's not around the *Urusei Yatsura* movies lose much of their

---

21 T. Ledoux, 1997, 62.
22 There are all sorts of gods and demons (*oni, yokai*) in Japanese religion and spirituality, and they often crop up in *manga* and *animé* (often in updated or contemporary dress): *Oh! My Goddess, Urusei Yatsura, Ogre Slayer, Legend of the Overfiend, Akira, Vampire Princess Miyu, Negima: Magister Negi Magi* and most of the movies of Hayao Miyazaki contain many demons and spirits.

entertainment value. The lithe figure of Lum in her tiger-stripe bikini is one of the classic images of contemporary Japanese *manga*. But it's also very light-hearted and wispy – the *Urusei Yatsura* series is not about seething passions but irritating jealousies and desires shaped like little, pink hearts.

The point, I guess, is that Ataru Moroboshi *doesn't* deserve all of this devotion from Lum and the alien babes in *Urusei Yatsura* (and Lum is only interested in him). Because he is *such* a loser. For instance, he'll have Lum floating in the air right next to him, but he'll still hit on another girl. You just don't do that when a super-babe with superpowers is right next to you! But Ataru doesn't learn, and thinks with his libido all the time.

Trish Ledoux and Doug Ranny sum up the appeal of Ataru in *The Complete Anime Guide* (we can see why Lum is appealing):

> By presenting Ataru as a loser among losers, not necessarily a bad person but definitely one who can't seem to help making all the wrong choices, Takahashi creates a story which is touching and somehow resonant to anyone who's ever wished for an attractive, unconditionally loving mate to appear from out of nowhere and change their life forever. (63)

In the *manga*, author Rumiko Takahashi gets a *lot* of mileage out of the romantic triangle between Ataru and the two women in his life: Lum and Shinobu. All three are subject to intense jealousies, and will fly off the handle at any opportunity. Altho' Ataru has apparently 'married' Lum, Shinobu seems to regard her and Ataru as still a couple. So Shinobu and Lum are frequently depicted snarling at each other, with their mouths grimacing like vampires (both Lum and Shinobu make formidable enemies!).

Meanwhile, Ataru's chums are either intrigued or bemused or irritated by their friend: Ataru remains a doofus in the *manga*. His family don't quite know what to make of Lum, either.

Each chapter in the *Urusei Yatsura manga* focusses on a single issue, very much like a TV sit-com show, which will typically present a problem to be solved in each episode. The scenarios are also like those in sit-coms, so that the comparison btn *manga* and popular television (which commentators such as Fred Schodt suggest) is completely right: a *manga* like *Urusei Yatsura* isn't like Western comicbooks, or graphic novels, or literature: it really is like a TV show. It's dumb-but-fun, it's utterly undemanding (it asks nothing more of you than you zip thru the story as light-hearted entertainment. It's not meant to be 'meaningful', or 'serious', or even – God forbid! – 'political'.)

Urusei Yatsura is pure *manga* fluff, a comic like candy, It's silly, it's superficial: yet don't let the apparent 'simplicity' or 'ease' of *Urusei Yatsura* deceive you: this is accomplished storytelling, by someone who knows every cliché of the romantic comedy format, and knows how to exploit them. And it is amusing seeing how the characters work themselves up into ridiculous misunderstandings and hysterical outbursts. Yes, *Urusei Yatsura* is predictable – the ending of each installment is always a foregone conclusion. We know where the story is going every time – and that, as with popular television, is part of its appeal (TV thrives on being predictable, on repeating the same piffle hour after hour. And that's a *big* reason why audiences tune in for an average of four hours a day in the Western world).

Similarly, the artwork by Rumiko Takahashi in *Urusei Yatsura* is functional and direct: it does the job, it delivers the comedy and the silly situations. It doesn't need (and we don't want it to be) clever and show-offy and detailed.

The animation in *Urusei Yatsura: Remember My Love* is broad and 'cartoony': that is, it's more like slapstick and physical comedy, with characters using out-size expressions and gestures. It's easy to see why Rumiko Takahashi's stories work well as both *manga* and *animé*: this sort of sex comedy is an area that *manga* delivers so well (*Love Hina* by Ken Akamatsu, 1998-2001, and *To Love Ru* by Hasemi Saki and Kentaro Yabuki, 2006-2009, are more recent, brilliant examples). You're orchestrating powerful erotic passions but in a social context of teenage insecurity, anxiety, and self-consciousness, where embarrassments, mis-understandings, incorrect perceptions and seething jealousies erupt all the time.

The social context of these stories of teen love and teen anxiety is crucial: these stories only work in social settings like schools and colleges and boarding houses and universities and workplaces and teams. Put the two or three lovers in a remote village, with only a grizzled, old coot and a wizened aunt for company, and you've got a scenario that'll easily slip into a Thomas Hardy rural romance which soon becomes melodrama or even tragedy.

ANGEL'S EGG

Is it rubbish? Is it art? Is it something? Or not really anything much at all? Is it worth talking about? Is it worth seeing? (Or has the movie laid an egg?).

Co-produced by Hayao Miyazaki's[23] regular producer, Toshio Suzuki, *Angel's Egg* (*Tenshi no Tamago*, 1985) was an unusual feature movie of 80 minutes.[24] Written by Mamoru Oshii and Yoshitaka Amano, produced by Hiroshi Hasegawa, Masao Kobayashi, Mitsunori Miura and Yutaka Wada for Studio Deen/ Tokuma Shoten/ Tokuma Japan, with

23 At this time, Mamoru Oshii was working with Miyazaki and Toshio Suzuki on an abandoned film project called *Anchor.*
24 Other sources say 71 minutes. Either length is still almost unendurable.

music by Yuhiro Kanno, animation by Yasuhiro Yukara, and design by Yoshitaka Amano, *Angel's Egg* comes across initially as a mood piece, a style piece, a let's-see-how-many-weird-backgrounds-we-can-create piece. It's twenty-some minutes before there's any dialogue, or any kind of meeting btn two characters. Instead, there are pink-and-purple-and-grey moody skies, shots of ripples in water, and images of an empty city street (echoes of the Italian painter Giorgio de Chirico). The town is Olde Worlde European, a dreamscape out of Ingmar Bergman and Tim Burton. Bizarre machinery stands gaunt against gloomy skies like the paintings of Yves Tanguy.

Angel's Egg is a picture that seems designed to travel to film festivals and wow the audiences with its earnest weirdness. It exudes artiness and self-consciousness in every frame. Some of it *is* beautiful. But it's a niche audience picture – a film for people who like looking at twelve very similar shots of ripples in water. For people who stare out of the window for, like, hours. For people who mope and loon about. For Goths. For 'emos'. For people who haunt cemeteries in the rain wearing long, black coats while listening to Joy Division, the Cure and Muse.

At the centre of *Angel's Egg* is a young Girl with long, blonde hair and a perpetual scowl/ frown (she resembles, at times, Mamoru Oshii himself! – minus the hair!). She's Alice in this Surrealist, *Alice's Adventures In Wonderland* sort of movie. But she's an Alice who doesn't meet a Cheshire Cat, a Mad Hatter or a White Rabbit (nothing as lively as that!): instead, she encounters a young man (who matches her in the sullen, staring-at-the-camera stakes). Two Sullens, made for each other. (She covets a large egg, which she keeps safe under her dress, as you do, and he carries a large, Christian cross, as you might well do in this sort of movie).

Nobody laughs, nobody smiles: there's a Samuel Beckettian atmosphere of desperation in *Angel's Egg*. Claustrophobia. Perpetual night. No sun. No moon. No stars. The skies're always filled with grey clouds, yet the buildings and squares in the town are lit with a bright, low level light (creating sharp shadows).

The Mamoru Oshii Curse (morose, silent staring) is allowed to infect the two main characters in *Angel's Egg*, so there is nothing they can do except to stare moodily at the viewer, or at the night sky, or at nothing in particular. As Samuel Beckett might put it, *empty eyes staring emptily, grey world, all the greys, void alone, endless nothingness, go void, omit.*

Trouble is, the film hasn't 'earned' the right to do that, so to speak – because there's no subtext, and no emotion in this bleak, blank movie. Even Ingmar Bergman or Carl-Theodor Dreyer give the viewer a few scraps to cling onto – a lonely vicar in a white-washed church interior in rural Sweden, say (Bergman)... or a windswept sand dune with long, marram grass and a bitter sky (Dreyer)... But it's better'n nothing!

In *Angel's Egg*, the viewer isn't offered any scraps to hang onto, and has to find their solace, their humanity, their joy elsewhere (i.e., primarily in the music). Occasionally something will 'happen' in *Angel's Egg* – a convoy of military trucks-'n'-guns trundles by (as if we're in WW2 Europe), or men emerge from the shadows (wearing suits and cloth caps), and wielding harpoons which they hurl (ineffectively) at enormous fish swimming as shadows along the buildings and the streets. (Images of more desperation, more pointless behaviour. Is this an oblique criticism of Japan's huge whaling industry?).

Sometimes, it seems as if the music (by Yoshihiro Kanno) is shoring up *Angel's Egg*: clearly the extraordinary score contributes hugely to this 1985 picture. As there are only minimal sound effects, the music is the main sound element in *Angel's Egg*. And yet it doesn't always gel with the images, or help the images, or the images don't help or work with the music. Partly because too many of the shots are lifeless. There's no life or energy in some of the shots in *Angel's Egg*.

The music also jars in *Angel's Egg*, as if it comes from a classical music concert taking place down the road. It's not part of this movie. Because the shots are often lacking energy, the movie relies on the music to provide the dramatic juice. But the continuity between the music and the imagery is fragmentary, inconclusive, and awkward (better, then, to use those fades to black and extend them to five minutes long. So we're just listening to the score, and aren't bothered by another shot of – wow! – a baroque, shadowy interior, or the hair of the Girl blowin' in the breeze).

For the Mamoru Oshii followers, there are Christian motifs, plenty of symbolism, and allusions (the *Bible* is solemnly quoted at length by the Boy, in his longest speech in *Angel's Egg*; and the Girl listens without vomiting). The Boy carries a crucifix.

Angel's Egg commits one of the common mistakes of student movies: it has numerous scenes of characters simply walking. Where? Why? Who cares? – so we have scenes where the Girl and/ or the Boy wander thru the streets of the deserted city at night. And they walk on... and then they walk on some more. If you like watching shots of people walking for no particular reason, going nowhere in particular, *Angel's Egg* is the movie for you!

Towards the end of *Angel's Egg*, the happy band of filmmakers have said all they want to say, shown all they want to show, and exploited the warbling, choral cues of Y. Kanno as much as they can. So they run out of ideas. Not uncommon, after all, in many a movie or artwork.

For instance, there's a shot that last *two and a half minutes*: it's a long shot of the Girl and the youth in a large room, with a fire burning nearby. She's asleep. He sits and watches (as he always does). Two and a half minutes is an *eternity* in animation, where every frame counts. For a shot where nothing happens, a lifeless, boring shot, it's unbearable for some viewers, no doubt.

So there's a flood in the city. So what? So the youth breaks the egg and it's empty. So what? So the Girl wakes, finds the smashed egg, and screams. So what? So the youth abandons the Girl and ambles to the coast. So what? So the youth is washed by waves. So what? So there's a strange circular thingie rising from the ocean. So what? So now the Girl appears to be one of the stone statuary arranged in rows on the thingie. So what?

In sum, *Angel's Egg* would be in any list of Top Ten Pretentious Animated Movies. Or the Top Ten Worst *Anime* Movies. It really is appalling.

PATLABOR

Mamoru Oshii was one of the directors of the *Patlabor* (*Kido Keisatsu Patoreiba*, a.k.a., *Mobile Police Patlabor*) animated TV series (Nippon TV, 1989), along with Naoyuki Yoshinaga, Fumihiko Takayama, and Yasunori Urata. Oshii also directed the two *Patlabor* movies (1990 and 1993). There is plenty of thematic crossover between *Patlabor* and Masamune Shirow's *Appleseed* and *Dominion: Tank Police*. And *Patlabor* was a significant forerunner of *Ghost In the Shell* in many ways, including many artists in the production team who went on to work on the *Ghost In the Shell* movies and TV series.

The *Patlabor* anime TV series was Mamoru Oshii's first big success. *Patlabor* began life as an Original Video Animation series (1987-88), then a TV series in 1989, and two movies (directed by Oshii), and more Original Video Animations in 1990-92. A third *Patlabor* movie appeared in 2001 (*WXIII*, dir. Fumihiko Takayama). Further entries in the franchise included the usual updates/ reboots, such as: *Patlabor Minimum* (a.k.a. *Minipato*) in 2002, a live-action version as a series and a movie in 2014-15, and a *Patlabor* reboot in 2016.

The original *Patlabor* TV series was seven 30-minute episodes; it was later animated as a series of 47 episodes for television, and 16 episodes for video. Headgear (a collective of fans whose chief members were Oshii and writer Kazunori Ito),[25] produced *Patlabor* (the *manga* based on the show was written and drawn by founder member Masami Yuki. The *manga* of *Patlabor* appeared in *Shonen Sunday* in 1988). There are also video games, novels, and parodies.

Also in the production of *Patlabor* were Kazunori Ito, screenwriter, Masami Yuki, *manga* artist, Yutaka Izubuchi, mechanical designer, and Akemi Takada, character designer.

Patlabor = *Patrol Labor*, the name for the mobile suits which the police use in a futuristic Tokyo. The S.V. 2 team in *Patlabor* are part of the Mobile Police Unit in Tokyo.

The comedy and humour in the *Patlabor* TV series is funnier and broader than in the two *Patlabor* movies, but they are all recognizably from the same source.[26] As in many of the finest *anime*, it's the evocation of the *team*, and how they interact, that provides much of the charm of this

---

25 Oshii, Yuki, Izubuchi, Takada and Ito were collectively known as Headgear.
26 There were some humorous send-ups of *Patlabor*, short animations called *Minipato*.

late 1980s TV show, as well as the obvious elements like the action and the *mecha*. In fact, as anyone knows who watches a lot of *animé* shows, the action usually occurs in the final five minutes: three-quarters of many shows is taken up with talk, humour, relationships, interactions (and exposition).

It may be a hi-tech, futuristic show about giant power suits, but *Patlabor* also explores Japanese folklore and ghost stories. There are monsters that lurk in the deeps of Tokyo Bay, there are ghosts that come back to haunt the division's complex, and there are mysteries that need solving. Meanwhile, the Patlabor team are as superstitious and wary as anybody in *animé*.

One of the finest stories in the *Patlabor* TV series takes place across two episodes, evoking a siege and civil war scenario, as a bunch of villains use Japan's Self Defence Forces to stage a coup. This looks forward to the second *Ghost In the Shell* series.

❖

PATLABOR 1.

The *Patlabor* (*Kido Keisatsu Patoreiba*) movies are stupendous pieces of animation in the classic *animé* action-adventure style: as Helen McCarthy and Jonathan Clements put it, the team who made *Patlabor* is probably 'the finest assembly of talents in modern *animé*, rivalled only by Hayao Miyazaki's cohorts at Studio Ghibli and the erratic Gainax collective' (294).

For the first *Patlabor* movie, the art direction was by the amazing Hiromasa Ogura (*Wings of Honneamise, Ninja Scroll, Ghost In the Shell*), Akemi Takada was animation director, Kazunori Ito was the writer, the concept was by Masami Yuki, and animation production was by Studio Deen.

It's giant robots (and mobile suits) again in *Patlabor*, with the police force and construction industry using them, and it's computers and viruses, and there's a lone terrorist-scientist who's going to mess everything up with an apocalyptic rampage of out-of-control robots laying waste to Tokyo (in the first *Patlabor* flick). So it's a riff on *Appleseed* by Masamune Shirow, and far more successful than the 1998 *animé* version of *Appleseed*.

Computers and operating systems, hardware and software, information systems, hacking and the like are all familiar elements in modern *animé*, and would lead directly on to Mamoru Oshii's work as director on the *Ghost In the Shell* movies.

But there're a host of elements that make *Patlabor* so enjoyable. For a start, *incredible action*: boy, can this animation team deliver action! And spectacle and visuals – vast vistas stuffed with intricate detail, and inventive designs, and hardware and machines to spare.

And plenty of atmosphere – once again in movies directed by Mamoru Oshii, there are lengthy interludes of pure visual poetry accompanied by a haunting percussive score (courtesy of Oshii's regular composer Kenji Kawai). Slabs of architecture slide across the screen, blocks of light and colour, seedy backwaters, dusty rooms lit by shafts of sunlight, sunny, empty canals (always with the water). Bird cages hanging from a ceiling. (The pretext for these poetic interludes were a couple of gumshoes on the trail of a missing scientist, but that's a mere sideshow for repeated dialogueless sequences which celebrate the backwaters and unremarkable corners of the Grand City of *Anime*, Tokyo. This is where the background artists (Hiromasa Ogura and Shuichi Hirata) shine, as they evoke the shabby, paint-peeling back alleys and hidden piazzas of Tokyo).

And there's a welter of visual effects animation, particularly in the stunning action climax of *Patlabor 1*, on a colossal platform (dubbed 'the Ark') in Tokyo Bay that's falling to pieces while giant robots battle it out. And it's right in the middle of a typhoon that ripping everything to shreds, with wind and rain and cloud effects tumbling thru the frame.

Of course, *Patlabor* being another police movie, there are numerous cop show genre elements, such as encounters with demanding bosses, repercussions from political manœuvrings, office and locker room camaraderie, investigations on foot and by computer, discussions of the case in progress, and the hero (Azuma) being sent on leave against his wishes.

But what really nails *Patlabor* as a classic is the group of misfits that Mamoru Oshii and the scriptwriters (Kazunori Ito and Michiko Yokote) and the Headgear group have developed from the TV series: they are grouped together as a Mobile Police unit: Azuma Shinohara, the techie millionaire's son, angry, with a chip on his shoulder, but determined to do well; the captain, Kiichi Goto, icy cool, middle-aged and pragmatic; his colleague, strait-laced, prim Shinobu Nagumo (and their prickly relationship and on-off romance); gentle giant Hiromi; the techhead Kanuka Clancy (a Japanese-American); the belligerent, macho Ota (who's always up for action); and the most appealing character, sweet, sensitive, red-haired Noah Izumi, a robot pilot.

The comedy and joshing among this group of oddballs takes up much more of *Patlabor* than one might think in an action-adventure *anime* TV series; but Mamoru Oshii is especially good at ensemble drama, at delineating quirky, goofy characters and bringing out how they interact. Alaso, this side of Oshii's works declines in his later career.

And *Patlabor* also contains some of Mamoru Oshii's grander themes – there are disquisitions on modern Tokyo, on the past, on how the city (and modern Japan) re-makes itself, on the endless expansion of advanced capitalism (this Tokyo is expanding into the ocean, reclaiming land or creating land, to be covered with homes), of the over-reliance of humans on technology, of the ambiguous relationship that people have with machines, and how technology creates isolation and distance as well as ease and luxury. (Oshii also weaves in his beloved Biblical references, to Yahweh, Noah, the Ark, the Tower of Babel, etc).

Patlabor is high quality *anime* on every level, in every department. The level of artistry on screen is staggering, way beyond what one might expect. The movies have a bigger budget than the TV shows and can cram the frame with ever-more detailed cityscapes and *mecha* and the paraphernalia of everyday life (Mamoru Oshii and Headgear's spaces always looked lived in and used). These are shows and movies to be seen at least twice.

There's plenty of talk in *Patlabor 1*, as characters ruminate sometimes for the sake of ruminating. But when the finale arrives, it is an all-out, giant spectacle, filled with wonderful gags, moments of suspense, and visceral, metal-on-metal action. Indeed, the finale of *Patlabor* is almost a separate movie, seeming to come out of nowhere with high speed hurricanes, power suits thundering down dark corridors lit by revolving red alarm lamps (more nods to *Alien*), and slamming action. It's really gripping, stops-all-out spectacle, and hugely enjoyable.

PATLABOR 2.

Patlabor 2 (1993) was more of the same – but not necessarily better. The character design (and character animation) – by Akemi Takeda and Masami Yuki – was less convincing, the interaction between the mobile police team far less enjoyable, and the whole thing was more downbeat (following a trend in Mamoru Oshii's cinema, it seemed).[27] Many of Oshii's characters spend whole scenes looking down sadly at the floor, or lost in contemplative trances. Fine, that's part of the Oshiian style, but in *Patlabor 2* that introspection attained near-depression levels (turning into the Mamoru Oshii Curse). It would be revisited big time in the two *Ghost In the Shell* movies of course (and even more so in the second *Ghost* movie). As would the unspoken and unreciprocated romance between Kiichi Goto and Shinobu Nagumo: this is the forerunner of the Major and Batou romance (or near-romance) in the *Ghost In the Shell* movies.

The static, depressive, melancholy scenes work OK on a first viewing, but on repeated viewings they become irritating. This is *animation*, guys! Making stuff *move*! It's as if the filmmakers attempted to deliberately subvert the tendency in most filmmaking to have things move.

But when *Patlabor 2* got going, boy, it was *incredible*. For *animé* action and spectacle, Mamoru Oshii and Headgear can be placed, at its finest, alongside Hayao Miyazaki, Katsuhiro Otomo, Shoji Kawamori, Noriyuki Abe and Isao Takahata; the filmmakers' sense of action can be just as astonishing. The density of the imagery, the intricacy of the details and the machinery, the flamboyance of the staging and layouts is superb.

The incredible detail in Japanese *animé* recalls Orson Welles' statement: get the details right, and the big things take care of themselves (all aspects of the design in *Patlabor 2* are impressive, with the art direction and the background art being especially distinctive – art dir. was Hiromasa Ogura, with background art by Kai, Arai, Kuroda *et al*). But the detail in the finest Japanese *animé* shows and movies goes beyond obsessive; the filmmakers devour whole textbooks full of research

27 The technical design team for *Patlabor 2* was dubbed 'one of the most awesome mecha teams in anime' by Helen McCarthy – because Shoji Kawamori and Hajime Katoki (*Gundam*) had joined *mecha* designer Yutaka Izunichi.

material, and transform it, and ladle it into their TV shows using giant ice cream scoops.

The Complete Anime Guide called the second *Patlabor* movie:

> Mamoru Oshii's masterpiece, and standing in the narrow circle of the very best anime films ever made... a brilliant, beautiful film visually, with realistic character design by Takada, and the dream-like landscape of the narrative, set in a winter Tokyo, from the master hand of art director Hiromasa Ogura.[28]

Stylistically, *Patlabor 2* was a *tour-de-force* of multi-layered animation: many scenes had heads-up displays and radar information superimposed over them; the emphasis on technology was everywhere (*Patlabor 2* is a movie of screens and data, of computers and monitors and video tapes); surveillance is all-pervasive, with cameras recording every aspect of contemporary, Japanese life; cars race along freeways glowing with lights at night;[29] and the ærial views of downtown, nighttime Tokyo were stupendous (and looked directly towards the portrayal of Newport City in the *Ghost In the Shell* movie of two years later).

Especially fine is the mobilization sequence in *Patlabor 2*, as the military machine goes into action, pitting the police against the Japan Self Defence Force, with the general public stuck in the middle.

The glossy, saturated animation in *Patlabor 2* overshadowed the human characters, who at times seemed lost in a hi-tech realm of the imagination (with the humans, as often in Mamoru Oshii's work, coming over as more robotic than the robots!).

Patlabor 2 is more a Mamoru Oshii movie than the first *Patlabor* outing. Or rather, Oshii's stamp is more easily discernible, as his later cinematic style developed. Numerous Oshiian concerns were featured in *Patlabor 2*: such as: the disquisitions on politics; the downbeat atmosphere; the introspective, uncommunicative characters; the use of symbols like animals (birds, fish, more birds,[30] etc); the fetishization of *mecha* (and of cars, and of the futuristic city); the function of the military and the Japan Self Defence Force in modern, Japanese society; and the role of technology and science in the contemporary era. (The background plot has a Japan Self Defence Force agent, Arakawa, secretly meeting with Kiichi Goto to tell him about the disgruntled businessman whose Patlabors had failed a test, who is undertaking terrorist acts; there's an emotional link, too: Arakawa was Shinobu's lover).

Sadly, the humorous and entertaining interactions among the cop team of the *Patlabor* TV series and the *manga* were hardly to be seen in *Patlabor 2* (it contains very few intentionally comic moments, for instance). Meanwhile, the lovely Noah Izumi took something of a backseat to the two middle-aged characters brought to the foreground: Kiichi Goto and

---

28 T. Ledoux, 1997, 133-4.
29 Yet there are daytime scenes where the sky is allowed to become nothing but white. No clouds, just flat, overcast days.
30 The filmmakers seem to have asked themselves, can we squeeze in some more symbolic birds in more shots?

Shinobu Nagumo (who also formed the usual unspoken, undemonstrative, super-repressed erotic relationship in the cinema of Mamoru Oshii).

There's a scene in *Patlabor 2* where Goto and Shinobu have escaped from government minders after being arrested; Tokyo is being bombed to bits by military helicopters; yet Goto and Shinobu sit in a car speeding thru the capital looking immobile and sullen as if they've just returned from burying their seventh cat in a rainy graveyard. You just want to slap them! Awful, awful, adolescent introspection and moroseness: the more I see of the work of Mamoru Oshii, the more his penchant for sad, lifeless, non- expressiveness in the characters becomes irksome and immature.

Yet again it was Tokyo in potential disarray from a disaffected former employee turned terrorist in *Patlabor 2*. Yet again, there was more quiet philosophizing about the nature of war, about the military and the police, about politics and political corruption, about Japan's uneasy relationship with the U.S.A. All par for the course with a Mamoru Oshii-directed movie, but *Patlabor 2* did seem unnecessarily talky, or the talk wended on too long (there are lengthy dialogue scenes in cars, an Oshii speciality, where pages of exposition are hurled at the audience under the guise of slick visuals of sliding backgrounds, winking red lights, and characters looming into close-up in rear-view mirrors. Or just as often, filmed from the back and below). In cars, and in a aquarium, and on telephones, and in voiceover on top of yet more pretty imagery of Tokyo at night, they talk.

Self-indulgent? Over-written? Yes – *Patlabor 2* is ridiculously over-cooked, from a script point-of-view. And the trouble is that some of the way too lengthy speeches become indigestible. They are like lectures being delivered by philosophy students at a political meeting in an after-school club in Tokyo. And sometimes with the camera on someone's face who's listening, while the speaker's is out of frame.

Where was the red pencil? the scissors? (the gun?!), when the producers met the writers and the director. Where was the executive producer in all this, who could've said NO to the filmmakers: *no*, we're not going to have *five* scenes of long, rambling political and philosophical discussions!

However, if you zone out of the pompous, political prattle about war and peace in contemporary Japan in *Patlabor 2*, you will see some remarkable animation. Not of action, not of storytelling, not of characterization, not of theme or issue, but purely animation-as-animation, which uses places and landscapes as its jumping-off point. Beautiful images slide over the screen, one after another: harbour views with red flashing lights of buoys and passing ships; distant skylines of skyscrapers; a slow drift past an abandoned shipworks... Especially fine is the evocation of a snowbound city, with piles of snow and drifting flakes in every image in the third act of *Patlabor 2*. A bunch of folk in the production team have gone to out-of-the-way corners of Tokyo Bay and taken 100s of photographs for reference (most of the images in the pretentious political speeches are essentially static images with partial animation).

So the pacing of *Patlabor 2* is cock-eyed, with too much of the third act stmbling back into introspection and interlude. Just when a *mecha*-heavy political thriller in Japanese animation would be ramping up to wall-to-wall action, *Patlabor 2* slows down again. It's a mistake, because the theme of war in an advanced capitalist society such as Japan has already been stated a few times. To keep going back to combining a studenty lecture on political theory with a hi-tech thriller doesn't work (and some of theses are simply banal, such as: 'war is always surreal'. *Ack!*).

The terrorism plot in *Patlabor 2* remains completely up-to-date: with the blowing up of the Bay Bridge halfway thru the first act of *Patlabor 2*, the spectre of terrorism is raised once again. Terrorism is a theme that has been used in most versions of the *Ghost In the Shell* world, in any media, and it remains as disturbing as ever (but even more so in the wake of 9/11).

That the North American military is implicated in the acts of terrorism (though unwittingly) further exacerbates the political aspects of the controversial issue in *Patlabor 2*. So that the troubled relations between Japan and the U.S.A. are once again brought into the foreground, with a focus on the military aspects (there is some talk of Japan's military capabilities, including references to historical events where Japan's defensive abilities were compromised).

JIN-ROH

Jin-Roh: The Wolf Brigade (*Jinro*, Hiroyuki Okiura, 2000) was scripted by Mamoru Oshii from his *Kerboros* saga *manga*. A deadly serious, prestige animation set in an alternative Japan of the 1950s, where Germany won the war, it employed elements from the famous *Little Red Riding Hood* fairy tale to tell the story of two doomed lovers caught in the political struggle between two rival government/ political/ military factions.

Like some of Mamoru Oshii's other movies as director, there is a distinctly European, and European New Wave, feel to *Jin-Roh:* the solemn, desperate mood evokes the cinema of Robert Bresson and Carl-Theodor Dreyer, while the chases in the sewers and the political machinations recalled the famous, Polish *Kanal* trilogy of the late 1950s.

The downbeat atmosphere of *Jin-Roh* also recalled the more serious movies of Kenji Mizoguchi and Yasujiro Ozu, two of Japan's masters of introspective, domestic cinema. Unfortunately, *Jin-Roh* didn't have an ounce of Mizoguchi's or Ozu's compassion, their humanity, their feeling for people and difficult situations. And referring to the *Ashes and Diamonds* trilogy makes *Jin-Roh* sound a lot more compelling than it actually is.

While many aspects of *Jin-Roh* were impressive (the settings, the layouts, the action, and some of the concepts), the 2000 movie was wrecked by the utterly dull, po-faced, mute characterizations of the two doomed lovers, Fuse Kazuki (Uoshikatsu Fujiki) and Kei Amemiya (Sumi Mutou), and the lifelessness and dopiness of their relationship. As with *The Sky Crawlers* and *Angel's Egg*, you don't care a damn about these ditzy, useless people, or their situation. You don't care that a young woman dies at the beginning and at the end of the piece (supposedly embodying the waste of war and the causalities of conspiracy), you don't care that Kazuki finds himself in a moral and political fix… you just don't care about anything the filmmakers are doing because the fundamentals of storytelling have been ditched.

Fuse Kazuki just sits there, for minute after minute in *Jin-Roh*, or he stands there, with his hands in his pockets – he's just wandered in from a failed audition for an amateur stage production in a suburb of Kobe for an adaptation of Existentialist writers Albert Camus or Knut Hamsun or Jean-Paul Sartre (talk about 'nausea'! *Jin-Roh* really does make you feel sick!). Meanwhile, Kei Amemiya, in her weedy, feeble way, tries to make conversation, and something happen.

Something indeed seems to have gone wrong with Production I.G. in 1999 and 2000, because two of their most important works, *Jin-Roh: The Boring Brigade* and *Blood: the Crappy Vampire*, come over like suicide notes: there are so many slow, downbeat moments in amongst dirty, drab colours (*Ghost In the Shell: Stand Alone Complex* retained some of the same colouration). These are *anime* that someone might watch before stepping off a Shinjuku skyscraper to their death. (At least Ingmar Bergman's movies, often cited as manic depressive and suicidal, have gorgeous people like Harriet Andersson, Liv Ullmann and Ingrid Thulin to look at! Oh yes, and astonishing performance. And brilliant storytelling. Yes, and probably finest scripts ever written for the screen).

Jin-Roh: The Wolf Brigade lacks, for instance, an all-important emotional and psychological catharsis. So that Kei Amemiya's death at the end is only pathetic, having no meaning and no value. Erwan Higuinen called *Jin-Roh* 'a profound and fundamentally pessimistic interrogation of identity, subjectivity and otherness'.[31]

No: it's rubbish.[32]

I reckon that Production I.G. should've made another movie at the same time, using the visual, backgrounds and research elements of *Jin-Roh: The Wolf Brigade*: so those lovely backgrounds of 1950s Tokyo (which are the best bit of the show), could've been employed for the settings of a completely different story. A time travel comedy, say, or a sweet, tender family adventure in the manner of *My Neighbor Totoro*.

Yes, it's unfair to mention what for many is still the finest *anime* ever made – *My Neighbor Totoro* – in conjunction with *Jin-Roh*, which's a car

31 In C. Chatrian, 105.
32 Brian Camp (in *Zettai*) also drew attention to the unsatisfying script: 'the basic story line could be pared down to its strict narrative elements and be adapted into a very good episode of *Ghost In the Shell: Stand Alone Complex*, but it wouldn't add up to much more than that' (175).

crash of a movie. And that, considering the talents involved, is very sad. (Some of the team who worked on *Jin-Roh: The Wolf Brigade* went on to contribute to *Ghost In the Shell: Stand Alone Complex* – most notably Kenji Kamiyama, here the animation director).

AVALON

Avalon (*Avaron*, a.k.a. *Gate To Avalon*, 2001) was a Japanese (and part-Polish) production about video games. It is a truly dreadful film. Wait, surely a movie about shoot-em-up video games, complete with guns and tanks and all, can't possibly be boring? This one is!

Avalon was prod. by Shigeru Watanabe, Atsushi Kubo, Tetsu Kayama, Naoyuki Tohya and Toru Shiobara, for Dentsu/ Nippon Herald/ Media Factory/ Bandai Visual/ Deiz, wr. by Kazunori Ito, music by Kenji Kawai (of course), and featured Malgorzata Foremniak, Dariusz Biskupski, Wladyslaw Kowalski, Jerzy Gudejko, and Bartek Swiderski in the cast. Released Jan 20, 2001. 106 mins (106 *very* long minutes).

M. Oshii is usually emphasized in film criticism of *Avalon*, because he's the most well-known name here (none of the actors are names in Western or Japanese cinema). But it was Kazunori Ito who wrote *Avalon*.

Being a film about video games and virtual reality, *Avalon* evoked the usual sliding between 'reality' and 'virtual reality' of Japanese pop culture – between the 'real world' and the 'video game world', how the two affect each other, etc (as in *animé* such as *.Hack, Gantz* and *Sakura Wars*).

Is the video game in *Avalon* about forming a pop idol band? Is it about how to win in the *pachinko* parlours? Is it a step-by-step guide to working in the animation industry in Japan? Of course not! It's a *war game*, folks! Well, *duh*!

And a war-based video game means the filmmakers can stage scenes involving all of the toys and scenarios that boys who refuse to grow up adore: land battles, tanks, helicopters, machine guns, soldiers, snipers, and *ronin* (lone warriors). Thus, *Avalon* opens, as *Garm Wars* later does, with a stops-all-out conflict featuring all of the *mecha* that the filmmakers could get their hands on (and anything that couldn't be rustled up in Eastern Europa could be added later, back in Nihon, using – what else? – computers).

An intriguing aspect of *Avalon* is that the production filmed partly in Poland, instead of Japan (locations included Wroclaw[33]). One issue was that getting hold of tanks and military hardware was easier in a former Eastern Bloc country (where invasion from the tanks of the Red Bear was

33 So this is Oshii's Andrzej Wajda movie.

a possibility for decades before the Wall came down). Thus, *Avalon* is sort of exotic with a double whammy: it's Japanese/ Asian, plus it's made in Poland, it's filmed in Polish, with a mainly Polish cast, and some Poles in the crew. (Surely the translators on set should be given a big credit, alongside the usual producers and technicians).

The budget of *Avalon* was apparently $8 million. In the Polish film industry, it could've been made for under $1 million (even at 2001 prices). The great film directors of Poland – Andrzej Wajda, Wojciech Has, Andrzej Munk, Jerzy Skolimowski, Krzysztof Zanussi, Walerian Boro-wczyk, Roman Polanski, Agnieszka Holland and Krzysztof Kieslowski – were used to working with tiny budgets (and operating under State censorship. Making films in Poland meant being part of the centralized, State-run, socialist industry, with the government administ-ering the whole film business, from production to distribution – the State owned or ran film distributors, theatres, etc).

According to David Cook in *A History of Narrative Film*, the Polish film industry in the 1980s operated on a low budget: film stock was hard to come by, so that going for more than two takes was seldom allowed, actors often worked on several films at the same time to make a living (as also in the Hong Kong film industry), and productions were turned around in 30 days because equipment was so scarce. Yet the film industry in Poland employed 30,000 people.

Poland boasts one of the richest film cultures in the world. If you want to see some really great Polish films, start with the key works of Wajda, Kieslowski, Borowczyk, Polanski, Holland, Zanussi *et al.*

٭

Avalon comes across as if a think-tank in Tokyo has put together a confection of the usual Oshiian ingredients: 1. War scenarios and *mecha*. 2. Cyber/ computer/ virtual reality. 3. European art movies. 4. Animation. And 5. Philosophical/ metaphysical musings. Or as if M. Oshii told screenwriter K. Ito that he fancied doing something about computer games and virtual reality, in the wake of *Ghost In the Shell* and *The Matrix* (released two years earlier in 1999), and Ito went away and wrote this film.

The familiar po-faced, miserable main character in a Mamoru Oshii film comes striding through the mayhem in the komputah world. Our heroine is Ash[34] (Malgorzata Foremniak), and she's told not to act: this is once agian the Antonioni-Dreyer-Bresson approach to film acting that Oshii is enslaved to. Ash barely emotes, and about the only time she smiles is when she comes home to her dawg (once again it's the faithful Oshii pooch, a basset hound). The scenes where Ash returns to her dingy, dank, dirty digs and fixes her doggie some *meshi* then has a drink was directly, shamelessly reprised in the second *Ghost In the Shell* movie.

In *Avalon*, Ash is not really a character (as often in a Mamoru Oshii picture), but a set of attributes, or a bunch of observations or political

---

34 The name Ash might be a nod to *Ashes and Diamonds* (Andrzej Wajda, 1958). Or Ash in *Alien*.

views. All we need to know is that she is the bog standard Alienated Outsider of modernist, European literature (Hamsun, Camus, Gide, Kafka, Durrell, Huxley, Huysmans, Sartre, Goethe *et al*). And she is sexually objectified: like, when she's put the virtual reality head-set on, lying down and exploring hyperspace, she's in her underwear, for no good reason. (And when she dresses, as if to hide her beauty, she's given a horrible, too-big overcoat as her regular-world costume[35]).

A lonely (but beautiful) female heroine in a computer realm playing war games (in part for real) recalls of course Motoko Kusanagi in *Ghost In the Shell*. Indeed, *Avalon* is a kind of live-action version of Masamune Shirow's *Ghostly* comic (tho' with plenty of animated elements. Like later films directed by Mamoru Oshii, such as *Garm Wars*, *Avalon* is a curious hybrid of animation and live-action footage).

Self-conscious bits of actorly business are added for Ash: Lighting a Cigarette (mandatory in any Euro-art flick), and Putting On Glasses (mandatory in any nerd movie). Yet altho' Ash is in most every scene, this is not an actor's film, nor a star vehicle, and Miss Foremniak is not encouraged to own the movie, or run with it, or do much beyond your regular mannequin acting. (This is in part Cheekbones Acting – Foremniak's immaculately chiselled cheekbones arrive in a shot five minutes before the rest of her does).

Avalon features several scenes where a character sits at a computer. Not even a superstar *animé* filmmaker can make working with computers compelling. It looks just as boring as someone doing office work, or an Office Lady typing. Computers and the digital realm took cinematic flight in *Ghost In the Shell* because the narrative context was infinitely gripping (the story was certainly much richer), and due more to Masamune Shirow's unique view of cyberspace.

Looks-wise, *Avalon* is filmed in beaten-out hues of beige and amber, a selective colour approach which is favoured in the films helmed by Mamoru Oshii. It's a bit of Andrei Tarkovsky, a bit of Andrzej Wajda, a bit of Carl-Theodor Dreyer, and quite a lot of Franz Kafka, etc (and the production design – by Barbara Nowak and Takashi Watabe – self-consciously draws on the films of Terry Gilliam, such as *Brazil* and *Twelve Monkeys*. *La Jetée* is in there, too – a 1962 short film which had partly inspired *Twelve Monkeys*).

Avalon never comes alive. Not once.

It has its admirers (such as James *Avatar* Cameron), but it's still-born. The initial concept just isn't compelling. Or maybe its time has passed: in 2001, an exploration of virtual reality and the role of komputahs in contemporary society was relevant. But now it seems like a bad TV movie.

And the way that *Avalon* is delivered – by a catatonic leading lady in that disgusting overcoat – doesn't help, either. After the exciting opening battle sequence, *Avalon* slithers into pools of murky filmmaking which

---

35 In fact, several of the costumes in *Avalon* are dodgy, even if it is meant to be the usual oppressive, Kafkaesque environment. Cost. des. was by Magdalena Biernawska-Teslawska.

amount to not much at all, and which are interminable in several sections.

For actors to just sit there, something has to happen for the audience: either you have a great actor (which Malgorzata Foremniak, bless her, is not), who can portray levels and insights (of something or other), or you have fascinating themes and issues to ruminate on, or you have a riveting dramatic situation. There has to be some connection with the viewer, some filmic juice flowing somewhere.

Avalon has none of that. In a Robert Bresson or Carl-Theodor Dreyer movie, for example, when actors stand and stare there is plenty going on to intrigue or move the audience. In films such as *The Sacrifice* or *Stalker*, helmed by Andrei Tarkovsky, many scenes feature actors standing still, but the effect gripping. In a Mamoru Oshii film, it hardly ever works. (Jean-Luc Godard talked about shots that were empty – there was nothing in them. Most of *Avalon* comprises empty shots).

As with some other Mamoru Oshii films, the most attractive element in the *Avalon* package was Kenji Kawai's music. *Avalon* is a thoroughly underwhelming outing, but we do get to a new soundtrack by Kawai-sensei (Shigeru Otake was music co-ordinator; Kawai was music producer and arranger; the choir was the Warsaw Choir). We have heard this choir and orchestra in other *animé*, of course (Polish musicians and orchestras have been used by many Japanese composers, including Yoko Kanno with the *Ghost In the Shell: Stand Alone Complex* series and Michiru Oshima with *Fullmetal Alchemist*).

The score of *Avalon* features some powerful cues: for one scene a solemn strings piece surges up, yet the scene itself is utterly banal – Ash cooks some food in her kitchen. The completely vacant images are beside the point, instantly discarded by the viewer,, because the music might accompany a tragic death scene of a hero on a battlefield.

The finale features a big concert scene, where the music is rightly allowed to dominate for part of the time. It's a Kenji Kawai sequence, featuring a live orchestra and choir on stage (it's a pity that Kawai himself wasn't the conductor!).

The finale of *Avalon* is excruciatingly humdrum. Who knew that the virtual realm of a shoot-em-up computer game could be depicted as so grey and flat and nothingy? We've already seen what seems like thousands of empty, worthless shots, but in the climax, they continue! There's a battle with a giant tank (in a warehouse/ factory setting), followed by interminable images of Ms. Foremniak drifting around nowhere in particular, followed by a city setting. A musical concert (the stand-out scene in *Avalon*) is next, and then the Big Finish, the lamest stand-off between two armed opponents you've ever seen.

The Sky Crawlers (*Suka Kurora,* 2008), produced by many of Mamoru Oshii's regular collaborators (including the Production I.G. team), and based on a novel by Hiroshi Mori, is a total failure.

Produced by Nippon Television/ D-Rights/ Chuokoron-Shinsha/ Hochi Shimbun/ Production I.G./ Hakuhodo D.Y. Media Partners/ D.N. Dream Partners/ Tokuyuki Matsutake/ Yomiuri Shimbun/ V.A.P./ Yomiuri Telecasting Corporation/ Warner Bros./ Bandai Visual (13 compannies!); producers: Tomohiko Ishi and Koji Morimoto; exec. producers: Mitsuhisa Ishikawa and Seiji Okuda; script: Chihiro Ito; char. des.: Tetsuya Mishio; music: Kenji Kawai; art dir.: Nazuo Nagai; and ani. dir: Toshihiko Nishikubo. Released Aug 2, 2008. 121 mins.

The Sky Crawlers is a very odd movie:

• the design of the main characters (by Tetsuya Nishio) is deliberately unsettling, with very peculiar eyes. These characters are more like androids than any of the robots or dolls in *Ghost In the Shell*.[36]

• very under-written characterizations, with the main character, Yuichi Kannami, a blank youth out of a Scandinavian suicide pact novel.

• the slow pace – even by Mamoru Oshii's standards, the editing (by Junichi Uematsu), crawls along. After a two-minute burst of action in the air after the credits, *The Sky Crawlers* grinds down to s-l-o-w scenes where nothing much happens. Yes, we are going to watch characters stand there and do bugger all.

• it drags on for 121 minutes!

• the script (by Chihiro Ito) is junk.

Let's remember that Mamoru Oshii is only the director. He didn't write *The Sky Crawlers* – Chihiro Ito did. He didn't write the novel, either – Hiroshi Mori did. So Oshii is not responsible for the concept, the story, the characters, the situations, and all the rest. Other people are.[37] Ditto with the designs, the animation, the photography, the editing, the sound, the music, etc. So when I attack *The Sky Crawlers*, I'm not attacking Mamoru Oshii, I'm merely saying that for one of Japan's most celebrated directors in animation, *The Sky Crawlers* is terrible.

Throughout *The Sky Clappers*, there is an atmosphere of disturbing melancholy and alienation: not one of the characters has any deep relationship with any of the others. Everything is at one remove of blankness and emptiness. Emotions are reined in to the point of catatonia (so that when the creepy boss character, Suito Kusanagi, unleashes some anger, it appears very weird – but it's not, that's normal!).

An aura of solitude and 'don't come near me' surrounds every character in this awful 2008 picture. Yeah, whatever, uhh, err, ahh, umm, errr, well, you could wheel in Albert Camus/ Knut Hamsun/ Jean-Paul

---

36 Yes, there is a reference to *Ghost In the Shell*, with the female boss character called Kusanagi.
37 But *The Sky Crawlers* is also a Mamoru Oshii movie in more obvious ways: dogs!, characters named after dogs (terriers), musical box music (by Kenji Kawai), hardware (planes), s-l-o-w contemplative montages, etc.

Sartre/ Friedrich Nietzsche, or whoever your favourite Existential, modernist philosopher is, and discuss alienation, outsiderness, solitude and all the rest in the light of modern and contemporary philosophy.

You *could* make *The Sky Trawlers* much more than it is.

I can't be bothered. Can you?

The Sky Crudders, despite its 3-D, computer-finangled skillism and gimmickry, its show-off technofetishism and glorification of planes and ærial dogfights, its high budget, is simply not worth the trouble. Luckily I only paid £3 ($4.50) for *The Sky Bawlers* from an H.M.V. store.

The Sky Crawlers is an ærial combat movie, the genre which usually focusses on World War Two (which's also the obvious historical starting-point for *The Sky Crawlers* – it is Japan fighting the Pacific War all over again, as has occurred in many *animé*). It's an air-base drama, too (like Production I.G.'s earlier *Blood: The Boring Vampire*).

The challenge with the ærial combat genre is to balance and fuse the ærial dogfight scenes and the drama on the ground. Typically, ærial combat movies go for a really soapy, cheesy melodrama (*Top Gun, Pearl Harbour, Battle of Britain, Wings*), or for some drama involving pushing the technology of flight to the limits (*The Right Stuff, 633 Squadron, The Dam Busters*).

Unfortunately, in *The Sky Crawlers* the two realms – air and ground – don't mix, and seem to come from completely different movies (Mamoru Oshii explained how the ærial scenes were all computer manufactured, in 3-D, while the earthbound scenes were in traditional, 2-D animation. Well, that wasn't quite true – the scenes on Earth were full of computer-aided elements).

The Sky Crawlers is hampered by a ground-based melodrama which's so boring and predictable it has no resonance whatsoever with anything. You'd be better off walking outside and looking up at the real sky and the real clouds.

The Sky Crawlers isn't *Macross Plus* or *Gunbuster* or *Evangelion* (if only!). Yes, there is a mystery plot, which the hero Yuichi Kannami is determined to unravel – exactly what happened with the dead pilot of his plane? What happened with creepo boss Suito Kusanagi and her lover? He won't leave the topic alone.

As in a Jean-Luc Godard flick, in *every single scene*, characters are lighting up cigarettes. Mamoru Oshii and his team want to bring back the 1960s with vengeance: they want every pause and beat in a movie to be filled with someone lighting up a cig or swigging some beer. And when they're not chugging cancer sticks or alcohol, the pilots're hanging out with the local whores – children getting laid in a brothel. (Lighting up another cigarette becomes repetitive to the point of nausea in *The Sky Crawlers,* but in a Godard movie, it works – especially when you've got the irrepressible, charismatic and key face of the Sixties, Jean-Pierre Léaud, trying to look cool by flicking a cig into his mouth. Oh, if only someone as marvellous as Léaud was in *The Sky Crawlers*!).

For once, I reckon the slowness and quietness of a Mamoru Oshii movie, the blankness and the impassiveness, and the visualness and imageness of a Mamoru Oshii movie, has totally backfired, and *The Sky Crawlers* amounts to *absolutely nothing*. It's positively Samuel Beckettian in its evocation of nothingness and nothing-happeningness (but although *The Sky Crawlers* is Oshii's *Waiting For Godot*, it has not a millionth of the wit or spikiness of Beckett's classic, 1950s play *Waiting for Godot*).

No, *The Sky Crawlers* is not Robert Bresson, not Carl-Theodor Dreyer, not Ingmar Bergman, and not Yasujiro Ozu (and certainly it isn't Jean-Luc Godard!). Those are (some of) the masters of Nothing Happening Cinema. But *The Sky Crawlers* is not like that.[38]

GARM WARS: THE LAST DRUID

Garm Wars: The Last Druid (2014) was a silly, tech-heavy fantasy adventure movie, an uneven and sometimes clunky mishmash of mediaeval/ Celtic folklore, Japanese-style *anime* action, ponderous filosofizin', and Hollywood theatrics. Culturally, *Garm Wars: The Last Druid* is a curious[39] hybrid of filmmaking styles and pop culture references, an uneasy and superficial blend of East and West, Asian and American, old and new.

Among the credits, many in the production were regulars in the Mamoru Oshii Circus,[40] including composer Kenji Kawai, Atsuki Sato, and Mitshuhisa Ishikawa. It was prod. by Makoto Asanuma, Michiru Ishikawa, Ken Nakamura, Peter Tuovi, Shin Unozawa, Nancy Welsh, Tetsu Fujimara, Toshio Suzuki, Lyse Lafontaine and Mitshuhisa Ishikawa (plus a further 8 co-/ assoc./ line producers)[41] for Bandai/ Lyla/ Nakamura/ Production I.G./ Bandai Visual, and wr. by Gen Urobuchi, Geoffrey Gunn and Mamoru Oshii. Released Oct 25, 2014. 102 mins.

The film was made in English (*American* English, that is), tho' a Japanese dub was also produced (released: May 20, 2016). It was a Canadian-Japanese co-production (with production based in the 'Hollywood of the North', Vancouver, and filming taking place in the by-now-very-familiar Canadian forests).

✻

Garm Wars: The Last Druid boasts the usual raft of Oshiian filmic motifs: dogs, red and amber colours, quirky, organic *mecha*, philosophizing, and ponderous interludes.

As a design piece, *Garm Wars: The Last Druid* has many entertaining

---

38 With those poignant pauses, Simon Richmond calls Mamoru Oshii 'the Harold Pinter of anime' (159). Maybe the Carl-Theodor Dreyer of *anime* or the Robert Bresson of *anime* is more accurate.
39 Curious only if you're *really* bored.
40 A circus where everybody is a sad clown – Mamoru Oshii was born to play a melancholy, white-faced Pierrot.
41 Does a movie like this *really* require *nineteen* film producers?!

ideas, including the eccentric costume design by Nicole Pelletier and Dango Takeda, the props and sets by David Blanchard and Ted Samuels, and the tonnage of *mecha* (concept designers included: Slav Kravchenko, Mujia Liao and Tory Miles. The *mecha* boasts an impressive array of flying machines with 'organic' forms – it's Hayao Miyazakian steam-punk achieved with shiny, digital techniques).

The evocation of ancient British/ Celtic/ European folklore and mythology in the work of Mamoru Oshii is a curious element. It pops up in *Avalon* and *Garm Wars*, for example, with talk about druids, Goddesses, magic and the sacred isle of Avalon. However, like the use of Christianity in Japanese pop culture, the Celtic-British mythopoeia isn't assimilated at anything other than a very superifical level. (It looks as if Oshii and screenwriters Ito, Urobuchi and Gunn have bought a few books by the usual suspects but not really absorbed them: Geoffrey Ashe, John and Caitlin Matthews, Mircea Eliade, Joseph Campbell, M.-L. von Franz, Monica Sjoo, Robert Graves, Marija Gimbutas, C.G. Jung, etc).

Garm Wars: The Last Druid is one of those hybrid productions which combines live-action footage with enormous amounts of digitally-aided material. If you've got a studio and a green screen, you can create anything, right? Sort of – if you have access to a state-of-the-art *animé* house like Production I.G. and its many affilitiates in the world of visual effects animation. So in *Garm Wars: The Last Druid* we have actors in partial sets with everything else cobbled together on the fami-com.

In one respect *Garm Wars: The Last Druid* soared: Kenji Kawai's score (as with *Avalon*). A new Oshii movie means a new score by Kawai. As expected of the highly individual Kawai, the music featured the customary choirs, but not always used as Hollywood composers use them. The most satisfying parts of the movie were when it allowed the music to dominate (as at the start of act two, when the heroine is recovering from a crash). Second unit shots of an actor walking in a wilderness isn't particularly gripping cinema (that was the basis of too many shots in *Angel's Egg*, for example). But when you add Kawai's score, who cares what the visuals are doing?

Garm Wars: The Last Druid is Mamoru Oshii's *Star Wars*[42] as well as his Hayao Miyazaki action-adventure film. But the worlds of *Star Wars* and Miyazaki (*Laputa* or *Porco Rosso*) were convincingly and forcefully laid out for the audience; *Garm Wars: The Last Druid* has all of the pieces in its toybox, but it can't quite put them together coherently.

❋

Too often *Garm Wars: The Last Druid* comes across as a higher budget version of a run-of-the-mill, TV sci-fi show, the sort of television drama that's churned out of L.A., New York, Vancouver, wherever, by the ton every month. With its garbled exposition and inconclusive plots, it also appears as a pilot episode that never led to a full-blown TV series. Instead, it was screened to studio executives in Burbank and immediately

42 Or maybe his *Willow,* a Lucasfilm fantasy movie which also raided the Celtic Magic *grimoire.*

axed.

However, a television show is (usually) much more concise and clear in its exposition. *Garm Wars: The Last Druid* opened with an outstanding aerial battle sequence, with the animators letting rip with all of their favourite moments from sky-high dogfights in cinema. The designs of aircraft were marvels of semi-organic shapes, insect forms, and shiny, metallic surfaces.

But the battle was followed with awkward and indigestible chunks of exposition (all about the communities of the planet, their wars, blah blah blah). Lance Henriksen pops up as the voice of authority, Melanie St-Pierre plays a cloned warrior, and, incredibly, *Garm Wars: The Last Druid* features a dog as a mystical, revered being.

Yes, a *dog*. Only Mamoru Oshii would have the guts and wilful eccentricity to feature a pooch (!) prominently in a movie as a special creature (even more than the druid!). And, yes, it's the same dawg from the *Ghost In the Shell* sequel and most of Oshii's work: a doggone basset hound! (So that the whole of *Garm Wars: The Last Druid* and its overly-intricate visuals seems created for the sole purpose of inserting a doggie into the narrative as a spiritual guide! We don't have a shaman, a wizard or a dog, we've got a dog!).

For Mamoru Oshii, a dog is more alive than any human being (and more precious, too). *Garm Wars: The Last Druid* is proof of that view: the hound – *bless it to the gods!, all praise the dog!* – is by far the most alive character in this flick.

When the exposition has finally been delivered (by the close of the shoddily edited and paced first act), *Garm Wars: The Last Druid* shifts into the usual quest narrative, depicting a bunch of misfits heading off to Oz (or Narnia or Wonderland or someplace strangely, oddly, curiously similar).

Like some of Mamoru Oshii's other works, *Garm Wars: The Last Druid* has taken up religious/ spiritual elements and applied them in the manner of Japanese animation. That is, in a superficial and trite manner. The film, needless to say, has nothing to do with Druidism, and knows nothing about the beliefs in Druidry.

❋

Garm Wars: The Last Druid looks as if sections were dropped in the writing or in the editing: what would usually be a two-hour, four-act movie is a 100-minute, three-act movie. Some critics said it felt like a prequel to a movie or series that didn't exist, or like the leftovers of a video game. The finale of *Garm Wars: The Last Druid*, for example, is underwhelming: it's face-off between Khara and Wydd for the Truth. Khara wants some answers, but altho' Wydd blethers plenty, the Truth is not forthcoming. Only that war is madness. Or a waste. Or stupid. Or something.

Following that very dissatisfying climax, there's a montage of another war (with an unhelpful voiceover added). The visuals are stupendous – of tanks and aircraft and ground troops battling giants –

but after two or three minutes of white-hot animation, the film's over!

Garm Wars: The Last Druid features characters telling us things, but lacks the ability to develop their visual correlative, to make those ideas and themes and issues resonate cinematically. So only half of it is cinema – the other half is radio (i.e., talk and more talk).

Sadly, *Garm Wars: The Last Druid* comes across, apart from its music and visual design, as fatally derivative of many much finer movies and TV shows.

A key flaw is that none of the characters – including Khara (Mélanie St-Pierre) – are especially appealing; add to that the way that they are played and directed, and it means that we don't root for them or feel for them.

And there aren't enough of them: a fantasy adventure movie of this kind requires more characters. At least a comic sidekick! No, no, this is Mamoru Oshii, the deadly serious, Japanese 'visionary' (however, I guess the dawg functions a little like a sidekick).

And *Garm Wars: The Last Druid* is humourless.

Garm Wars: The Lost Fluid looks, from the outset, as if it has something to say, or if it has a new spin on old material. But it doesn't – apart from notions such as:

'war is naughty and bad and evil and people really shouldn't do it'.

Or: 'dogs are cool'.

Some of Mamoru Oshii's films as director.
Above: two Urusei Yatsura animations.
Below: Angel's Egg.

Clockwise from right: Patlabor. The Sky Crawlers. Garm Wars: The Last Druid. Avalon.

05

GHOST IN THE SHELL,
THE LIVE-ACTION MOVIE (2017)

Produced by Paramount/[1] DreamWorks/ Reliance/ Shanghai Film Group/ Huahua Media/ Arad Productions, the much-rumoured live-action[2] version of the *Ghost In the Shell* story reached movie theatres in 2017.

Ultimately, it is a mere footnote to the *Ghost In the Shell* franchise.

But the Western, live-action movie has an impossible task – to follow two masterpiece movies and two seasons of an outstanding TV series.

However, it is significant in being the first big budget, live-action interpretation of Masamune Shirow's fiction, and the first movie aimed at a global audience of Shirow's work that was made by a (mainly) Western team (tho' the money, as so often, came from several sources).

The 2017 movie is also significant, of course, in raising the awareness of Masamune Shirow's work outside Japan, and also important in being a high budget adaptation of a Japanese *manga* and *animé* aimed at an international audience. Most adaptations of Japanese comics are made in Japan by Japanese for Japanese (*Death Note, Fullmetal Alchemist, Bleach, Silver Spoon*, etc). Western-Japanese co-productions or Western/ Hollywood versions of Japanese pop culture are much rarer (the *Death Note* movie, for example).

◆

Script: Jamie Moss, William Wheeler and Ehren Kruger (Wheeler said there were at least 6 or 7 writers who worked on it; Laeta Kalogridis, Jonathan Herman and others were also some of the scriptwriters over the years). The producers were: Ray Angelic, Avi Arad, Holly Bario, Michael Costigan, Jane Evans, Steven Pauland and Maki Terashima-Furuta. Executive producers: Tetsuya Fujimura, Mitsuhisa Ishikawa, Yoshinobu Noma, and Jeffrey Silver (that's – count 'em! –

---

1 Disney were originally going to distribute the movie, with their deal with DreamWorks.
2 'Live-action', sure – but actually, as with many expensive Western movies, much of this *Ghost In the Shell* is actually animation.

eleven producers!).[3] Director: Rupert Sanders. Music: Lorne Balfe and Clint Mansell. Costumes: Kurt and Bart. Hair: Vinnie Ashton. Make-up supervisor: Stefan Knight. DP: Jess Hall. Casting: Lucy Bevan, Liz Mullane and Miranda Rivers. Editors: Billy Rich and Neil Smith. Prod. des.: Jan Roelfs. Sound designers: Odin Benitez, Peter Staubli, and Jon Title. Stunt co-ordinators: Sean Graham, Glenn Suter and Guy Norris. Vfx super-visors: John Dykstra, Asregadoo Arundi, Axel Bonami, Ryan Jefferson Hays, Greg McKneally, Ivan Moran *et al*. Plus a vast army of visual effects people (the fx houses included M.P.C., Weta, Territory, Method, Framestore, Iloura, Atomic Fiction, Prime Focus, Halon, Lola, Pixo-mondo, Clear Angle and Digital Art).

In the cast were: Scarlett Johansson, Pilou Asbæk, Michael Pitt, Juliette Binoche, Takeshi Kitano, Chin Han, Danusia Samal, Peter Ferdinando and Anamaria Marinca. Released: Mch 16, 2017. 107 mins.

The budget was rumoured to be $110 million. It was filmed in L.A., Hong Kong and New Zealand. It was released in 3-D as well as 2-D (plus I.M.A.X. versions).

◆

A movie which was optioned years ago will typically have had several writers turning in scripts; directors will come and go; actors will be interested then do something else. Some scenes might survive, but many will fall by the wayside (often the pricier sequences). Tests might be filmed (of costumes, make-up, props, etc); locations might be scouted (then dropped); costumes and sets might be created – the process can go on forever, it seems. Some producers will ask for this or that element or theme to be emphasized; the next set of producers or writers will go for something else.

Thus, the cast and the writers of the 2017 *Ghost In the Shell* movie will be simply the latest in a long line of people who've worked on the project. (Notice that, with the inclusion of characters such as Hideo Kuze, the producers bought up the rights not only to remake the 1995 movie, and the 1989 *manga*, but also the *Ghost In the Shell: Stand Alone Complex* series, and the *Innocence* sequel).

◆

The choice of Scarlett Johansson caused some controversy – for the casting of a white American in an Asian story. Hollywood has done that since, well, the 1910s – sometimes with grotesque caricatures of Oriental types (such as Fu Manchu and Charlie Chan). And it goes the other way: Yanks are regularly satirized in Asian movies, for instance (in the *Once Upon a Time In China* films, starring Jet Li, Americans are portrayed as crude, boorish, aggressive imperialists and slave traders). But the brouhaha brought to light how the very Japanese flavour of Masamune Shirow's work is interpreted in the West. (The criticism of the casting choice highlighted, in a roundabout way, the very issues of identity and origins in Shirow-sensei's vision of cyborgization).

Anyway, the movie cast – as the second-billed actor – a big Japanese

---

3 Yes, the no. of producers on movies has increased significantly since the 1990s.

star (Beat Kitano), and other characters were (or were played as) Japanese (such as Togusa). (But the Public Security Section 9 team included other non-Asian characters/ actors, including a woman played with a Brit accent).

Scarlett Johansson is a sensational actor, but not right for this part.[4] No one believes that Johansson is capable of being an action heroine (despite her role in the *Avengers* series, for instance), or an accomplished military commander; also she's too small, too short, a little dumpy, and (sad to say) too old (at 32).[5] The villain, Cutter (Peter Ferdinando), insists in the film that she is not 'a machine', but 'a weapon'.[6] A 'weapon' for what? For a video game of supermodel pouting, shopping and angsting? How can someone as sensitive and unthreatening as Scarlett Johansson be a 'weapon' of any kind?

But Scarlett Johansson does bring glamorous star power to the production.[7] (Johansson convinces as a neurotic woman searching for her roots and her identity, but not as a ruthless warrior).[8]

Besides, none of the Western actors in the 2017 version of *Ghost* come anywhere near the truly wonderful trio from the animated *Ghost In the Shell* films and shows. Nobody can be Motoko Kusanagi other than Atsuko Tanaka – and it's the same with Batou – played by Akio Otsuka – and Togusa – played by Koichi Yamadera. (Actually, Tanaka, Otsuka and Yamadera were the voices for the Japanese version of the 2017 *Ghost In the Shell*. Thus, the movie would've seemed more like the rest of the *Ghost In the Shell* outings when screened in Nihon.)

Beat Kitano (b. 1947) was surprising casting, perhaps – however, he's a huge celebrity in Japan, appearing in numerous TV shows, in comedy acts (with an emphasis on crude, near-offensive material), and is also known for his *yakuza* roles and as a director of serious films.[9] Takeshi certainly looked the part at the end when he takes out his ancient pistol[10] and sets about the henchmen sent to nobble him, and later when he tackles the villain, Cutter (even tho' he seems as if he's acting in a different movie for most of the time).

◆

Essentially, the 2017 *Ghost In the Shell* was a remake of (and *hommage* to) the 1995 *Ghost In the Shell* animation, with the same main plot of the Puppeteer, with the Existential identity issue (of 'who am I?) as a subplot or subtext (thus, in this movie, the heroine goes by the name of Mira Killian, and receives her famous name in the finale). Typically in an action or thriller movie, the main subplot is romance, but not in the Shirowworld.

---

4 Mamoru Oshii visited the set and said he thought that Johansson was great as Motoko.
5 That does follow the *animé* adaptations, however: the Motoko Kusanagi in the *manga* is younger than in the animated versions (aside from *Arise*).
6 It doesn't make sense that the Major has been designed as a 'weapon', according to Cutter, when she's short and plump.
7 Despite that silly, quasi-Japanese-style, black wig.
8 Johansson's one-note tone, in the 2nd half of *Ghost*, perpetually grumpy and downbeat, gets a little tiresome.
9 I can't be the only cyborg who'd prefer Kitano to have helmed this film.
10 A nod to Togusa, and also to Deunan in *Appleseed*.

The Public Security Section 9 team working as a professional group barely makes an impression in the 2017 outing;[11] the live-action movie doesn't understand or deliver the subtle interactions in Public Security Section 9, or the precisely-defined hierarchy of the *Ghost manga* (or other Japanese *manga*). Most outrageously, Togusa hardly features at all. Most of the emphasis is on Batou and Aramaki, amongst the Public Security Section 9-ers. Many scenes comprise either Killian plus Batou, or Killian plus Aramaki. Was this, one wonders, because of the emphasis on the character of the Major? – and, by extension, on creating a script which was a star vehicle? (Scarlett Johansson dominates this movie).

So the Hollywood version of *Ghost In the Shell* opts for the familiar configuration:

1. Heroine (Killian/ Kusanagi). 2. Boss (Aramaki). 3. Sidekick (Batou). 4. Helper (the doctor, Ouelet). 5. Villain (Cutter). 6. Rival (Kuze/ Hideo).[12]

As expected, the Hollywood version of *Ghost In the Shell* added Western psychology – the 'who am I?' plot is given a Westernized slant: so li'l Killian is now on a quest to uncover her past (there's even time to meet her mom). Cute and angsty in the modernist, Existential manner – but it departs from the 1995 movie, and of course from Masamune Shirow's *manga*, which isn't remotely interested in scenes where Motoko hugs her mom in a cemetery![13]

◆

The 2017 live-action flick is, you have to admit, a fascinating but flawed attempt at rendering a quintessentially *Japanese* franchise in Western/ Hollywood terms. Ironic, of course, because, as Masamune Shirow admits, much of *Ghost In the Shell* is already Westernized (from the cop show format to the elements of big business and cyberization).

Composers Clint Mansell and Lorne Balfe had one of the toughest assignments in the live-action adaptation of *Ghost In the Shell:* how in •••• do you follow the two greatest composers in Japanese animation? – Yoko Kanno and Kenji Kawai?[14] At least when it comprised busy electronica, the Mansell & Balfe score was far more successful than the so-ambient-it's-almost-non-existent score of Cornelius for the *Arise* series.

Unfortunately, Mansell & Balfe also delivered too many very boring low drones which any kid can concoct on a laptop computer:

Drone <1>: ambient and s-l-o-w, for talky scenes (can be played in loops dribbling on for hours, turning music into a sludge of boring muzak).

Drone <2>: as drone 1, with some zingy fly-bys and glissandos added (for tense build-ups to action scenes).

Drone <3>: a bass rumble drone, loud, for right after an action scene or an important plot point. (The score is partly an *hommage*, once again, to

---

11 The Hollywood version added a female chara to the team.
12 Kuze takes on the role of the Puppeteer, and bits of Kuze and the Laughing Man.
13 However, there are a surprising number of scenes set in graveyards in Japanese pop culture. Every major *animé* series, for instance, features at least one.
14 And the movie plays out with a Kenji Kawai cue.

the Vangelis score for *Blade Runner* – which was also remade/ sequelized in 2017. The new *Blade Runner* soundtrack – by Hans Zimmer and Benjamin Wallfisch – is more accomplished. But it still trots out ominous drones by the ton). If drones were outlawed from sci-fi movie soundtracks, there'd be almost nothing left.

As to the action, the 2017 *Ghost* movie is never more than run-of-the-mill[15] – and far less compelling compared to even a minor Hong Kong action movie (from the *real* Hong Kong!). Action bristling with invention and humour, Hong Kong-style, could've elevated this movie so much higher. Forget the thriller plot, where big business is the nefarious and all-pervading influence in postmodern society, just give us some imaginative action already! (Tsui Hark, Tony Ching Siu-tung, Yuen Woo-ping, Corey Yuen *et al* are the go-to guys for spectacular action).

Parts of *Ghost In the Shell* seemed soulless – in a movie all about bodies and spirits and brains and minds. The picture seemed to be more concerned with recreating a fancypants futuristic world, with the design, the look, the gadgets.

It's one of those films that never quite comes to life, like a botched cyborgization: all of the pieces are there (it's in focus, it has music, sound fx, a script, actors, costumes and all), but it's still-born.

And too much of *Ghost In the Shell* runs by with the same tone.[16] Here we miss the comedy of Masamune Shirow's comic, and the *Ghost In the Shell: Stand Alone Complex* TV series.

On the plus side, it was surprising, perhaps, that the live-action *Ghost In the Shell* kept so many Asian elements, including the setting of a Hong Kong-ish city[17] (which's from the 1995 movie, not Shirow's *manga*), and to the casting of Motoko's mom (Kaori Momoi), and also Takeshi Kitano as Aramaki (and having him speak in Japanese, with subtitles). The cemetery, Motoko's mom's *aparto*, the street life, the *geishas*, all are Asian.

And there's one big plus with the live-action *Ghost*: it is 107 minutes long. Far too many similar movies recently run to 2h 20m or longer, adding a fourth act and sometimes a fifth act to a three-act structure.

◆

Of the 100s of omissions in the 2017 movie from the *Ghost In the Shell* franchise as authored by Masamune Shirow, humour was a major failing. The 2017 *Ghost In the Shell* is gloomy and straight all the way thru, with perhaps 2 or 3 attempts at humour (coming mainly from Batou).[18] As with the 1995 and the 2004 movies, the live-action flick misses the essence of the cop team format of Shirow's *manga* (which the three TV series were far more successful at capturing[19]). Scarlett Johansson drifts about the movie with a sour, po-faced[20] expression like she's just discovered she isn't

---

15 Guy Norris was action unit director.
16 Every scene begins with a slow, boring establishing shot.
17 Yet the *Ghost In the Shell* of 2017 seemed to get lost in the evocation of yet another *Blade Runner*-inspired futuristic metropolis. While it looked amazing, the visual overkill didn't quite fit this take on the story.
18 Thus, elements such as the child-like robots were not included.
19 The 4th series, *2045* reverted to the Gloom.
20 Her cyborg face has not been built to smile.

getting paid as much as initially agreed (look at the screenshots included in this book. So miserable! Motoko in Shirowland is *not* like this!).

Connecting in cyberspace isn't portrayed much, a huge element in the *manga* and the *Ghost In the Shell: Stand Alone Complex* series. (The movie jettisoned Shirow's dense, layered cyberspace (and the digital interfaces), for voiceovers, and a spectral realm in which the Major drifts about with her face in a perpetual frown). Indeed, the cybernetic elements of the Shirowworld were portrayed rather sketchily: important concepts were not quite delivered clearly and punchily (such as diving into someone else's brain, communicating via the net, travelling in cyberspace, etc).

The theme of sexuality, so prominent in Shirow-sensei's later work, is addressed in the 2017 film only in passing. Scarlett Johansson doesn't shed her clothing for the thermoptic camo, tho' the movie teases with glimpses of the heroine's artificial body. A scene where the Major picks up a hooker and examines her freckled face is a nod to the lesbian clinches in the *Ghost manga*, but cuts away before anything like the explicit scenes in Masamune Shirow's art can occur. (Instead, it's another 'who am I?', 'what am I?' scene).

The addition of a mother for Motoko (and a visit to her home) is the sort of ingredient that might've been added way back in the development process. It has the feel of an element that Steven Spielberg is fond of (consider the additions of similar familial and psychological elements in *Minority Report*, for instance, the movie that's closest to *Ghost In the Shell* from Spielberg as a director). We know that DreamWorks was a co-producer of *Ghost In the Shell*, and that Spielberg is famous for pitching suggestions to scripts in development at his company. (The addition of a *mother* rather than a father was added perhaps to emphasize the theme of origins and birth, and to bump up the female presence in this very boysy outing (the casting of a well-known face like Juliet Binoche as the cyborg doctor was also part of this trend). However, all of Uncle Shirow's female characters are father complex girls – like all women in fantasy and science fiction literature).

Now we discover that Motoko was a wild and rebellious girl with outspoken political views that led her to run away with a bunch of anti-government activists. It's a very different take on previous interpretations of the Major. So now she's switched ideologically and practically from being a critic and rebel opposing the State to a State-manufactured weapon (weapon or not, in working for Public Security Section 9 she is an emissary of the government: *she's a cop*).

From peacenik to cop is a striking turnaround of ideology and politics – it's part of the flashback that the Major uncovers as the film progresses (her memories have been tampered with, of course, and the old memories, aided by Doctor Ouelet, eventually materialize).

This is where Hideo Kuze[21] fits in – back then, he wasn't a resentful Frankenstein's-monster-cum-botched-cyborg. No, he was Moto-chan's

---

21 Kuze, and the way that Pitt plays him (with his patchwork body), evokes Frankenstein's monster, the bungled scientific experiment, the artificially created being who wants to be whole and human.

buddy in their fight against the Man (where they were snatched off the streets by Cutter's company to be used in those experiments). They were Dickensian street urchins who became political agitators – until the authorities stamped them out (in a scene of police aggression amid fiery carnage, which, this flashback boasting a traditional, Chinese setting, inevitably comes across as a critique of the political suppression of radicals by the government of the People's Republic of China).

A significant alteration from the *manga* and the *animé* versions of *Ghost In the Shell* was dispensing with the numerous political conflicts: in the comic of *Ghost In the Shell*, departments within the government are at odds with each other (sometimes escalating to civil war). In the 2017 movie it boils down to big business versus the government (personalized in the figures of Aramaki and Cutter, in scenes where they growl at each other).

As well as the 1995 *Ghost In the Shell* movie, the 2017 live-action adaptation took plenty from the second *Ghost In the Shell* movie (of 2004), and the two *Ghost In the Shell: Stand Alone Complex* series and three spin-off *Ghost In the Shell: Stand Alone Complex* movies. Really, the writers of the two *Ghost In the Shell* TV series (Saito, Sakurai, Kamiyama, Suga, Fujisaku *et al*) should receive credit here, as so many bits were lifted from them.

For instance, the break-up of the Public Security Section 9 team comes from the ending of the 1st *Ghost In the Shell: Stand Alone Complex* season; geisha robots attacking guests at a swanky dinner from the top of the 1st series; Project 2571 developing a quasi-religious union of ghosts or spirits in the cyber network is from the 2nd *Ghost In the Shell: Stand Alone Complex* series (he's also called Kuze); the motorcycle on the freeway is from the 3rd (*Arise*) series; the multiple visits to the cyber doctors is also from *Arise* (by way of the *manga*[22]); the smoking cyber specialist is from *Innocence,* as is the raid on the *yakuza* nightclub (the dogs, including good ol' Gabriel, are also from *Innocence*).

A more appealing prospect would be to adapt the *manga* by Shirow-sensei, not the 1995 movie (marvellous as that is). None of the *Ghost In the Shell* adaptations have truly grappled with Shirow's comic.

There are numerous Shirowian elements in the live-action version of *Ghost In the Shell,* however, despite carping from fans. The finale is pure Masamune Shirow – a female cyborg versus a spider-shaped tank. (However, Aramaki would *not* kill Cutter, nor ask for the Major's permission to do so! It works in hokey Hollywood terms ('Kill the Bad Guy! Yeah! All right!'), but Shirow's Aramaki is by-the-rulebook all the way. It should be the Major, of course, who blows Cutter away. However, as played by Beat Kitano, I guess Aramaki has to pull the trigger).

Yet the finale of the '17 flick, for a movie costing $110 million, doesn't seem big enough. Batou, for ex, is out of the loop (as are the rest of the Public Security team – they have their moment in the 'Burn Section 9'

---

22 Tho' Juliet Binoche doesn't appear in half-naked stockings like the nurses in Uncle Shirow's comic.

sequence). You're expecting Batou (or Boma) to hurry in carrying a mega-gun to blast the bejesus out of the tank. But as Kuze is part of the tank battle, Batou only appears at the end, to carry off the New Motoko in his arms.

◆

You have to admit that the 2017 *Ghost In the Shell* turned the *Ghost In the Shell* franchise into a run-of-the-mill action thriller with an Existential, 'who am I?' subplot. At times, despite its visual intensity and invention, the 2017 *Ghost In the Shell* is underwhelming and even – gasp! – boring.

And *Ghost In the Shell* should never be boring! Is it boring because it's a remake? Because, rather, it's a remake of a remake? (The 1995 movie, *plus* the 2002-2005 TV series, *plus* the *Ghost In the Shell: Stand Alone Complex* spin-off movies, *plus* the *Arise* prequel series – not forgetting the three installments of Shirow-sensei's comic!).

Yes – there *is* a feeling of *déja vu* with the Paramount/ DreamWorks flick. We *have* seen this movie before, even if we're not rabid *Ghost In the Shell* and Masamune Shirow fans. And there is a feeling that the 2017 movie didn't add enough of its own material, its own take on the *Ghost In the Shell* franchise.

◆

Reaction from fans has been mixed. My initial reaction to the prospect of a live-action remake of a classic movie is the usual one:

Why bother?

The *Ghost In the Shell* franchise *already* consists of two classic movies, two classic TV series, several spin-off movies, and a third TV series.

Why not spend that budget of $110 million (plus millions more for P. & A., marketing, etc) on financing 100 new films from young filmmakers, at $1 million a piece?

Or, how about using that $100 million to fund 20 new animated series, at $5 million per series? Oh yes, for that money you could have 20 or 30 entire *animé* series!

Needless to say, the reaction of the one person we'd love to hear from to the 2017 film – Shirow-sensei – was not forthcoming. (Altho' he has voiced his opinion of previous adaptations, such as the 2004 *Appleseed*). However, the idea that Uncle Shirow would've hated the live-action movie because so much of his beloved comic was changed is wrong: Shirow accepts – and embraces – the adaptation process. A work in a new medium has to be something else, he reckons.

Mamoru Hosoda (*Wolf Children, The Girl Who Leapt Through Time*) derides the whole concept of making live-action movies from animated movies:

> I have gotten asked if I want to turn any of my films into live action, but I simply think that's just meaningless... I actually do get frustrated about live action versions of animation because the general concept, probably, is that live action films are superior to animation.

So by making a live action version, they think they are trying to improve the animated movie. No, that's not true. Or people think live action may be better for being accepted by a general audience. I don't think that's true. It's all about good stories, good movies.[23]

The response in the critical community ranged from raves (in *Variety*: 'this is smart, hard-lacquered entertainment that may just trump the original films for galloping storytelling momentum and sheer, coruscating visual excitement'), and enthusiasm (in *Total Film*: 'It's the most staggeringly detailed and impressively realised sci-fi location since James Cameron welcomed audiences to Pandora'), to raspberries (*USA Today*: '*Ghost in the Shell* is a defective mess with lifeless characters, missed chances for thematic exploration and a minefield of political incorrectness'; and Roger Moore in *Movie Nation*: '*Ghost in the Shell* can't escape its own ghosts, the movies, stories, characters and even settings of truly original work that predates it').

Some critics simply don't know their *manga* and their *animé*. For ex, Michael Phillips, writing in the *Chicago Tribune*, asserted that 'this isn't jokey, quippy science fiction; true to the source material, it's fairly grave about the implications of an android-dominated culture'.

Wrong! In fact, the 'source material' is *very* quippy (Shirow loves sarcastic quips!), is full of humour, and has a heroine who's joshing with her Public Security Section 9 pals and robot underlings *all the time*.

---

23 Hosoda in J. Slater-Williams, *The Skinny*, Oct 26, 2018.

Ghost In the Shell (2017)
(This page and over)

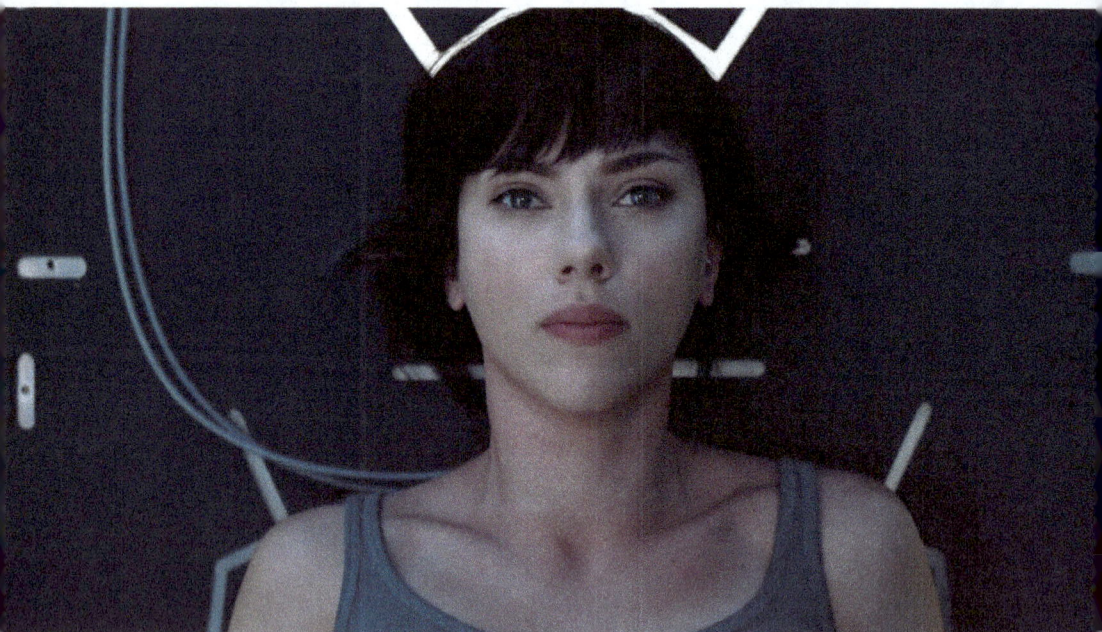

RESOURCES

WEBSITES

Masamune Shirow's own website is Shirowledge: shirowledge.com
Useful websites for the *Ghost In the Shell* franchise include:
• ghostintheshell.tv
• manga.com
• kenjikawai.com
• productionig.com.
• motorballer.org/shirow
• shirowsama.blogspot.com.es (Spanish)

One of the best sources on the internet for *animé* information is Anime News Network: animenewsnetwork.com. It is excellent, and the first stop for any online research on *animé*. Anime News Network has the fullest credits on the web for animation, and each entry is linked, so you can follow your favourite actors, directors, producers and artists, across numerous shows.

Also:
Japanese Cinema Database.
Japanese Movie Data Base.
Anime Web Turnpike: anipike.com.
Gilles Poitras's site: koyagi.com.
Fred L. Schodt's site: jai2.com.
Otaku News: otakunews.com.
Midnight Eye (for Japanese cinema): midnight eyec.com.
There are fan sites, of course. See the list of websites in the bibliography.

BOOKS ON *ANIMÉ*

Books by Frederik Schodt, Helen McCarthy, Trish Ledoux, Patrick Drazen, Fred Patten, Jonathan Clements, Simon Richmond, Antonia Levi, Susan Napier, Jason Thompson and Gilles Poitras are standard works. But apart from those key authors, there is surprisingly little available on *animé* in English.

And most film critics tend to focus on characters, stories, and the biographies of the filmmakers. So many books on *animé* simply tell us the stories. Very few critics grapple with the industrial, social and cultural aspects of *animé* (and even less with theory and philosophy). Which's why critics such as Fred Schodt and Helen McCarthy are so important, because they address issues such as the modes of production, the audience and the market, and social-cultural contexts.

The single most useful book on *animé* is *The Animé Encyclopedia* (2001/ 2006/ 2015) by Jonathan Clements and Helen McCarthy. If you buy one book on Japanese animation, get this one. *The Animé Encyclopedia* provides entries on pretty much every important *animé* show, Original Video Animation and movie to come out of the Japanese animation industry, as well as numerous minor shows and oddities. This is the equivalent of a Leonard Maltin/ *Time Out*/ *Virgin*/ *Oxford*/ *Variety* guide to cinema. Clements and McCarthy are *animé* experts as well as fans (I would also recommend any of Clements' other books, including his history of *animé*, and his entertaining account of working in the *animé* business in translation and dubbing, *Schoolgirl Milky Crisis*).

All of Helen McCarthy's books have become standard works: *Anime! A*

Beginner's Guide To Japanese Animation, The Animé Movie Guide, The Erotic Animé Movie Guide, 500 Manga Heroes & Villains and *500 Essential Anime Movies* (some of these were co-authored with Jonathan Clements). They contain facts, credits and background to *animé* and *manga* which will greatly enhance your studies (and enjoyment) of Japanese comics and cartoons.

Other standard works on *animé* include: *The Art of Japanese Animation* (from Animage, 1988-89), and the *Dictionary of Animation Works* (2010).

Fred Schodt is one of the most valuable commentators on Japanese *animé* and *manga* in the West. His pioneering study of *manga, Manga! Manga! The World of Japanese Magazines*, is a marvellous book. Before it, there was virtually nothing. Because of the huge crossover between *manga* and *animé*, many of the chapters on *manga* in Schodt's studies also apply to *animé*. Schodt also offers one of the fullest and most detailed accounts of the history of *manga* and visual art in Japan. (*Manga! Manga!* also includes samples from some famous *manga*, including *Barefoot Gen* and *The Rose of Versailles*, and the illustrations – from the history of Japanese art as well as from *manga* – are stunning).

Fred Schodt's follow-up, *Dreamland Japan: Writings On Modern Manga*, is equally riveting. It includes a huge number of illuminating studies of individual artists and their works (with illustrations), as well as another history of *manga*. *Dreamland Japan* is also probably the finest, most intelligent and best-informed analysis of the *manga* market in both Japan and overseas. As well as Osamu Tezuka, Frederik Schodt also discusses Hayao Miyazaki, the relation of *manga* to *animé*, artistic styles, Japanese publishers, and the big *manga* magazines. It enhances Schodt's books that he has also interviewed many of the chief artists of *manga*, including the 'god of manga' himself, Osamu Tezuka.

Trish Ledoux and Doug Ranney edited an early guide to *animé, The Complete Anime Guide*, that is now a standard work. It is packed with fascinating snippets, as well as hard information, credits, etc. The companion volume, *Anime Interviews*, culled from *Animerica* magazine, is wonderful, featuring many of the key practitioners in animation (such as Masamune Shirow, Shoji Kawamori, Mamoru Oshii, Leiji Matsumoto, Rumiko Takahashi and Hayao Miyazaki).

Gilles Poitras has produced a number of works on *animé*, including *The Animé Companion* and *Animé Essentials*. Poitras offers vital links between Japanese animation and Japanese culture and society. There are objects, gestures, words and customs in *animé* that often surprise or bemuse Western viewers: Poitras' books help to explain them. You will find yourself recognizing all sorts of elements in *animé* that Poitras includes in his books (which contain many illustrations).

Antonia Levi's *Samurai From Outer Space* is stuffed with information on Japanese society as well as Japanese animation. Clearly written and with an appealing sense of humour, Levi's book is a lesser-known but invaluable work. *Samurai From Outer Space* discusses all of the celebrated *animé* shows that've made the leap across the Pacific to the Western world. Published in 1996, you wish that Levi (like many other authors whose books came out in the 1990s), was able to update it. Many great shows have been released since 1996!

Simon Richmond's *The Rough Guide To Anime* is a superb, general introduction to the wild world of *animé*. Like other *Rough Guides*, it selects fifty must-see TV shows and movies, plus providing discussions of related topics like *manga,* adaptations of *animé*, and a history of animation.

Jason Yadao's *The Rough Guide To Manga* is a companion guide to the *Rough Guide To Animé*. It has the same format and is a terrific general introduction to the world of Japanese comics. Yadao's enthusiasm is infectious: you will want to hunt out many of his recommendations. Both *Rough Guides* were published in the 2000s, so they're able to include recent classics like *Fullmetal Alchemist, Cowboy Bebop, Love Hina* and the masterpieces of Satoshi Kon.

Manga: The Complete Guide (Jason Thompson and others) is another illuminating book, packed with short reviews and longer pieces on topics like games, sci-fi, martial arts, sport, religion, crime, *mecha, shojo*, and *yaoi*.

Zettai! Anime Classics is another of those books that looks at 100 classic movies: Brian Camp and Julie Davis spend more time, however, on each of the familiar masterpieces of Japanese animation, exploring the films, Original Video Animations and TV shows in much more detail than the usual single paragraph review.

Manga Impact! from Phaidon is an entertaining survey of Japanese animation, with a format focussing on characters and personnel. *Manga Impact!* has short text entries, but features numerous wonderful illustrations in colour.

Susan Napier's *Anime: From Akira To Princess Mononoke* is much more theoretical, and somewhat dry. (If you are familiar with the theoretical approaches to Western animation (see the studies noted below), you will find nothing new in Western authors exploring Japanese animation from a theoretical or philosophical point-of-view).

The guides to the art of comics by Scott McCloud (including *Understanding Comics*), are highly recommended general introductions to how comics work (delivered in the form of a comic, with plenty of humour).

BOOKS ON ANIMATION

On animation in general, I would recommend the following studies: P. Wells' *Understanding Animation*; E. Smoodin's *Animating Culture: Hollywood Cartoons From the Sound Era*; Leonard Maltin's *Of Mice and Magic: A History of American Animated Cartoons*; James Clarke's *Animated Films*; *From Mouse To Mermaid: The Politics of Film, Gender and Culture* (edited by E. Bell *et al*); *Animation Art* (edited by J. Beck); and *Reading the Rabbit: Explorations in Warner Bros. Animation* (edited by K. Sandler).

For information on Walt Disney, the standard works include: Leonard Maltin's *The Disney Films*; Richard Schickel's *The Disney Version: The Life, Times, Art, and Commerce of Walt Disney*; R. Grover's *The Disney Touch*; Project on Disney's *Inside the Mouse: Work and Play at Disney World*; *Disney Discourse: Producing the Magic Kingdom* (edited by E. Smoodin); and *Walt Disney: A Guide to References and Resources* (edited by E. Leebron *et al*).

BOOKS ON CINEMA

For a study of cinema, there is one book that towers above *every other book* on film (even tho' the competition is fierce!): David A. Cook's *A History of Narrative Film*. If you want one book that covers everything, this is it.

David Bordwell and Kristin Thompson have written many meticulously researched and beautifully crafted books on cinema: *Film Art: An Introduction, Narration In the Fiction Film, Film History: An Introduction, The Classical Hollywood Cinema: Film Style and Mode of Production to 1960* and *Storytelling In the New Hollywood*. Anything by Bordwell and/ or Thompson is excellent.

I would also recommend Bruce Kawin's *How Movies Work*, Gerald Mast's *Film Theory and Criticism: Introductory Readings*, and Mast & Kawin's *A Short History of the Movies*.

David Cook, David Bordwell, Kristin Thompson, Gerald Mast and Bruce Kawin will give you all you could need for an in-depth study of cinema. Read their books: it's the equivalent of a degree or PhD in cinema!

MASAMUNE SHIROW

KEY WORKS

ART

Black Magic, 1983.
Appleseed, 1985-89.
Dominion, 1986.
Appleseed Databook, 1990.
Ghost in the Shell, 1989/ 1991.
Orion, 1991.
Neuro Hard, 1992-94.
Intron Depot 1, 1992. *2,* 1998. *3,* 2003. *4,* 2004. *5,* 2012. *6,* 2013. *7,* 2013. *8,* 2018. *9,*
2019.
Appleseed Databook, 1994.
Dominion: Conflict 1 (No More Noise), 1995.
Cybergirls Portfolio, 2000.
Ghost in the Shell 2: Man-Machine Interface, 2001.
Galgrease, 2002.
Galhound, 2003. *2,* 2004.
Ghost in the Shell 1.5: Human-Error Processor, 2003.
Appleseed: Illustration and Data, 2007.
Pieces 1, 2009. *2,* 2010. *3,* 2010. *4,* 2010. *5,* 2011. *6,* 2011. *7,* 2011. *8,* 2012. *9,* 2012.
W-Tails Cat 1, 2012. *2,* 2013. *3,* 2016.
Pieces Gem 1, 2014. *2,* 2015. *3,* 2016.
Greaseberries 1, 2014. *2,* 2014. *3,* 2018. *4,* 2019.

ADAPTATIONS

Black Magic, 1987.
Appleseed, 1988.
Dominion: Tank Police, 1988.
New Dominion: Tank Police, 1994.
Ghost In the Shell, 1995.
Ghost In the Shell: Stand Alone Complex, 2002-05.
Ghost In the Shell 2: Innocence, 2004.
Appleseed, 2004, 2007, 2014.
Ghost In the Shell: Stand Alone Complex: The Laughing Man, 2005.
Ghost In the Shell: Stand Alone Complex: 2nd G.I.G.: Individual Eleven, 2006.
Ghost In the Shell: Stand Alone Complex: Solid State Society, 2006.
Ghost Hound, 2007.
Real Drive, 2008.
Ghost In the Shell: Arise, 2013-15.
Ghost In the Shell: The New Movie, 2015.
Pandora in the Crimson Shell: Ghost Urn, 2015-16.
Ghost In the Shell, 2017.
Ghost In the Shell: S.A.C. 2045, 2020.

FILMOGRAPHIES

GHOST IN THE SHELL (1995)

Kôkaku Kidôtai. 88 mins.

CREW

Produced by Makoto Ibuki, Mitsuhisa Ishikawa, Ken Iyadomi, Ken Matsumoto, Teruo Miyahara, Yoshimasa Mizuo, Takashi Mogi, Yasushi Sukeof, Shigeru Watanabe, Hiroshi Yamazaki, Andy Frain, Laurence Guinness
Written by Kazunori Itô and Masamune Shirow (*manga*)
Directed by Mamoru Oshii
Music by Kenji Kawai
Cinematography by Hisao Shirai
Film Editing by Shûichi Kakesu
Production Design by Takashi Watabe
Art Direction by Hiromasa Ogura
Production Manager – Ryuji Mitsumoto
Shuji Inoue – sound recording engineer
Kurt Kassulke – sound re-recording mixer
Kazutoshi Satou – sound effects
Kazuhiro Wakabayashi – sound director
Mutsu Murakami – special effects
Hiroyuki Okiura – key animation supervisor and character designer
Shôji Kawamori – mechanical designer
Kazuchika Kise – key animation supervisor
Toshihiko Nishikubo – animation director
Atsushi Takeuchi – animator and mechanical designer
Mamoru Akimoto – production scheduler
Paul C. Halbert – translator: English
Taro Yoshida – translation coordinator

JAPANESE VOICE CAST

Atsuko Tanaka – Major Motoko Kusanagi
Akio Otsuka – Batou
Kôichi Yamadera – Togusa
Tamio Ôki – Chief Aramaki
Iemasa Kayumi – Project 2501 a.k.a. 'the Puppet Master'
Tesshô Genda – Section 6 Department Chief Nakamura
Kazuhiro Yamaji – Garbage Collector A
Shigeru Chiba – Garbage Collector B
Namaki Masakazu – Dr.Willis

Takashi Matsuyama – Terrorist
Mitsuru Miyamoto – Daita Mizuho
Shinji Ogawa – Notorious Diplomat
Maaya Sakamoto – Motoko (Girl)
Masato Yamanouchi – Foreign Minister

GHOST IN THE SHELL 2: INNOCENCE (2004)

Kôkaku Kidôtai: Inosensu 99 mins.

CREW

Produced by Mitsuhisa Ishikawa, Ryuji Mitsumoto, Toshio Suzuki, and Maki Terashima-Furuta
Written and directed by Mamoru Oshii
Based on Masamune Shirow's *manga Koukaku Kidoutai*
Original Music by Kenji Kawai
Cinematography by Miki Sakuma
Film Editing by Sachiko Miki, Chihiro Nakano, Junichi Uematsu
Production Design by Yohei Taneda
Art Direction by Shuichi Hirata
Tetsuya Nishio – supervising animator, weaponry designer and sub character designer
Hiroyuki Okiura – supervising animator and character designer
Atsushi Takeuchi – key animator, layout artist and mechanical designer
Shuji Inoue – mixing supervisor
Randy Thom – sound designer
Hiroyuki Hayashi – special effects supervisor
Hisashi Ezura – visual effects supervisor
Masashi Ando – key animator
Richard Epcar – voice director

JAPANESE VOICE CAST

Atsuko Tanaka – Major Motoko Kusanagi
Akio Otsuka – Batou
Kôichi Yamadera – Togusa
Tamio Ôki – Chief Aramaki
Yutaka Nakano – Ishikawa
Naoto Takenaka – Kim
Hiroaki Hirata – Koga
Yoshiko Sakakibara – Haraway
Sumi Mutoh – On'na no ko
Masaki Terasoma – Azuma
Gou Aoba
Eisuke Asakura
Yuzuru Fujimoto
Emiko Fuku
Masao Harada
Minoru Hirano
Katsunosuke Hori
Sukekiyo Kameyama
Eriko Kigawa
Hiroyuki Kinosha

Shuji Kishida
Kenichi Mochizuki
Ryûji Nakagi
Yasushi Niko
Yu Sugimoto
Fumihiko Tachiki
Akino Watanabe
Makoto Yasumura

GHOST IN THE SHELL
LIVE-ACTION (2017)

Kôkaku Kidôtai. 107 mins.

CREW

Produced by Paramount/ DreamWorks/ Reliance/ Shanghai Film Group/ Huahua Media/ Arad Productions

Producers – Ray Angelic, Ari Arad, Holly Bario, Michael Costigan, Jane Evans, Steven Paul, Maki Terashima-Furuta

Exec. producers – Tetsuya Fujimura, Mitsuhisa Ishikawa, Yoshinobu Noma, Jeffrey Silver

Script – Jamie Moss, William Wheeler, Ehren Kruger

Director – Rupert Sanders

Music – Lorne Balfe, Clint Mansell

Cinematography – Jess Hall

Film Editing – Billy Rich, Neil Smith

Casting – Lucy Bevan, Liz Mullane, Miranda Rivers

Production Design – Jan Roelfs

Art Direction – Matt Austin, Simon Bright, Miro Harre, Andy McLaren, Ken Turner, Erik Polczwartek

Richard L. Johnson – supervising art director

Costume Design – Kurt and Bart

Vinnie Ashton – key hair stylist

Special makeup effects artists – Mathieu Baptista, Barbara Broucke, Mike Smithson

Make-up artists – Michele Perry, Kate Biscoe, Deborah La Mia Denaver, Cody Dysart, Natalie Henderson

Stefan Knight – makeup supervisor

Jane O'Kane – makeup/hair designer

Sarah Rubano – makeup and hair co-designer

Claire Rutledge – prosthetic make up and hair artist

Simon Warnock – first assistant director

Guy Norris – action unit director and supervising stunt co-ordinator

Stunt coordinators – Glenn Suter, Sean Graham

Sound designers – Odin Benitez, Peter Staubli, Jon Title

Per Hallberg – supervising sound editor

John Dykstra – visual effects supervisor

Visual effects supervisors – Asregadoo Arundi, Axel Bonami, Jason Billington, Ryan Jefferson Hays, Greg McKneally, Ivan Moran, Guillaume Rocheron, Doug Spilatro, Ryan Tudhope

Kenn McDonald – animation supervisor

Matt Dunkley – conductor / lead orchestrator

Queenie Li – music production/coordination

Orchestrators – Òscar Senén, Tony Blondal

CAST

Scarlett Johansson – Major
Pilou Asbæk – Batou
Takeshi Kitano – Aramaki
Juliette Binoche – Dr. Ouelet
Michael Pitt – Kuze
Chin Han – Togusa
Danusia Samal – Ladriya
Lasarus Ratuere – Ishikawa
Yutaka Izumihara – Saito
Tawanda Manyimo – Boma
Peter Ferdinando – Cutter
Anamaria Marinca – Dr. Dahlin
Daniel Henshall – Skinny Man
Mana Hira Davis – Bearded Man
Erroll Anderson – Hanka Security Agent
Kai Fung Rieck – Diamond Face
Andrew Stehlin – No Pupils
Matthias Luafutu – Thick Built Yakuza
John Luafutu – Barkeep
Kaori Momoi – Hairi
Kaori Yamamoto – Motoko
Andrew Morris – Hideo
Adwoa Aboah – Lia
Chris Obi – Ambassador
Rila Fukushima – Red Robed Geisha
Makoto Murata – Yakuza Gunman
Natarsha Orsman – Ouelet's Assistant
Joseph Naufahu – Police Commander Johns
Vinnie Bennett – Rookie Cop
Pete Teo – Tony
David Johnson Wood – Section Six Leader
Xavier Horan – Section Six Soldier
Allan Henry – Section Six Soldier
Bowie Chan Wing Wai – Yakuza
Kirt Kishita – Street Hustler
Kate Venables – Geisha
Emma Coppersmith – Geisha
Tanya Drewery – Geisha
Hannah Tasker-Poland – Geisha
Jacqueline Lee Geurts – Geisha

BIBLIOGRAPHY

MASAMUNE SHIROW

MANGA WORKS

Areopagus Arther, published in *Atlas*, 1980
Yellow Hawk, published in *Atlas*, 1981
Colosseum Pick, published in *Funya*, 1982/ *Comic Fusion Atlas*, 1990
Pursuit, published in *Kintalion*, 1982
Black Magic, Seishinsha, 1983
Optional Orientation, published in *Atlas*, 1984
Battle On Mechanism, published in *Atlas*, 1984
Metamorphosis In Amazoness, published in *Atlas*, 1984
Alice In Jargon, published in *Atlas*, 1984
Appleseed, Seishinsha, 1985-89/ Dark Horse, 1995
Bike Nut, published in *Dorothy*, 1985
Dominion, Hakusensha, 1986
Gun Dancing, published in *Young Magazine Kaizokuban*, Kodansha, 1986
Pile Up, published in *Young Magazine Kaizokuban*, Kodansha, 1987
Ghost in the Shell, Kodansha, 1991/ Dark Horse, 2007
Orion, Seishinsha, 1991
Neuro Hard - The planet of a bee, published in *Comic Dragon*, 1992-94
Appleseed Databook, 1994
Interview, *Manga Mania*, Feb, 1994
Interview, Dark Horse, 1995
Dominion: Conflict 1 (No More Noise), Hakusensha, 1995
Appleseed Databook, Dark Horse, 1994/ 1995
Ghost in the Shell 2: Man-Machine Interface, Kodansha, 2001
Ghost in the Shell 1.5: Human-Error Processor, Kodansha, 2003
Appleseed: Illustration and Data (a.k.a. *Hypernotes*), Dark Horse, 2007
Pandora In the Crimson Shell: Ghost Urn, *Newtype Ace* magazine, 2012 (art by Koshi Rikudo)

ART BOOKS

Intron Depot 1 Seishinsha, 1992
Intron Depot 2: Blades, Seishinsha, 1998
Cybergirls Portfolio, Norma/ Dark Horse, 2000
Intron Depot 3: Ballistics, Seishinsha, 2003
Intron Depot 4: Bullets, Seishinsha, 2004
Kokin Toguihime Zowshi Shu, Seishinsha, 2009
W-Tails Cat 1, G.O.T., 2012
Intron Depot 5: Battalion, Seishinsha, 2012
Intron Depot 6: Barb Wire 1, Seishinsha, 2013
Intron Depot 7: Barb Wire 2, Seishinsha, 2013

W-Tails Cat 2, G.O.T., 2013
W-Tails Cat 3, G.O.T., 2016
Intron Depot 8: Bomb Bay, Seishinsha, 2018
Intron Depot 9: Barrage Fire, Seishinsha, 2019

GREASEBERRIES/ GALGREASE/ PIECES

Galgrease, *Uppers Magazine*, 2002
Galhound 1, Kodansha, 2003
Galhound 2, Kodansha, 2004
Pieces 1 - Premium Gallery, Kodansha, 2009
Pieces 2 - Phantom Cats, Kodansha, 2010
Pieces 3 - Wild Wet Quest, Kodansha, 2010
Pieces 4 - Hellhound 1, Kodansha, 2010
Pieces 5 - Hellhound 2, Kodansha, 2011
Pieces 6 - Hell Cat, Kodansha, 2011
Pieces 7 - Hellhound 1 & 2, Kodansha, 2011
Pieces 8 - Wild Wet West, Kodansha, 2012
Pieces 9 - Kokon Otogizoshi Shu Hiden, Kodansha, 2012
Pieces Gem 1: Ghost In the Shell Data, Seishinsha, 2014
Greaseberries 1, G.O.T., 2014
Greaseberries 2, G.O.T., 2014
Pieces Gem 2: Neuro Hard, Seishinsha, 2015
Pieces Gem 3, Kodansha, 2016
Greaseberries 3, G.O.T., 2018
Greaseberries 4, G.O.T., 2019

TIE-IN *MANGA*, NOVELS AND RELATED WORKS

Dominion: Tank Police by Nemuruanzu, Kadokawa Shoten, 1994
Ghost In the Shell by Akinori Endo, Kodansha, 1995, 1998
Ghost In the Shell: Stand Alone Complex by Junichi Fujisaku, 3 novels, Tokuma Shoten, 2004-05
Black Magic by Hideki Kakinuma, Softbank Creative, 2005-08
Real Drive by Yoshinobu Akita, Kodansha, 2008
Ghost In the Shell: Stand Alone Complex by Yu Kinutani, Kodansha, 2009
Ghost In the Shell: Stand Alone Complex: Tachikoma na Hibi by Yoshiki Sakurai and Mayasuki Yamamoto, Kodansha, 2009
Appleseed XIII by Yoshiki Sakurai, T.O. Entertainment, 2012
Ghost In the Shell: Arise: Sleepless Eye by Junichi Fujisaku and Takumi Ooyama, Kodansha, 2013
Appleseed: Alpha by Iou Kuroda, 2014
Ghost In the Shell: Comic Tribute, Kodansha, 2017
Ghost In the Shell: Perfect Book, Kodansha, 2017
Ghost In the Shell: The Human Alogorithm by Yuki Yoshitomo and Junichi Fujisaku, Kodansha, 2019

BIBLIOGRAPHY

OTHERS

Animage. *The Art of Japanese Animation*, Tokuma Shoten, 1988-89
—. *Best of Animage*, Tokuma Shoten, 1998
L. Armitt, ed. *Where No Man Has Gone Before: Women and Science Fiction*, Routledge,
    1991
A. Balsamo. *Technologies of the Gendered Body: Reading Cyborg Women*, Duke
    University Press, Durham, N.C., 1996
—. "Reading Cyborgs Writing Feminism", in J. Wolmark, 1999
M. Barr, ed. *Future Females, the Next Generation: New Voices and Velocities In Feminist
    Science Fiction Criticism* , Rowman & Littlefield, Lanham, M.D., 2000
R. Barringer: "Skinjobs, Humans and Radical Coding", *Jump Cut*, 41, 1997
J. Baxter. *Science Fiction In the Cinema* , Tantivy Press, 1970
J. Beck, ed. *Animation Art*, Flame Tree Publishing, London, 2004
D. Bell & B. Kennedy, eds. *The Cybercultures Reader*, Routledge, 2000
E. Bell *et al*, eds. *From Mouse To Mermaid: The Politics of Film, Gender and Culture*,
    Indiana University Press, Bloomington, I.N., 1995
G. Bender & T. Druckrey, eds. *Cultures On the Brink*, Bay Press, Seattle, 1994
M. Benedikt, ed. *Cyberspace: First Steps*, M.I.T. Press, Cambridge, M.A., 1991
I. Bergman. *The Magic Lantern: An Autobiography*, London, 1988
J. Bergstrom: "Androids and Androgyny", *Camera Obscura*, 15, 1986
J. Berndt, ed. *Global Manga Studies*, Seika University International Manga Research
    Center, Kyoto, 2010
C. Bloom, ed. *Gothic Horror*, Macmillan, 1998
D. Bordwell & K. Thompson. *Film Art: An Introduction*, McGraw-Hill Publishing
    Company, New York, N.Y., 1979
—. *Narration In the Fiction Film*, Routledge, London, 1988
—. *The Way Hollywood Tells It*, University of California Press, Berkeley, C.A., 2006
F. Botting. *Gothic*, Routledge, 1996
—. *Sex, Machines and Navels: Fiction, Fantasy and History In the Future Present*,
    Manchester University Press, Manchester, 1999
J. Bower, ed. *The Cinema of Japan and Korea*, Wallflower Press, London, 2004
S. Brewster *et al*, eds. *Inhuman Reflections: Thinking the Limits of the Human*,
    Manchester University Press, Manchester, 2000
R. Brody. *Everything Is Cinema: The Working Life of Jean-Luc Godard*, Faber, London,
    2008
J. Brook & I. Boal, eds. *Resisting the Virtual Life: The Culture and Politics of Information*,
    City Lights, San Francisco, 1995
P. Brophy, ed. *Kaboom! Explosive Animation From America and Japan*, Museum of
    Contemporary Art, Sydney, 1994
—. *100 Anime*, British Film Institute, London, 2005
—. ed. *Tezuka*, National Gallery of Victoria, 2006
J. Brosnan. *Future Tense: The Cinema of Science Fiction* , St Martin's Press, New York,
    N.Y., 1978
—. *Primal Screen: A History of Science Fiction Film* , Orbit, London, 1991

S. Bukatman. *Terminal Identity: The Virtual Subject In Postmodern Science Fiction*, Duke University Press, Durham, N.C., 1993
—. *Blade Runner*, British Film Institute, London, 1997
—. "The Ultimate Trip: Special Effects and Kaleidoscopic Perception", *Iris*, 25, 1998
J. Butler. *Gender Trouble: Feminism and the Subversion of Identity*, Routledge, 1990
—. & J.W. Scott, eds. *Feminists Theorise the Political*, Routledge, 1992
—. *Bodies That Matter*, Routledge, 1993
—. *Subjects of Desire: Hegelian Reflections In 20th Century France*, Columbia University Press, N.Y., 1999
D. Cartmell *et al*, eds. *Alien Identities: Exploring Differences In Film and Fiction*, Pluto, 1999
J. Caughie & A. Kuhn, eds. *The Sexual Subject: A* Screen *Reader In Sexuality*, Routledge, 1992
D. Cavallaro. *The Cinema of Mamoru Oshii: Fantasy, Technology and Politics*, McFarland & Company, 2006
—. *The Animé Art of Hayao Miyazaki*, McFarland, Jefferson, N.C., 2006
C. Chatrian & G. Paganelli, *Manga Impact!*, Phaidon, London, 2010
L. Cherny & E.R. Weise, eds. *Wired Women: Gender and New Realities In Cyberspace*, Seal Press, Seattle, 1996
J. Clarke. *Animated Films*, Virgin, London, 2007
J. Clements & H. McCarthy. *The Animé Encyclopedia*, Stone Bridge Press, Berkeley, C.A., 2001/ 2006/ 2015
—. *The Development of the U.K. Anime and Manga Market*, Muramasa Industries, London, 2003
—. *Schoolgirl Milky Crisis*, Titan Books, London, 2009
—. *Anime: A History*, British Film Institute, London, 2013
C. Clover. *Men, Women and Chain Saws: Gender In the Modern Horror Film*, Princeton University Press, N.J., 1992
J. Collins *et al*, eds. *Film Theory Goes To the Movies*, Routledge, N.Y., 1993
I. Condry. *The Soul of Anime*, Duke University Press, Durham, N.C., 2013
D.A. Cook. *A History of Narrative Film*, W.W. Norton, New York, N.Y., 1981, 1990, 1996
L. Cooke & P. Wollen, eds. *Visual Display*, Bay Press, Seattle, 1995
J.C. Cooper: *Fairy Tales: Allegories of the Inner Life*, Aquarian Press, 1983
J. Crary, ed. *Incorporations*, Zone Books, 1992
B. Creed. *The Monstrous-Feminine*, Routledge, 1993
C. Degli-Esposti, ed. *Postmodernism In the Cinema*, Berghahn Books, N.Y., 1998
T. de Lauretis & S. Heath, eds. *The Cinematic Apparatus*, St Martin's Press, N.Y., 1980
—. *Alice Doesn't: Feminism, Semiotics, Cinema*, Indiana University Press, Bloomington, 1984
—. *Technologies of Gender*, Macmillan, 1987
M. Dery, ed. *Flame Wars: The Discourse of Cyberculture*, Duke University Press, Durham, N.C., 1994
—. *Escape Velocity: Cyberculture At the End of the Century*, Hodder, 1996
C. Desjardins. *Outlaw Masters of Japanese Film,* I.B. Tauris, London, 2005
J. Dixon & E. Cassidy, eds. *Virtual Futures: Cyberotics, Technology and Post-human Pragmatism*, Routledge, 1998
J. Donald, ed. *Fantasy and the Cinema*, British Film Institute, London, 1989
P. Drazen. *Animé Explosion*, Stone Bridge Press, Berkeley, C.A., 2003
Mircea Eliade. *Ordeal by Labyrinth*, University of Chicago Press, Chicago, I.L., 1984
—. *Symbolism, the Sacred and the Arts*, Crossroad, New York, N.Y., 1985
P. Evans. "Future Tense", *Manga Mania*, Feb 1994
M. Featherstone & R. Burrows, eds. *Cyberspace/ Cyberbodies/ Cyberpunk*, Sage, 1995
D. Fingeroth. *The Rough Guide To Graphic Novels*, Rough Guides, 2008
T. Foster. "Meat Puppets or Robopaths?", *Genders*, 18, 1983
C. Fuchs: "Death Is Irrelevant: Cyborgs, Re-production, and the Future of Male Hysteria", *Gender*, 18, 1993
H. Garcia. *A Geek In Japan*, Tuttle, North Clarendon, V.T., 2011
P.C. Gibson & R. Gibson, eds. *Dirty Looks: Women, Pornography, Power*, British Film Institute, 1993
W. Gibson. *Neuromancer*, Grafton, 1986
Ghost In the Shell: Stand Alone Complex Official Log, ed. R. Napton, Bandai Entertainment, 2005

F. Glass: "The 'New Bad Future': *Robocop* and 1980s Sci-Fi Films", *Science as Culture*, 5, 1989

L. Goldberg *et al*, eds. *Science Fiction Filmmaking In the 1980s*, McFarland, Jefferson, 1995

J.-L. Godard. *Godard on Godard*, eds. J. Narobi & T. Milne, Da Capo, New York, N.Y., 1986

J. González. "Envisioning Cyborg Bodies", in C. Gray, 1995

J. Goodwin, ed. *Perspectives On Akira Kurosawa*, G.K. Hall, Boston, M.A., 1994

B.K. Grant, ed. *Planks of Reason: Essays On the Horror Film*, Scarecrow Press, N.J., 1984

—. ed. *Crisis Cinema: The Apocalyptic Idea In Postmodern Narrative Film*, Maisonneuve Press, 1993

—. ed. *The Dread of Difference: Gender and the Horror Film*, University of Texas Press, Austin, 1996

P. Gravett. *Manga*, L. King, London, 2004

—. ed. *1001 Comics You Must Read Before You Die*, Cassell, London 2011

C. Gray, ed. *The Cyborg Handbook*, Routledge, 1995

E. Grosz. *Sexual Subversions*, Allen & Unwin, 1989

—. *Volatile Bodies*, Indiana University Press, Bloomington, 1994

—. *Space, Time and Perversion*, Routledge, 1995

J. Halberstam. *Skin Shows: Gothic Horror and the Technology of Monsters*, Duke University Press, Durham, N.C., 1995

D. Haraway. "A Manifesto For Cyborgs", *Socialist Review*, 15, 2, 1985

—. *Primate Visions: Gender, Race and Nature In the World of Modern Science*, Routledge, 1989

—. *Simians, Cyborgs, and Women*, Routledge, 1991

—. "The Promises of Monsters", in J. Wolmark, 1999

P. Hardy, ed. *The Aurum Encyclopedia of Science Fiction*, Aurum, London, 1991

N.K. Hayles: "The Life of Cyborgs", in M. Benjamin, ed: *A Question of Identity*, Rutgers University Press, N.J., 1993

E.R. Helford, ed. *Fantasy Girls: Gender In the New Universe of Science Fiction and Fantasy TV*, Rowman & Littlefield, Lanham, M.D., 2000

H. Hitoshi. *Mecha World*, in *Appleseed Databook*, 1990

V. Hollinger: "Cybernetic Deconstructions", *Mosaic*, 1990

D. Holmes, ed. *Virtual Politics*, Sage, 1997

Tze-yue Hu. *Frames of Anime*, Hong Kong University Press, H.K., 2010

J. Hunter. *Eros In Hell: Sex, Blood and Madness In Japanese Cinema*, Creation Books, London, 1998

E. James. *Science Fiction In the 20th Century*, Oxford University Press, Oxford, 1994

F. Jameson. *Signatures of the Visible*, Routledge, N.Y., 1990

—. *Postmodernism, or the Cultural Logic of Late Capitalism*, Verso, 1991

S. Jeffords. *Hard Bodies: Hollywood Masculinity In the Reagan Era*, Rutgers University Press New Brunswick, 1994

R. Johnson. "Kawaii and kirei: Navigating the identities of women in *Laputa: Castle in the Sky* by Hayao Miyazaki and *Ghost in the Shell* by Mamoru Oshii", *Rhizomes: Cultural Studies in Emerging Knowledge*, 14, 2007

S. Jones, ed. *Virtual Culture*, Sage, 1997

E. Ann Kaplan, ed. *Psychoanalysis and Cinema*, Routledge, 1990

B.F. Kawin. *Mindscreen: Bergman, Godard and First-Person Film*, Princeton University Press, N.J., 1978

—. *How Movies Work*, Macmillan, N.Y., 1987

R. Keith. *Japanamerica*, Palgrave Macmillan, London, 2007

A. Kibbey *et al*. *Sexual Artifice: Persons, Images, Politics*, New York University Press, 1994

B. King. *Women of the Future: The Female Main Character In Science Fiction*, Scarecrow Press, 1984

G. King. *Science Fiction Cinema*, Wallflower, 2000

Sharon Kinsella. *Adult Manga*, University of Hawaii Press, Honolulu, 2002

P. Kirkham & J. Thumim, eds. *Me Jane: Masculinity, Movies and Women*, Lawrence & Wishart, 1995

P. Kramer. *The Big Picture: Hollywood Cinema From Star Wars To Titanic*, British Film Institute, 2001

J. Kristeva. *Desire In Language: A Semiotic Approach To Literature and Art*, ed. L.S.

Roudiez, tr. T. Gora *et al*, Blackwell, Oxford, 1982

—. *Powers of Horror: An Essay On Abjection*, tr. L.S. Roudiez, Columbia University Press, N.Y., 1982

—. *Revolution In Poetic Language*, tr. M. Walker, Columbia University Press, N.Y., 1984

—. *The Kristeva Reader*, ed. T. Moi, Blackwell, Oxford, 1986

—. *Tales of Love*, tr. L.S. Roudiez, Columbia University Press, N.Y., 1987

—. *Black Sun: Depression and Melancholy*, tr. L.S. Roudiez, Columbia University Press, N.Y., 1989

A. & M. Kroker, eds. *Hacking the Future*. New World Perspectives, Montreal, 1996

—. *Digital Delirium*, New World Perspectives, Montreal, 1997

A. Kuhn, ed. *Alien Zone: Cultural Theory and Contemporary Science Fiction*, Verso, London, 1990

—. ed. *Alien Zone 2*, Verso, London, 1999

F. Ladd & H. Deneroff. *Astro Boy and Anime Come To the Americas*, McFarland, Jefferson, N.C., 2009

T. Lamare. *The Anime Machine*, University of Minnesota Press, Minneapolis, M.N., 2009

B. Landon. *The Aesthetics of Ambivalence: Rethinking Science Fiction Film*, Greenwood Press, 1992

—. *Science Fiction After 1900*, Twayne, N.Y., 1997

T. Ledoux & D. Ranney. *The Complete Animé Guide*, Tiger Mountain Press, Washington, D.C., 1997

—. ed. *Anime Interviews*, Cadence Books, San Francisco, C.A., 1997

S. Lefanu. *In the Chinks of the World Machine: Feminism and Science Fiction*, Women's Press, 1988

T. Lehmann. *Manga: Masters of the Art*, HarperCollins, London, 2005

J. Lent, ed. *Animation in Asia and the Pacific*, John Libbey, 2001

A. Levi. *Samurai From Outer Space: Understanding Japanese Animation*, Open Court, Chicago, I.L., 1996

L. Levidow & K. Robins, eds. *Cyborg Worlds: The Military Information Society*, Columbia University Press, N.Y., 1989

P. Macias. *The Japanese Cult Film Companion*, Cadence Books, San Francisco, C.A., 2001

—. & T. Machiyama. *Cruising the Anime City* , Stone Bridge Press, C.A., 2004

M. MacWilliams, ed. *Japanese Visual Culture: Explorations In the World of Manga and Anime*, M.E. Sharpe, Armonk, N.Y., 2008

L. Maltin. *Of Mice and Magic: A History of American Animated Cartoons*, New American Library, New York, N.Y., 1987

—. *The Disney Films*, 3rd ed., Hyperion, New York, N.Y., 1995

A. Masano & J. Wiedermann, eds. *Manga Design*, Taschen, 2004

G. Mast *et al*, eds. *Film Theory and Criticism: Introductory Readings*, Oxford University Press, New York, N.Y., 1992a

—. & B. Kawin. *A Short History of the Movies*, Macmillan, New York, N.Y., 1992b

L. McCaffery, ed. *Storming the Reality Studio: A Casebook of Cyberpunk and Postmodern Fiction*, Duke University Press, Durham, N.C., 1991

H. McCarthy. *Anime! A Beginner's Guide To Japanese Animation*, Titan Books, 1993

—. *The Animé Movie Guide*, Titan Books, London, 1996

—. & J. Clements. *The Erotic Animé Movie Guide*, Titan Books, London, 1998

—. *Hayao Miyazaki: Master of Japanese Animation*, Stone Bridge Press, Berkeley, C.A., 2002

—. *500 Manga Heroes & Villains*, Barron's, Hauppauge, New York, 2006

—. *500 Essential Anime Movies*, Collins Design, New York, N.Y., 2008

S. McCloud. *Understanding Comics*, Harper, London, 1994

—. *Reinventing Comics*, Harper, London, 2000

—. *Making Comics*, Harper, London, 2006

H. Miyazaki. *Points of Departure, 1979-1996*, Tokuma Shoten, Tokyo, 1997

—. *Starting Point, 1979-1996,* tr. B. Cary & F. Schodt, Viz Media, San Francisco, C.A., 2009

—. *Turning Point, 1997-2008,* tr. B. Cary & F. Schodt, Viz Media/ Shogakukan, San Francisco, C.A., 2014

T. Moi. *Sexual/Textual Politics: Feminist Literary Theory*, Methuen, 1985

A. Morton. *The Complete Directory To Science Fiction, Fantasy and Horror Television*

Series, Other Worlds, 1997

J. Murray. *Hamlet On the Holodeck: The Future of Narrative In Cyberspace* , M.I.T. Press, Cambridge, M.A., 1997

C. Napier. *"Ghost In the Shell S.A.C.-2045* is a dead end of an adaptation", Polygon, June 9, 2022

S. Napier. *Anime: From Akira To Princess Mononoke*, Palgrave, New York, 2001

—. "Excuse Me, Who Are You?", in S. Brown, 2006

—. "Interviewing Hayao Miyazaki", *Huffington Post*, Jan, 2014

S. Neale & M. Smith, eds. *Contemporary Hollywood Cinema*, Routledge, London, 1998

E. Niskanen. "Untouched nature: Mediated animals in Japanese anime", *Wide Screen*, 2007

C. Odell & M. Le Blanc. *Studio Ghibli: The Films of Hayao Miyazaki and Isao Takahata*, Kamera Books, Herts., 2009

—. *Anime*, Kamera Books, Herts., 2013

I. & P. Opie: *The Classic Fairy Tales*, Paladin, 1980

T. Oshiguchi. "The Whimsy and Wonder of Hayao Miyazaki', *Animerica*, 1, 5 & 6, July, 1993

Oshii Mamoru, Kawade shobo shinsha, Tokyo, 2004

M. Oshii. Interview, in T. Ledoux, 1997

A. Osmond. *"Nausicaä* and the Fantasy of Hayao Miyazaki", *SF Journal Foundation*, 73, Spring, 1998

—. "Hayao Miyazaki", *Cinescape*, 72, 1999

—. "Will the Real Joe Hisaishi Please Stand Up?", *Animation World Magazine*, 5.01, April, 2000

— *Spirited Away*, British Film Institute, London, 2003a

—. "Gods and Monsters", *Sight & Sound*, Sept, 2003b

—. *Satoshi Kon*, Stone Bridge Press, San Francisco, 2009

K. Ott *et al. Artificial Parts, Practical Lives: Modern Histories of Prosthetics*, New York University Press, 2001

L. Pearce, ed. *Romance Revisited*, Lawrence & Wishart, London, 1995

D. Peary & G. Peary, eds. *The American Animated Cartoon*, Dutton, New York, N.Y., 1980

C. Penley, ed. *Feminism and Film Theory* , Routledge, 1988

—. *et al*, eds. *Close Encounters: Film, Feminism and Science Fiction*, University of Minnesota Press, Minneapolis, M.N., 1991

—. & A. Ross, eds. *Technoculture*, University of Minnesota Press, Minneapolis, 1991

A. Phillips & J. Stringer, eds. *Japanese Cinema: Texts and Contexts,* Routledge, London, 2007

C. Platt. *Dreammakers: Science Fiction and Fantasy Writers At Work*, Xanadu, 1987

G. Poitras. *The Animé Companion*, Stone Bridge Press, Berkeley, C.A., 1999

—. *Animé Essentials*, Stone Bridge Press, Berkeley, C.A., 2001

D. Porter, ed. *Internet Culture*, Routledge, 1997

N. Power. *God of Comics: Osamu Tezuka and the Creation of Post-World War II*, University of Mississippi Press, 2009

K. Quigley. *Comics Underground Japan*, Blast Books, New York, N.Y., 1996

E. Rabkin & G. Slusser, eds. *Shadows of the Magic Lamp: Fantasy and Science Fiction In Film* , Southern Illinois University Press, 1985

—. *Aliens: The Anthropology of Science Fiction*, Southern Illinois University Press, 1987

D. Richie. *The Films of Akira Kurosawa*, University of California Press, Berkeley, C.A., 1965

K. Robins & L. Levidow. "Soldier, Cyborg, Citizen", in J. Brook, 1995

J.M. Robinson. *The Cinema of Hayao Miyazaki*, Crescent Moon, 2015

—. *Cowboy Bebop: The Animé TV Series and Movie,* Crescent Moon, 2015

—. *Spirited Away*, Crescent Moon, 2016

—. *Princess Mononoke*, Crescent Moon, 2016

— *The Akira Book: Katsuhiro Otomo,* Crescent Moon, 2018

—. *The Art of Katsuhiro Otomo*, Crescent Moon, 2018

—. *The Art of Masamune Shirow*, 3 vols., Crescent Moon, 2020/ 2023

M. Rose. *Alien Encounters*, Cambridge University Press, Cambridge, 1981

P. Rosenthal. "Jacked In: Fordism, Cyberpunk, Marxism", *Socialist Review*, Spring, 1991

A. Ross. *Strange Weather: Culture, Science and Technology In an Age of Limits,* Verso, 1991

C. Rowthorn. *Japan*, Lonely Planet, 2007

N. Ruddick, ed. *State of the Fantastic*, Greenwood Press, 1992

B. Ruh. *Stray Dog of Anime: The Films of Mamoru Oshii*, Palgrave Macmillan, 2004

J. Rusher & T. Frentz. *Projecting the Shadow: The Cyborg Hero In American Film*, University of Chicago Press, 1995

D. Rushkoff. *Cyberia: Life In the Trenches of Cyberspace*, HarperCollins, 1994

K. Sandler. *Reading the Rabbit: Explorations In Warner Bros. Animation*, Rutgers University Press, Brunswick, N.J., 1998

C. Sandoval. "New Sciences: Cyborg Feminism and the Methodology of the Oppressed", in C. Gray, 1995

Z. Sardar & J. Ravetz, eds. *Cyberfutures*, Pluto, 1996

—. "Alt.Civilizations.FAQ: Cyberspace As the Darker Side of the West", in Z. Sardar, 1996

P. Schelde. *Androids, Humanoids and Other Science Fiction Monsters*, New York University Press, 1993

R. Schickel. *The Disney Version: The Life, Times, Art, and Commerce of Walt Disney*, Pavilion, London, 1986

R. Shields, ed. *Cultures of the Internet*, Sage, 1996

M. Schilling. *The Encyclopedia of Japanese Pop Culture*, Weatherhill, Boston, M.A., 1997

—. *Contemporary Japanese Film*, Weatherhill, New York, N.Y., 1999

F. Schodt. *Manga! Manga! The World of Japanese Magazines*, Kodansha International, London, 1997

—. *Dreamland Japan: Writings On Modern Manga*, Stone Bridge Press, Berkeley, C.A., 2002

—. *The Astro Boy Essays*, Stone Bridge Press, C.A., 2007

G. Schwab: "Cyborgs", *Discourse*, 9, 1987

C. Shiratori, ed. *Secret Comics Japan*, Cadence Books, San Francisco, C.A., 2000

K. Silverman. *The Subject of Semiotics*, Oxford University Press, N.Y., 1983

—. *The Acoustic Mirror: The Female Voice In Psychoanalysis and Cinema*, Indiana University Press, Bloomington, 1988

C. Sinclair. *Net Chicks: A Small Girl Guide To the Wired World*, Henry Holt, N.Y., 1996

T. Smith. "Miso Horny: Sex In Japanese Comics", *Comics Journal*, Apl, 1991

E. Smoodin. *Animating Culture: Hollywood Cartoons From the Sound Era*, Roundhouse, 1993

—. ed. *Disney Discourse: Producing the Magic Kingdom*, Routledge, London, 1994

V. Sobchack. *The Limits of Infinity: The American Science Fiction Film*, A.S. Barnes, N.Y., 1980

—. *Screening Space: The American Science Fiction Film*, Ungar, N.Y., 1987/ 1993

—. "Cities On the Edge of Time: The Urban Science Fiction Film", *East-West Film Journal*, 3, 1, Dec, 1988

—. *The Address of the Eye: A Phenomenology of Film Experience*, Princeton University Press, N.J., 1992

—. ed. *The Persistence of History: Cinema, Television, and the Modern Event*, Routledge, 1995

—. "New Age Mutant Ninja Hackers", in D. Bell, 2000

Z. Sofia. "Virtual Corporeality", *Australian Feminist Studies*, 15, Adelaide, 1992

C. Springer. "The Pleasure of the Interface", *Screen*, 32, 3, 1991

—. *Electronic Eros*, Athlone, 1996

G. Stewart. *Between Film and Screen: Modernism's Photo Synthesis*, University of Chicago Press, Chicago, I.L., 1999

J. Stieff & A. Barkman, eds. *Manga and Philosophy*, Open Court, Chicago, I.L., 2010

Y. Tasker. *Spectacular Bodies: Gender, Genre and the Action Cinema*, Routledge, 1993

J. Telotte: "*The Terminator, Terminator 2* and the Exposed Body", *Journal of Popular Film & Television*, 20, 2, 1992

—. *Replications: A Robotic History of the Science Fiction Film*, University of Illinois Press, Urbana, 1996

—. *A Distant Technology: Science Fiction Film and the Machine Age*, Wesleyan University Press, Hanover, 1999

J. Thompson. *Manga: The Complete Guide*, Del Rey, New York, N.Y., 2007

K. Thompson & D. Bordwell. *Film History: An Introduction*, McGraw-Hill, New York, N.Y., 1994

—. *Storytelling In the New Hollywood*, Harvard University Press, Cambridge, M.A.,

1999

Tokyo Otaku Mode. "Anime Site Collaboration Project Vol. 17: Production I.G.", July 22, 2019

A. Tudor. *Monsters and Mad Scientists*, Blackwell, Oxford, 1989

B. Vincent. "Stream It Or Skip It: *Ghost In the Shell: S.A.C.-2045*", Decider, July 2, 2022

P. Virilio & S. Lotringer. *Pure War*, Semiotext(e), N.Y., 1983

—. *Lost Dimensions*, tr. D. Moshenberg, Semiotext(e), N.Y., 1991a

—. *The Aesthetics of Disappearance*, tr. P. Beitchman, Semiotext(e), N.Y., 1991b

—. *War and Cinema*, Verso, 1992a

—. "Aliens", in J. Crary, 1992b

—. *The Vision Machine*, tr. J. Rose, Indiana University Press, Bloomington, 1994a

—. "Cyberwar, God and Television", *CTHEORY*, http:// www/aec/at/ctheory/a-cyberwar_god. html, 1994b

—. *The Art of the Motor*, tr. J. Rose, University Press, Minnesota, 1995a

—. "Speed and Information", *CTHEORY*, http:// www/aec/at/ctheorya30-cyberspace_alarm.html, 1995b

P. Warrick: *The Cybernetic Imagination In Science Fiction* , M.I.T. Press, 1980

J. Wasko. *Hollywood In the Information Age*, Polity Press, 1994

P. Webb. *The Erotic Arts*, Secker & Warburg, London, 1983

P. Wells. *Understanding Animation*, Routledge, London, 1998

C. Winstanley, ed. *SFX Collection: Animé Special* , Future Publishing, London

J. Wolmark. *Aliens and Others: Science Fiction, Feminism and Postmodernism*, Harvester Wheatsheaf, 1993

—. "The Postmodern Romances of Feminist Science Fiction", in L. Pearce, 1995

—. ed. *Cybersexualities: A Reader On Feminist Theory, Cyborgs and Cyberspace*, Edinburgh University Press, Edinburgh, 1999

T. Woods. *Beginning Postmodernism*, Manchester University Press, Manchester, 1999

K. Woodward. "From Virtual Cyborgs To Biological Time Bombs", in G. Bender, 1994

S. Zizek. *Looking Awry*, Verso, 1991

—. *Enjoy Your Symptom: Jacques Lacan In Hollywood and Out*, Routledge, N.Y., 1992

—. *Tarrying With the Negative: Kant, Hegel, and the Critique of Ideology*, Duke University Press, Durham, N.C., 1993

—. *The Metastases of Enjoyment*, Verso, 1994

—. *The Indivisible Remainder*, Verso, 1996

—. *The Fright of Real Tears: The Uses and Misuses of Lacan In Film Theory* , British Film Institute, 1999

J. Zipes. *Fairy Tales and the Art of Subversion: The Classical Genre for Children and the Process of Civilization*, Heinemann, London, 1983

—. *The Brothers Grimm: From Enchanted Forests To the Modern World*, Routledge, New York, N.Y., 1989

—. ed. *The Oxford Companion To Fairy Tales*, Oxford University Press, 2000

—. *Breaking the Spell: Radical Theories of Folk and Fairy Tales*, University of Kentucky Press, Lexington, 2002

—. *Sticks and Stones: The Troublesome Success of Children's Literature from Slovenly Peter To Harry Potter*, Routledge, London, 2002

—. *The Enchanted Screen: The Unknown History of Fairy-tale Films*, Routledge, New York, N.Y., 2011

—. *The Irresistible Fairy Tale*, Princeton University Press, Princeton, N.J., 2012

WEBSITES

MASAMUNE SHIROW

Shirowledge (Shirow's own website): shirowledge.com
gallery.shirow.net
mshirow.free.fr

GHOST IN THE SHELL

ghostintheshell.tv
production-ig.com
kenjikawai.com
darkhorse.com
appleseed13.jp
worldwide-yk.com (Yoko Kanno)

ANIMÉ

manga.com
animenewsnetwork.com
anipike.com
koyagi.com
jai2.com
otakunews.com
midnighteyec.com
www.moribito.com
www3.nhk.or.jp/anime/moribito

JEREMY ROBINSON has published poetry, fiction, and studies of J.R.R. Tolkien, Samuel Beckett, Thomas Hardy, André Gide and D.H. Lawrence. Robinson has edited poetry books by Novalis, Ursula Le Guin, Friedrich Hölderlin, Francesco Petrarch, Dante Alighieri, Arseny Tarkovsky, and Rainer Maria Rilke.

Books on film and animation include: *The Akira Book* • *The Art of Katsuhiro Otomo* • *The Art of Masamune Shirow* • *The Ghost In the Shell Book* • *Fullmetal Alchemist* • *Cowboy Bebop: The Anime and Movie* • *The Cinema of Hayao Miyazaki* • *Hayao Miyazaki: Pocket Guide* • *Princess Mononoke: Pocket Movie Guide* • *Spirited Away: Pocket Movie Guide* • *Blade Runner and the Cinema of Philip K. Dick* • *Blade Runner: Pocket Movie Guide* • *The Cinema of Donald Cammell* • *Performance: Donald Cammell: Nic Roeg: Pocket Movie Guide* • *Pasolini: Il Cinema di Poesia/ The Cinema of Poetry* • *Salo: Pocket Movie Guide* • *The Trilogy of Life Movies: Pocket Movie Guide* • *The Gospel According To Matthew: Pocket Movie Guide* • *The Ecstatic Cinema of Tony Ching Siu-tung* • *Tsui Hark: The Dragon Master of Chinese Cinema* • *The Swordsman: Pocket Movie Guide* • *A Chinese Ghost Story: Pocket Movie Guide* • *Ken Russell: England's Great Visionary Film Director and Music Lover* • *Tommy: Ken Russell: The Who: Pocket Movie Guide* • *Women In Love: Ken Russell: D.H. Lawrence: Pocket Movie Guide* • *The Devils: Ken Russell: Pocket Movie Guide* • *Walerian Borowczyk: Cinema of Erotic Dreams* • *The Beast: Pocket Movie Guide* • *The Lord of the Rings Movies* • *The Fellowship of the Ring: Pocket Movie Guide* • *The Two Towers: Pocket Movie Guide* • *The Return of the King: Pocket Movie Guide* • *Jean-Luc Godard: The Passion of Cinema* • *The Sacred Cinema of Andrei Tarkovsky* • *Andrei Tarkovsky: Pocket Guide.*

'It's amazing for me to see my work treated with such passion and respect. There is nothing resembling it in the U.S. in relation to my work.'
(Andrea Dworkin)

'This model monograph – it is an exemplary job, and I'm very proud that he has accorded me a couple of mentions… The subject matter of his book is beautifully organised and dead on beam.'
(Lawrence Durrell, on *The Light Eternal: A Study of J.M.W. Turner*)

'Jeremy Robinson's poetry is certainly jammed with ideas, and I find it very interesting for that reason. It's certainly a strong imprint of his personality.'
(Colin Wilson)

'*Sex-Magic-Poetry-Cornwall* is a very rich essay... It is a very good piece… vastly stimulating and insightful.'
(Peter Redgrove)

CRESCENT MOON PUBLISHING

web: www.crmoon.com e-mail: cresmopub@yahoo.co.uk

ARTS, PAINTING, SCULPTURE

The Art of Andy Goldsworthy
Andy Goldsworthy: Touching Nature
Andy Goldsworthy in Close-Up
Andy Goldsworthy: Pocket Guide
Andy Goldsworthy In America
Land Art: A Complete Guide
The Art of Richard Long
Richard Long: Pocket Guide
Land Art In the UK
Land Art in Close-Up
Land Art In the U.S.A.
Land Art: Pocket Guide
Installation Art in Close-Up
Minimal Art and Artists In the 1960s and After
Colourfield Painting
Land Art DVD, TV documentary
Andy Goldsworthy DVD, TV documentary
The Erotic Object: Sexuality in Sculpture From Prehistory to the Present Day
Sex in Art: Pornography and Pleasure in Painting and Sculpture
Postwar Art
Sacred Gardens: The Garden in Myth, Religion and Art
Glorification: Religious Abstraction in Renaissance and 20th Century Art
Early Netherlandish Painting
Leonardo da Vinci
Piero della Francesca
Giovanni Bellini
Fra Angelico: Art and Religion in the Renaissance
Mark Rothko: The Art of Transcendence
Frank Stella: American Abstract Artist
Jasper Johns
Brice Marden
Alison Wilding: The Embrace of Sculpture
Vincent van Gogh: Visionary Landscapes
Eric Gill: Nuptials of God
Constantin Brancusi: Sculpting the Essence of Things
Max Beckmann
Caravaggio
Gustave Moreau
Egon Schiele: Sex and Death In Purple Stockings
Delizioso Fotografico Fervore: Works In Process 1
Sacro Cuore: Works In Process 2
The Light Eternal: J.M.W. Turner
The Madonna Glorified: Karen Arthurs

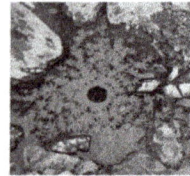

LITERATURE

J.R.R. Tolkien: The Books, The Films, The Whole Cultural Phenomenon
J.R.R. Tolkien: Pocket Guide
Tolkien's Heroic Quest
The *Earthsea* Books of Ursula Le Guin
Beauties, Beasts and Enchantment: Classic French Fairy Tales
German Popular Stories by the Brothers Grimm
Philip Pullman and *His Dark Materials*
Sexing Hardy: Thomas Hardy and Feminism
Thomas Hardy's *Tess of the d'Urbervilles*
Thomas Hardy's *Jude the Obscure*
Thomas Hardy: The Tragic Novels
Love and Tragedy: Thomas Hardy
The Poetry of Landscape in Hardy
Wessex Revisited: Thomas Hardy and John Cowper Powys
Wolfgang Iser: Essays and Interviews
Petrarch, Dante and the Troubadours
Maurice Sendak and the Art of Children's Book Illustration
Andrea Dworkin
Cixous, Irigaray, Kristeva: The *Jouissance* of French Feminism
Julia Kristeva: Art, Love, Melancholy, Philosophy, Semiotics and Psychoanalysis
Hélene Cixous I Love You: The *Jouissance* of Writing
Luce Irigaray: Lips, Kissing, and the Politics of Sexual Difference
Peter Redgrove: Here Comes the Flood
Peter Redgrove: Sex-Magic-Poetry-Cornwall
Lawrence Durrell: Between Love and Death, East and West
Love, Culture & Poetry: Lawrence Durrell
Cavafy: Anatomy of a Soul
German Romantic Poetry: Goethe, Novalis, Heine, Hölderlin
Feminism and Shakespeare
Shakespeare: Love, Poetry & Magic
The Passion of D.H. Lawrence
D.H. Lawrence: Symbolic Landscapes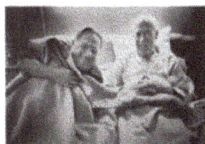
D.H. Lawrence: Infinite Sensual Violence
Rimbaud: Arthur Rimbaud and the Magic of Poetry
The Ecstasies of John Cowper Powys
Sensualism and Mythology: The Wessex Novels of John Cowper Powys
Amorous Life: John Cowper Powys and the Manifestation of Affectivity (H.W. Fawkner)
Postmodern Powys: New Essays on John Cowper Powys (Joe Boulter)
Rethinking Powys: Critical Essays on John Cowper Powys
Paul Bowles & Bernardo Bertolucci
Rainer Maria Rilke
Joseph Conrad: *Heart of Darkness*
In the Dim Void: Samuel Beckett
Samuel Beckett Goes into the Silence
André Gide: Fiction and Fervour
Jackie Collins and the Blockbuster Novel
Blinded By Her Light: The Love-Poetry of Robert Graves
The Passion of Colours: Travels In Mediterranean Lands
Poetic Forms

POETRY

Ursula Le Guin: Walking In Cornwall
Peter Redgrove: Here Comes The Flood
Peter Redgrove: Sex-Magic-Poetry-Cornwall
Dante: Selections From the Vita Nuova
Petrarch, Dante and the Troubadours
William Shakespeare: Sonnets
William Shakespeare: Complete Poems
Blinded By Her Light: The Love-Poetry of Robert Graves
Emily Dickinson: Selected Poems
Emily Brontë: Poems
Thomas Hardy: Selected Poems
Percy Bysshe Shelley: Poems
John Keats: Selected Poems
Joh n Keats: Poems of 1820
D.H. Lawrence: Selected Poems
Edmund Spenser: Poems
Edmund Spenser: Amoretti
John Donne: Poems
Henry Vaughan: Poems
Sir Thomas Wyatt: Poems
Robert Herrick: Selected Poems
Rilke: Space, Essence and Angels in the Poetry of Rainer Maria Rilke
Rainer Maria Rilke: Selected Poems
Friedrich Hölderlin: Selected Poems
Arseny Tarkovsky: Selected Poems
Arthur Rimbaud: Selected Poems
Arthur Rimbaud: A Season in Hell
Arthur Rimbaud and the Magic of Poetry
Novalis: Hymns To the Night
German Romantic Poetry
Paul Verlaine: Selected Poems
Elizaethan Sonnet Cycles
D.J. Enright: By-Blows
Jeremy Reed: Brigitte's Blue Heart
Jeremy Reed: Claudia Schiffer's Red Shoes
Gorgeous Little Orpheus
Radiance: New Poems
Crescent Moon Book of Nature Poetry
Crescent Moon Book of Love Poetry
Crescent Moon Book of Mystical Poetry
Crescent Moon Book of Elizabethan Love Poetry
Crescent Moon Book of Metaphysical Poetry
Crescent Moon Book of Romantic Poetry
Pagan America: New American Poetry

MEDIA, CINEMA, FEMINISM and CULTURAL STUDIES

J.R.R. Tolkien: The Books, The Films, The Whole Cultural Phenomenon
J.R.R. Tolkien: Pocket Guide
The *Lord of the Rings* Movies: Pocket Guide
The Cinema of Hayao Miyazaki
Hayao Miyazaki: *Princess Mononoke*: Pocket Movie Guide
Hayao Miyazaki: *Spirited Away*: Pocket Movie Guide
Tim Burton : Hallowe'en For Hollywood
Ken Russell
Ken Russell: *Tommy*: Pocket Movie Guide
The Ghost Dance: The Origins of Religion
The Peyote Cult
Cixous, Irigaray, Kristeva: The *Jouissance* of French Feminism
Julia Kristeva: Art, Love, Melancholy, Philosophy, Semiotics and Psychoanalysis
Luce Irigaray: Lips, Kissing, and the Politics of Sexual Difference
Hélène Cixous I Love You: The *Jouissance* of Writing
Andrea Dworkin
'Cosmo Woman': The World of Women's Magazines
Women in Pop Music
HomeGround: The Kate Bush Anthology
Discovering the Goddess (Geoffrey Ashe)
The Poetry of Cinema
The Sacred Cinema of Andrei Tarkovsky
Andrei Tarkovsky: Pocket Guide
Andrei Tarkovsky: *Mirror*: Pocket Movie Guide
Andrei Tarkovsky: *The Sacrifice*: Pocket Movie Guide
Walerian Borowczyk: Cinema of Erotic Dreams
Jean-Luc Godard: The Passion of Cinema
Jean-Luc Godard: *Hail Mary*: Pocket Movie Guide
Jean-Luc Godard: *Contempt*: Pocket Movie Guide
Jean-Luc Godard: *Pierrot le Fou*: Pocket Movie Guide
John Hughes and Eighties Cinema
Ferris Bueller's Day Off: Pocket Movie Guide
Jean-Luc Godard: Pocket Guide
The Cinema of Richard Linklater
Liv Tyler: Star In Ascendance
Blade Runner and the Films of Philip K. Dick
Paul Bowles and Bernardo Bertolucci
Media Hell: Radio, TV and the Press
An Open Letter to the BBC
Detonation Britain: Nuclear War in the UK
Feminism and Shakespeare
Wild Zones: Pornography, Art and Feminism
Sex in Art: Pornography and Pleasure in Painting and Sculpture
Sexing Hardy: Thomas Hardy and Feminism

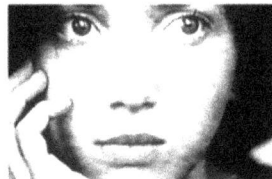

The Light Eternal is a model monograph, an exemplary job. The subject matter of the book is beautifully organised and dead on beam. (Lawrence Durrell)
It is amazing for me to see my work treated with such passion and respect. (Andrea Dworkin)

CRESCENT MOON PUBLISHING
P.O. Box 1312, Maidstone, Kent, ME14 5XU, Great Britain. www.crmoon.com

cresmopub@yahoo.co.uk   www.crescentmoon.org.uk

www.ingramcontent.com/pod-product-compliance
Lightning Source LLC
Chambersburg PA
CBHW060347100426
42812CB00003B/1161